THE SACRED AND THE FEMININE
IN ANCIENT GREECE

THE SACRED AND THE FEMININE IN ANCIENT GREECE

Edited by Sue Blundell and Margaret Williamson

London and New York

First published 1998
by Routledge
11 New Fetter Lane, London EC4P 4EE

Simultaneously published in the USA and Canada
by Routledge
29 West 35th Street, New York, NY10001

© 1998 selection and editorial matter, Sue Blundell and Margaret Williamson; individual chapters, the contributors to be identified as the Author of this Work has been asserted by them in accordance with the Copyright, Designs and Patents Act 1988

Typeset in Garamond by RefineCatch Limited, Bungay, Suffolk
Printed and bound in Great Britain by Biddles Ltd, Guildford and King's Lynn

All rights reserved. No part of this book may be reprinted or reproduced or utilised in any form or by any electronic, mechanical, or other means, now known or hereafter invented, including photocopying and recording, or in any information storage or retrieval system, without permission in writing from the publishers.

British Library Cataloguing in Publication Data
A catalogue record for this book is available from the British Library

Library of Congress Cataloging in Publication Data
The Sacred and the Feminine in Ancient Greece.
Edited by Sue Blundell and Margaret Williamson.
p. cm.
Includes bibliographical references and index.
1. Women and religion–Greece–History. 2. Greece–Religion.
I. Blundell, Sue. II. Williamson, Margaret.
BL795.W65S23   1998
292.08′082–dc21   97–25099
CIP

ISBN 0-415-12662-2 (hbk)
ISBN 0-415-12663-0 (pbk)

CONTENTS

List of illustrations		vii
List of contributors		ix
1	Introduction	1

PART I
Deities and their worshippers 11

2	The gamos of Hera: myth and ritual ISABELLE CLARK	13
3	Domesticating Artemis SUSAN GUETTEL COLE	27

PART II
Objects of worship 45

4	Marriage and the maiden: narratives on the Parthenon SUE BLUNDELL	47
5	Born old or never young? Femininity, childhood and the goddesses of ancient Greece LESLEY BEAUMONT	71
6	The nature of heroines EMILY KEARNS	96

CONTENTS

PART III
Ritual and gender   111

7   Death becomes her: gender and Athenian death ritual   113
    KAREN STEARS

8   In the mirror of Dionysos   128
    RICHARD SEAFORD

PART IV
Sources and interpreters   147

9   Thesmophoria and Haloa: myth, physics and mysteries   149
    N. J. LOWE

Bibliography   174
Index   187

ILLUSTRATIONS

3.1 A mother presents her baby to Artemis, Lamia, Department of Prehistoric and Classical Antiquities, Inv. 1041. 35
4.1 A wedding procession, London, British Museum, 1920.12–21.1. 50
4.2 Plan of the Parthenon. After a drawing by Sue Bird. 52
4.3 Plan of the Athenian Acropolis. After J. Travlos. 54
4.4 A centaur carries off a Lapith woman, London, British Museum, south metope 29. 59
4.5 The birth of Athene, Henry Lillie Pierce Fund, courtesy of the Museum of Fine Arts, Boston, 00.330. 61
4.6 Women in the Panathenaic procession, London, British Museum, east section of the Parthenon frieze: slab VIII. 63
4.7 Female attendant carrying stool; priestess; priest and child, Athene; Hephaistos, London, British Museum, east section of the Parthenon frieze: slab V. 64
4.8 Nike, Hera and Zeus, London, British Museum, east section of the Parthenon frieze: slab V. 65
4.9 The 'Varvakeion' Athene, Athens, National Archaeological Museum, 129. 66
5.1 Marble group of Hermes with the baby Dionysos, Olympia Museum. (Photo: DAI, Athens). 73
5.2 The infant Hermes in his cradle, Rome, Vatican Museum, 16582. 75
5.3 The newborn Athene at the knee of her father Zeus, Vienna, Kunsthistorisches Museum, IV 728. (Photo: Kunsthistorisches Museum, Nr. II 10416). 77
5.4 Aphrodite rising from the sea at her birth, Rome, Museo Nazionale Romano, 8570. 78
5.5 Leto, the infant Apollo and Artemis flee from the Python, once Naples, Second Hamilton Collection, now lost. (Photo: reproduced from *Jahrbuch des Deutschen Archäologischen Instituts* 47 [1932], p. 65, fig. 18). 79

ILLUSTRATIONS

5.6	Attic red-figure chous depicting a mortal baby girl, Athens, National Archaeological Museum, 1739.	81
5.7	Marble figure of a mortal female child, Athens, National Archaeological Museum, 695.	82
5.8	Attic grave stele depicting a little girl at the knee of a woman, Athens, National Archaeological Museum, 3289.	83
7.1	Attic black-figure pinax depicting a prothesis and chariots, New York, the Metropolitan Museum of Art, Rogers Fund, 1954 (54.11.5).	114
8.1	Dionysiac scene on Apulian bell-krater, Archaeological Institute of the University of Zurich, Inv. 3585.	130

CONTRIBUTORS

Lesley Beaumont is Assistant Director of the British School at Athens. She has published articles on the iconography, archaeology and social history of children and childhood in Classical Athens.

Sue Blundell lectures in Classical Civilization at Birkbeck College, University of London, and at the Open University, and is also a tutor at the Architectural Association in London. She is the author of *The Origins of Civilization in Greek and Roman Thought* (1986) and of *Women in Ancient Greece* (1995).

Isabelle Clark completed her D.Phil. thesis on the subject of Hera and marriage in Greek myth and cult in 1994 at Magdalen College, Oxford. She has since left full-time Classics for the world of finance.

Susan Guettel Cole is Associate Professor of Classics and History at the State University of New York at Buffalo. She has published articles and books on a variety of subjects, including the (il)literacy of Greek women, rituals of maturation, the cult of Dionysos, and the placement of sanctuaries of Demeter in the territory of the Greek city.

Emily Kearns is Lecturer in Classics at St Hilda's College, Oxford. She is the author of *The Heroes of Attica* (1989), and of articles on various aspects of Greek religion.

N. J. Lowe is a lecturer in Classics at Royal Holloway and Bedford New College, University of London.

Richard Seaford is Professor of Greek Literature at the University of Exeter. He is the author of *Pompeii* (1978), of commentaries on Euripides' *Cyclops* (1984) and *Bacchae* (1996), of *Reciprocity and Ritual: Homer and Tragedy in the Developing City-State* (1994) and of numerous articles on Greek literature and religion.

Karen Stears lectures in Classics and Ancient History at the University of Edinburgh.

CONTRIBUTORS

Margaret Williamson is Senior Lecturer in Classical Studies at St Mary's University College, University of Surrey. She is the author of *Sappho's Immortal Daughters* (1995), and of various articles on Greek literature and culture.

1

INTRODUCTION

'So it is seemly for a woman to remain at home and not be out of doors; but for a man to stay inside instead of devoting himself to outdoor pursuits is disgraceful' (Xenophon, *Oeconomicus* 7.30). These words, uttered by an Athenian citizen during a discussion of household management, neatly illustrate what has long been a commonplace about the women of ancient Athens and, as far as we know, of other cities of the time: that in sharp contrast to their male counterparts, female citizens were excluded from public affairs. Equally commonplace, however, is the observation that there is one major exception to this generalisation. In one crucial area, that of religious practice, the barriers between women and public life were conspicuously breached. Debarred entirely from public debate, from law-making and political processes, women nonetheless participated fully in the city's religious life. They were involved in religious ritual at all levels, from private and informal celebrations to state-sponsored occasions; the part they played was often of acknowledged importance to the community as a whole, and it could take them into public spaces otherwise reserved for men. In the public symbolism of religion, too, the female was often accorded equal importance with the male, with goddesses displaying power, and commanding respect, equal to that of gods. The role of priestess was the only public office open to women, and there are indications that women were regarded as having a closer intrinsic connection with the divine than men.[1]

The connection between the feminine and divine spheres of life and thought was, then, a particularly rich one. The purpose of this book, originating in a series of papers presented at the Institute of Classical Studies in London in 1993, is to examine some of the multifarious links involved. We shall be considering not only the ways in which real-life women related, or were thought to relate, to divine beings, but also the cultural constructions shaping the categories of the feminine and of the divine. Thus, these essays are concerned with goddesses and heroines as well as with human females, and even with rituals involving gender inversion by male participants.

We begin, however, with some brief contextualising information. Greek religion can be divided into two principal components: ritual and myth.

INTRODUCTION

Although it would be wrong to assume that Greek religious systems were devoid of beliefs or ideas, they were not constructed around a uniform and authoritative set of doctrines; rather, it was through actions and through mythical representations that the Greeks sought to establish a relationship with the divine. The actions, or rituals, were of many different types but, whether performed in private or in public, their focus was generally on acknowledging and honouring a divinity or set of divinities. The main medium for representing divinity was myth, a body of traditional tales in which the human condition was explored through narratives featuring superhuman beings. These myths could be sung, spoken, written or visually conveyed in sculpture and vase-paintings. Narratives and representations such as these would often be presented in close conjunction with ritual, for example in hymns sung at religious festivals, but this was not always the case: statues of heroes and gods, for example, functioned in several different contexts.

The divine powers worshipped by the Greeks can be divided into two main types, both of which receive detailed attention in this volume: deities, and heroes and heroines. The deities were immortal beings who had been born, but would never die. There were many of them, and their numbers were fluid, with the possibility of introducing new cults in response to changing priorities in the culture. Individual gods and goddesses, too, were honoured under a range of titles which could be used to emphasise and call upon particular facets of their power on different occasions. To a large extent, the behaviour of deities is modelled on that of their human worshippers: they are often conceived of as responding and acting like exceptionally powerful human beings. But they also differ from humans in crucial ways, and many of these essays are concerned with the defining differences between mortals and deities. The differences are especially significant in the case of goddesses, who are seen as wielding great power in a period when real-life women were, in general, socially and politically subordinate to men.

The significance of deities was, however, not purely individual. They also had a corporate identity, in that they belonged both to a divine universe and to various sub-groups within it; and they could be worshipped collectively. The most prominent of the sub-groups was that of the Olympians, an elite which consisted of six goddesses (Hera, Athene, Artemis, Aphrodite, Demeter, Hestia) and six gods (Zeus, Poseidon, Apollo, Hermes, Ares, Hephaestus). Even here, though, fixity of personnel was not an essential feature; in Athens, for example, Hestia, goddess of the hearth, was sometimes replaced by Dionysus, who as god of drama was of particular importance to the Athenians. The Olympian group was both an extended family and a kind of governing council, headed by Zeus. It was thus capable of functioning as a paradigm for institutions within Greek society on several levels, and provided a framework for exploring issues of cohesion and conflict, order and disorder within and between human communities.

The second major category is that of heroes, who differed from gods in having had an existence as human beings who had lived and died. Some were real historical personalities, but most were imagined as having lived in the distant past. All had performed deeds benefiting their communities, which had earned them the right to be worshipped after their deaths; in most cases hero cults were local, and it was rare for a hero to receive recognition outside the region in which he was thought to have operated. Heroes, and their rarer female counterparts, heroines, could intervene in human affairs independently, conferring rewards and exacting punishments in the manner of deities. Their status is best described, though, as intermediate between that of deity and mortal; thus they can move between human and divine realms, and may for example be mortal women loved by male gods or the children (normally male) of such unions. Their intermediate position makes heroines in particular a rich source for exploring the paradoxes inherent in the conjunction of the idea of divinity with that of the feminine.

There is no privileged source of information for Greek religion, which had nothing equivalent to the Christian Bible; however, so integral was it to Greek life and thought that most of the written and material remains of the culture provide information about it. Literature includes many descriptions of religious practice, and epic, lyric and tragic poetry are based largely on mythical narratives about gods and heroes – narratives which were reworked at each retelling. Our two major sources apart from literature are inscriptions and archaeological material. The inscriptions relate particularly to religious practices in the public sphere, recording such things as religious calendars, dedications to deities, correct ritual procedures, oracular pronouncements and the financial accounts of sanctuaries. Archaeological material from cemeteries, sanctuaries and temples tells us about rituals, about the organisation of religious space and about objects offered to deities; relief sculptures from temples are also, together with vase-paintings, important texts in the transmission of myth.

This book focuses mainly on the archaic and classical periods of Greek history (approximately 750 to 330 BCE). Some aspects of Greek cults and of the divine beings who were honoured in them can be traced back to well before that time; but it was within the context of the *polis*, usually translated as 'city-state', that the religious practices and representations with which these essays are concerned achieved their characteristic form. In physical terms, the *polis* (plural *poleis*) was an area of arable land containing a number of small agricultural settlements; it was fringed by hill country which was used for pasture and hunting, and had an urban centre which, as well as housing much of the population, also functioned as a market and meeting-place. Though generally small in size, with a population in the low thousands, each *polis* was an autonomous state. This form of political organisation developed rapidly during the early part of the archaic period, so that by about 600 BCE the Greek world was divided into literally hundreds of *poleis*. Religion had played an important part in their formation, since the establishment of sanctuaries and cults in rural areas was crucial to the definition and defence of each *polis*'s territorial frontiers.[2] The continuing link between religious practices and the life of the *polis*, in which each both determines and is determined by the other, is a theme that recurs in many of the discussions that follow.

We begin with a pair of case-studies that link the two defining elements of Greek religion: myth and ritual. In the opening section (Part I, 'Deities and their worshippers') Isabelle Clark in Chapter 1 and Susan Guettel Cole in Chapter 2 study some of the representations and practices associated with the worship of two goddesses whose spheres of influence were central to women's lives. Artemis, the goddess of wild nature and of hunting, was also associated with girls' rites of maturation and later with childbirth; Hera was traditionally regarded as a marriage deity. Both are panhellenic goddesses, members of the group of twelve Olympians; yet in both cases we see how much local diversity there could be in the practices associated with their worship. It is also clear that their spheres of influence are not neatly divided: each of these two is linked at some point both with maturation rites and with marriage.

Striking too is the range of different ways in which the worship of these two goddesses was important to the community as a whole. It is not just that, as both essays show, each was both a guarantor and to some extent also a paradigm for the behaviour of human females. Women's lives, properly ordered, were of central importance to the entire social group, not only because they were childbearers but also in more symbolically mediated ways. Thus, Artemis's far-flung sanctuaries and the women who worshipped in them were significant precisely because of their proximity to the boundaries of a city's territory. For as long as it was not attacked (and of course it sometimes was), vulnerable territory close to a border demonstrated the security of the whole community; and Cole also suggests that there is a symbolic link between the integrity of the bodies of female celebrants and that of the *polis*. The worship of Hera served another function again: her festival at Plataea, in which both sexes participated, helped to promote cohesion among the communities that took part.

Each of these goddesses is portrayed as having characteristics broadly similar to those of human females: Artemis is herself represented as a *parthenos*, an unmarried girl, and Hera as a bride or wife. Like mortal women, therefore, they are defined at least partly in terms of their sexual status. But we have already noted that deities also differ from their human counterparts, most obviously in the case of goddesses because of their power. These two goddesses exhibit other differences as well. Unlike her mortal counterparts, Artemis is able to remain a *parthenos*; Hera is not only party to an incestuous marriage (since Zeus is her brother), but she also displays a degree of independence, and vindictiveness towards her husband's paramours, that would not be tolerated in a mortal woman.

INTRODUCTION

The theme of divine females' difference, principally from humans but also from male deities, is explored further in the next section (Part II, 'Objects of worship'). Sue Blundell in Chapter 4 discusses the ways in which Athens, an unusually large and powerful *polis*, chose to represent its patron deity on the Parthenon, the largest and most splendid temple of its time and situated in the most prominent of the city's public spaces, the Acropolis. Like Artemis, Athena was a *parthenos*, and this presented the city with a double paradox. A virginal female presided over a city whose public institutions were all male, and which identified marriage as central to its claim to civilised values. This, Blundell argues, helped to determine the complex message of the Parthenon sculptures, structured as a discourse by the spectator's movement alongside and eventually into the building. Athena's difference from human females was central to this discourse, which not only counterposed Athena to Pandora, the first woman, but probably also contrived to suggest a structural link between the victory over Poseidon by which Athena was established as the city's patron and the disenfranchising of real Athenian women.

Visual representations of deities and the assumptions underpinning them are also the subject of Lesley Beaumont's discussion in Chapter 5, which focuses on the early stages of life. A contrast between male and female is immediately apparent as regards divine birth and infancy: scenes showing the birth of a goddess are far less frequent, and such as there are represent their subjects as fully grown – unlike, say, the infants Hermes or Apollo. Thus Athena springs fully armed from the head of her father, while Aphrodite emerges as an adult female from the sea or from a shell; and both, significantly, have only one, male, parent. The explanation for this, it is suggested, has to do with the polarities of power and powerlessness which are already uneasily combined in the notion of a female divinity. Adding the element of childhood, another fundamentally weak or incomplete condition, would destabilise the paradox to the point of untenability.

Intermediate between the categories of human and divine is, as we have seen, that of the heroic, and the female version of heroic identity is explored in Emily Kearns' essay (Chapter 6) on heroines. The range of roles performed by heroines is considerable, ranging from heroes' consorts to gods' paramours (and thus the mothers of heroes), priestesses and eponymous heroines. Heroes and heroines normally have a two-phase existence: before death, when they lead quasi-human lives, and after it, when they become the objects of cult. It might perhaps be expected that the dichotomy between human and divine would be neatly distributed between these two stages. The reality, however, turns out to be more complicated: not only do myth and ritual often (as the opening chapters also showed) pull in different directions, but they can do so in unpredictable ways. Like goddesses, heroines are both like and unlike mortals; but the degree of that difference varies considerably, and it is as likely to be found in the myths about a heroine's life as in the practices and myths linked with her worship. Thus, for example, heroines who are worshipped as heroes' consorts seem to know their place in much the same way as mortal women. Heroines worshipped by *parthenoi*, on the other hand, often show in their own life-stories a troubled relationship to the transition to adult status which their human devotees must accomplish. This case illustrates particularly well the heroine's intermediate status: goddesses can avoid the transition altogether and humans not at all, while heroines' attempts to achieve it either fail or are accompanied by disaster.

In the next section (Part III, 'Ritual and gender'), the focus moves from divinities to their human worshippers. Karen Stears in Chapter 7 explores the nature and significance of gender division in Athenian funerary practices. The procedures for laying out, lamenting and burying the dead were well established and involved a fairly clear division of labour between the sexes. As one might expect, women played an important role in the stages that took place in domestic space: the preparation of the body and the laments over it. They were also, however, involved in the next phase: female as well as male mourners would accompany the corpse on its way to burial. The importance of women at both stages is indicated by legislation from the archaic period limiting the permitted categories of female mourners and prohibiting excessive displays of grief. Since iconographical evidence shows women mourning in a less restrained way than men, it is possible to see in this legislation a reinforcement of the ideology that constructed women as in need of male control.

Yet this is not the whole story. Previous discussions of the division of labour in death ritual have focused on women's association with the private sphere, and their relative powerlessness and lack of status outside it. An important implication of Stears' discussion, however, is that this perspective is too limited. It is not simply that, as has already been observed, ritual is the one area of life in which women habitually crossed the divide between public and private with impunity. Even the most apparently private features of these family-based rituals could themselves have consequences in the public world, affecting not only the public standing of a household or kinship group in the wider world but ultimately also relationships between these groups in the *polis* as a whole: funerary legislation can, indeed, be made sense of only on the assumption that women's behaviour has consequences for the whole community. We may, therefore, need to revise our understanding of the notions of power and status in relation to women. Women's greater expressiveness in mourning is a case in point. No doubt it is true that the ideology of gender to which it both conforms and contributes reinforces women's subordination; yet women's mourning could simultaneously, and paradoxically, also enhance their own status and that of their kin group, and possibly even form the basis of legal claims on the deceased's estate. Once again we find that women's lives and religious practice, however closely they may be confined within the private sphere, are seen as essential to society as a whole.

Death ritual is only one of a number of rites of passage involving a temporarily marginal or liminal status for some or all of the participants. Others especially relevant to women which have already been discussed are those surrounding marriage and childbirth, linked particularly with Hera and Artemis. Another ritual in which women played a central role, and which explicitly involved such marginality, was maenadism, a type of cult honouring Dionysus. This typically involved groups of women performing cult for the god in the wild spaces outside the city, on the mountain. For female worshippers, Richard Seaford has argued that this period in the wild renewed the links thought to exist between unmarried women and wildness: in a maenadic group, married women were re-entering the wild state which Greek culture associated with human females before they were 'tamed' by marriage. Euripides' play *The Bacchae*, named after its maenadic chorus, suggests that this temporary reversion to an earlier state was accompanied by other departures from their normal identity: in the play the women's actions are compared to those of animals or of males.

The need for divine protection and patronage at such exceptional and defining moments in women's lives has already been demonstrated in the two opening chapters. The account of maenadism offered here, however, takes our understanding of the social definition of identity through ritual even further, focusing on gender identity itself as the product of an intrinsically social and dynamic process. In Chapter 8 in this volume Seaford extends his argument in relation to the male protagonist of the play, Pentheus, showing how he too repeatedly crosses boundaries in a way typical of Dionysiac worship – boundaries between male and female, life and death, and most crucially adulthood and infancy. In Pentheus' case, the process is dysfunctional and the outcome tragic, involving a regressive dissolution of his adult male identity which is never redeemed. Seaford suggestively links the dissolution (and literal fragmentation, when Pentheus is torn apart by the maenads) staged by Euripides with the psychoanalytic account of ego formation found in Lacan's account of the mirror phase – a link which is reinforced by his argument that the play itself alludes to the use of mirrors in Dionysiac ritual. Tragedy of course represents ritual patterns not directly but in a way mediated by its own preoccupations. Nonetheless, the links implicit in the play between individual identity, ritual practices and the wellbeing of the community as a whole echo those drawn by Susan Cole in her discussion of the worship of Artemis. We are reminded again, and from yet another angle, of the sometimes paradoxical centrality of both the sacred and the feminine to Greek culture.

The final chapter in the volume, while continuing to focus on human worshippers, also tackles a problem fundamental to the study of ancient religion: that of sources and their interpretation, particularly as regards the meanings attributed to rituals (Chapter 9 in Part IV, 'Sources and interpreters'). Nick Lowe's subject is two women-only festivals, the Haloa and the more widespread Thesmophoria, which were celebrated annually in honour of Demeter. The primary celebrants of the Thesmophoria seem to have been married citizen women, whose husbands were (in Athens at any rate) required to pay their wives' expenses during their three-day absence from home. In Athens the women spent this time camped out on the Pnyx in the centre of the city, displacing the Assembly business which was normally transacted there. Despite the festival's high profile and officially sponsored nature, however, the proceedings themselves were strictly secret.

Besides being among the best-known of ancient women's festivals, these two, especially the Thesmophoria, are also among the best-documented. But to say this, as Lowe demonstrates, is not to say very much. Our only detailed source for each consists of marginal notes to the work of a later author, Lucian, in a manuscript produced in the thirteenth century AD and thus closer in time to the present day than to antiquity. These are the only sources to offer any detail about the practices of the festival, telling of rituals involving pits, snakes, pigs and models of genitalia, all of which have a more or less marked sexual significance. They also offer explanations of the rituals' meaning and purpose. Like all such notes these are a compilation from earlier material, and they have often been attributed to a tenth-century scholar. Lowe, however, argues convincingly not only that the compilation must have taken place much earlier than this, but also that the ultimate source of the information they contain may go back to the third century BCE or earlier, to an informant close – in time at least – to the practices described.

Yet the point of this quest lies not in the pursuit of unattainable certainties, but in the questions that are raised along the way. The identity and dating of the original source of these passages, revealing as they do privileged knowledge of supposedly secret rituals, is only the beginning. More crucial still are the statements made in them about the meanings attached to the rituals, and the ways in which these statements have been understood by subsequent interpreters. In this complex history a key moment, Lowe argues, is the nineteenth century, when the idea of primitive religion as fertility magic, attempting to promote the productivity of the natural world by supernatural means, took hold. These passages, with their explicit reference to fertility, were eagerly seized upon by the proponents of this hypothesis, which though now largely discredited within anthropology, lives on in accounts of the Thesmophoria: it is still customary to say that the festival's overall purpose was to promote fertility.

The close reading offered here, however, does not support this view. It is true that reference is made to fertility: the already mentioned objects which were offered at the festival symbolise sexuality and reproduction, and those who later mix the rotting remains of snakes, pigs and models of genitalia with seedcorn do so, these notes tell us, in the belief that their crops will grow better as a result. Lowe points out, however, that the stated purpose of the offerings themselves is quite other: they are described as a thank-offering to Demeter, who in giving them agriculture also 'civilised the race of humans'.

INTRODUCTION

It is fitting that our collection should end on this note. Greek thought, echoed until very recently by many modern scholars, tended to relegate women to areas of life and thought outside the realm of the civilised – to the wild spaces outside the city, or to the dark and private recesses of the home. Time and again in these essays, however, we find women's ritual practices playing a central and irreplaceable role in relation to the wellbeing of the city. Women's marginality, even invisibility, in everyday public life did not render their activities marginal to the publicly self-defining city, even when those activities were performed in private space or in secret. Nowhere is this more evident than in the Thesmophoria, a festival whose rituals, though performed in public space, were literally invisible to the male citizens who normally regarded themselves as custodians of the social order. If our source is to be believed, the central gesture of this state-sponsored and yet strictly women-only festival celebrated the achievement on which Greeks, and especially Athenians, most prided themselves: civilisation.

Fitting too is this closing essay's reminder of a question which modern anthropology in particular has put on the agenda: the position of the observer. Ever since Aristophanes made comedy out of men's ignorance about it in the fifth century BCE, the Thesmophoria has generated a wide range of responses. Christian sources, shocked by what they saw as obscenity, handed down bowdlerised accounts of it; the nineteenth century, as we have seen, drafted it in to support a primitivising view of religion; and recent scholarship has again made it the focus of debate, this time about its significance for the worshippers themselves: did the festival work to keep them in their place, or did it have a counter-cultural aspect?[3] Lowe's essay leaves us with a salutary reminder of how far the enquirer's own agenda in all these cases has coloured the answers she or he receives from the ancient material.

The last few decades have been an exciting time for the study of women and gender; we hope this collection gives a glimpse of some of the secrets antiquity may still disclose to us if we can only find the right questions.

NOTES

1 This connection has been explored by Padel 1983, 1992, 1995.
2 See de Polignac 1995 [1984]: 32–88.
3 See, for example, Zeitlin 1982, Burkert 1985: 245, Detienne 1989 and Winkler 1990.

Part I

DEITIES AND THEIR WORSHIPPERS

2

THE GAMOS OF HERA
Myth and Ritual

Isabelle Clark

The subject of this chapter is the worship and the representation of a major female deity, the goddess Hera. A member of the panhellenic group of twelve Olympians, Hera is strongly associated in both myth and ritual with *gamos*, a term usually translated as 'wedding' or 'marriage'. In myth she herself was the wife of the supreme god, Zeus, and she figures prominently in rituals linked with human marriage: my title refers to both these levels. It is reasonable therefore to characterise her as a marriage deity. Yet both the nature and the extent of her links with marriage vary more widely than this simple description would suggest, and most of this essay is devoted to exploring that variety through a comparison of three festivals honouring her. I begin, however, with some brief remarks about the practices and the significance of marriage itself, and about Hera's role in cult and myth.

GREEK WOMEN AND MARRIAGE

Marriage in Greek society, as in others, was of central importance to society as a whole. Wedding ceremonies, however, were (unlike the preceding betrothal) an essentially female concern, with the focus almost entirely upon the bride and the female experience of marriage. The wedding was a major rite of passage for the bride, and was associated with a number of different deities and rituals. At the same time, the marital status of a Greek woman was important in determining some of the religious rites and festivals in which she could participate and the roles within these that she might play. The institution of marriage and its attendant rituals are therefore significant in more than one way in structuring women's experience of cult in Greek religion.

It has frequently been noted that the Greek word for 'woman', *gyne*, is the same as that for 'wife', reflecting the fact that the roles available to women in the Greek world were almost exclusively those of wife and mother. Since marriage was generally the only path available to Greek girls, the wedding was correspondingly one of the most significant life events. It marked the principal point of transition from childhood to adulthood, and a fundamental change in status from *parthenos* to *gyne*, the two most important categories of the female. The *parthenos* (plural *parthenoi*) is the marriageable virgin, the girl who has attained physical and sexual maturity, but has not yet married. The *gyne* is the wife, and is ideally also a mother. There is a third intermediate category, that of *nymphe*, the woman who is married but who has not yet had her first child. This is a period which is ideally as short as possible, since it is the birth of a child which makes a woman a true *gyne*. It is the change in status from *parthenos* to married *gyne*, celebrated by the wedding, which is the most radical.

The various perceptions of marriage and weddings include a range of positive and negative images of the process of becoming a *gyne*. We have considerable evidence from various parts of the Greek world for the existence of rituals for *parthenoi* which are frequently associated with myth.[1] These rites are associated particularly with girls who are on the brink of marriage, and therefore at a period of particular vulnerability. The girl is sexually mature and ready for marriage, yet still 'untamed' by the yoke of marriage. She is frequently perceived as wild and unpredictable, and reluctant and fearful to submit herself to the domination of the male and of civilised society. This model of the female is articulated in myths associated with *parthenoi* and nymphs who reject marriage or the embrace of a male deity in order to devote themselves to the band of Artemis, and a life of roaming free in the mountains outside the confines of 'normal' society. In these myths, marriage is associated with themes of rape and of violent subjugation. At the same time, the wedding is represented in other contexts as a romanticised event at which the bride and groom are attended by Eros and figures associated with beauty, harmony and concord. The ideology of marriage is therefore complex and includes a spectrum of different perceptions.[2]

Although the wedding is the most important part of the transition from childhood to adulthood, the process of attaining full wifehood extends far beyond the wedding ritual itself. We know of collective girls' rituals for children as young as five which are associated with the preliminary stages of acculturation and preparation for marriageability. These rituals can be linked with particular stages of biological and sexual development, and they form a continuum with the rituals for *parthenoi* that come at a later stage in the maturation process.

We are fortunate in having relatively full information about the rituals most frequently associated with the Greek wedding, and it is possible to draw some conclusions about the particular rituals and practices which were the most common and the most widespread.[3] A farewell to childhood appears to have been fairly common. This often took the form of a dedication to a deity, such as Artemis, who is particularly associated with childhood and the virginity which is to be left behind. The dedication could be a lock of hair, or some other symbol of past or future status. Pre-nuptial bathing also appears to have been a common theme, with water provided from a special local source or in a particular type of vessel. This is not a practice unique to the wedding. Ritual bathing is a common cult practice associated with other types of religious occasion, but in this context it appears to have been intended to enhance the bride's fertility as well as for purification. Special bridal clothes were prepared for the bride. We know of sacrifices to a number of different local gods and panhellenic deities which took place around the time of the wedding, and celebrations also included feasting and processions marking the metaphorical and physical passage of the bride from her old to her new home.

Of the various deities associated with marriage and the wedding, the most important is Hera; hence modern commentators frequently refer to her as 'the goddess of marriage', meaning among other things that she receives honours at weddings.[4] The term 'marriage' (*gamos*), however, may be used to denote not only getting married but also being married and a wide range of associated experiences, such as general preparation for female adulthood and, later, pregnancy and child-rearing. Hera's roles reflect the flexibility of the term. Not only is she seen as being involved in girls' rituals prior to marriageable age; she is often also linked with married women, and celebrated in festivals related to the married state.

HERA IN CULT AND MYTH

Hera's persona as wife of Zeus and as the pre-eminent marriage deity is well attested in panhellenic myth, and her importance as bride is particularly well-developed in the epics of Homer and Hesiod. However, she is not prominent to the same degree in all Greek cities and regions, nor is she always the principal marriage deity. Although worshippers at a given locality must have been familiar with the 'general', panhellenic personality of a deity, there were also local priorities. Different panhellenic figures might be privileged in different cult systems, and local deities might take on roles elsewhere reserved for others. In Laconia and Arcadia, for example, Hera is not particularly prominent and other deities are more closely associated with the rituals and preparation of brides. Nonetheless, the evidence suggests that it was Hera who had the widest currency as a marriage deity.

At the same time, Hera's importance as a deity extends far beyond her role in the context of marriage; she was also patron deity of several important communities. In these cities, notably Argos and Samos where she was mistress of the whole island, her cult importance was not confined to the female and the domestic but encompassed the protection of the city and the citizens. In these locations, she was closely linked with political and military functions. At the Argive Heraion, for example, Hera was portrayed in her cult statue as the bride of Zeus. She also had an important function as protector of Argos, and her principal festival, incorporating various military themes, included an armed procession from the city to the sanctuary.[5] However, worshippers at the Argive Heraion did not draw a sharp distinction between 'Hera the bride' and 'Hera who protects the city of Argos': Hera was a single cult personality but with multiple aspects and functions. Such multiplicity makes it problematic to describe her as a 'marriage deity', in the simplistic sense of the term which equates a deity with one main function. This can be further demonstrated by considering more closely some of the myths associated with Hera, especially that of the *gamos* of Zeus and Hera.

The many myths dealing with the *gamos* of Zeus and Hera demonstrate that the marriage of the pre-eminent marriage deity is not simply an idealised perception of marriage to which mortals may aspire. To a large extent they reflect the spectrum of perceptions of marriage, both positive and negative, which operated for the human plane. The most popular version of the *gamos* of Zeus and Hera presents it as a secret event which was not a formal wedding, but a sexual act. It is said to have taken place in a number of locations, usually in a remote and open setting in a meadow or on a mountain and without the knowledge of the other gods. In some versions, Zeus uses deceit to seduce the unwitting Hera, who is powerless to resist. The emphasis is on the *gamos* as a romanticised event, as we see in *Iliad* 14, where Hera arouses the irresistible desire of Zeus, and as they make love, the ground beneath them spontaneously sends up a carpet of flowers.[6] Other versions suggest that the couple had a formal wedding with guests, feasting and gifts, but this perception seems to have been less popular. Besides it being secret, we should also note that the *gamos* is incestuous since the couple are siblings who deceive their parents, and in that respect represent a negative paradigm.

The myths about Hera as wife present a rather different picture from those of Hera as bride. Hera and Zeus are the most important married pair of the pantheon, but the relationship is frequently portrayed as a problematic one. From the earliest sources we find myths about dissent, rebellion and anger. In the *Iliad* Hera uses devious means to borrow erotic charms and seduce her husband, which allows her to assert her own plans. In the *Homeric Hymn to Pythian Apollo*, Hera angrily withdraws from her husband and gives birth to her own parthenogenetic child, the monstrous Typhon, who grows up to threaten Zeus and the whole Olympian order.[7] Hera is certainly not an archetypal wife; she is independent, rebellious, and even threatening.[8]

In myth, much of the dissent between Hera and Zeus seems to be provoked by marital and sexual matters. The numerous infidelities of Zeus provoke the resentment and violent retribution of Hera. The persona of Hera is often characterised by vindictiveness; her anger is generally directed at those who represent a threat to her status as wife of Zeus. These are typically the lovers of Zeus, such as Io, or the children of Zeus' mistresses, such as Heracles. The myths of Hera as a bride and wife also focus on the threats to these roles, and on a type of reaction which would not be available to her mortal counterparts. The area of parenthood is also fraught with tension; the divine couple both produce children by parthenogenesis – Typhon, Hephaistos and Athena – and this becomes a further area of competition.

FESTIVALS OF HERA

I turn now to three festivals of Hera which may all be said to be 'about' Hera in some way. The tendency has often been for commentators to interpret festivals of Hera as a quasi-wedding ritual in which Hera is somehow married to Zeus. A recent book on the Sacred Marriage (*hieros gamos*), the wedding of Zeus and Hera, follows a similar pattern, and interprets a number of Hera festivals as wedding rituals.[9] Standard ritual practices such as processions are interpreted as wedding processions, and the ritual cleansing of cult statues is seen in terms of premarital bathing. However, this preoccupation with the *hieros gamos* of Hera and Zeus seems to lead to dangerous over-simplification and misinterpretation.

I The *hieros gamos* festival in Attica

First, a festival of Hera in Attica. The cult of Hera in Attica does not appear to have been particularly prominent; in fact, we know of only one temple. Nor is there much evidence of any major festivals of Hera apart from this one. The cult of Hera is far more prominent in areas outside Attica, especially Samos, Argos and Boiotia. The evidence for the cult of Hera in Attica comes from a variety of sources: literary, epigraphic and iconographic. For reasons of time and space, I will confine myself to evidence from texts and inscriptions.

In various parts of the Greek world, including Athens, the cult of Hera as marriage deity is linked with the cult epithet Teleia. This seems to be an allusion to the idea of marriage as a completion or fulfilment; *gamos* is said to be the *telos* and those who are married are called *teleioi*.[10] I am unable here to enter into detailed discussion of the whole range of meaning of the word *telos*, but it is sufficient to note that the basic sense seems to be 'fulfilment' or 'end' (in the sense of 'aim' or 'death'). It is also associated with sacrifice and especially marriage sacrifice, also known as *proteleia*. Those who are married are called *teleioi*, and thus Hera the marriage deity is known by the epithet Teleia. The sense of fulfilment in the epithet is both active and passive: Hera is fulfilled or made complete by marriage, and she also has the power to make complete those who get married.

The *locus classicus* for the function of Hera Teleia as goddess of marriage is found in Aristophanes' *Thesmophoriazusai*:[11] 'Let us hymn Hera Teleia as is appropriate; she delights in the chorus and guards the keys of marriage.' This is an important reference, since it explicitly links Hera Teleia with the specific role of protecting marriage as an institution. Aeschylus also refers to Hera Teleia and Zeus Teleios in the *Oresteia*, a cycle in which the theme of marriage plays a major role. Aeschylus exploits to the full the term *telos* and its compounds with all its implications, which include marriage, death, and sacrifice. It could be said to be one of the key words in the text; the ambiguities and implications of *telos* are highly significant.[12]

Hera Teleia and Zeus Teleios both appear in the trilogy. In *Eumenides*, Hera Teleia and Zeus Teleios are invoked as guardians of marriage, along with Aphrodite. Apollo accuses the Erinyes of disregarding marriage:[13] 'You have made worthless the pledges of Hera Teleia and Zeus.' The epithet Teleia is applied specifically to Hera, but it should also be understood as alluding to Hera's cult partner Zeus Teleios. Clytemnestra's crime of killing her husband is represented as a transgression of the pledges of Hera Teleia and Zeus Teleios and as a crime against the institution of marriage. The role of Zeus Teleios, husband of Hera and joint patron of marriage, is particularly significant in the *Agamemnon*. Before Clytemnestra enters the palace to murder her husband, it is to Zeus Teleios that she addresses her prayer for success:[14] 'Zeus, Zeus Teleios, accomplish my prayers. May you bring to pass that which is your will.'

The sense of 'fulfilment' is present in Zeus Teleios, but this title must also refer to Zeus the marriage god. Zeus is the Fulfiller of Clytemnestra's impious prayer, and he is also, ironically, 'Married' Zeus, who is being invoked for the murder of a husband. These references, together with others from later lexicographers, provide fairly good evidence for the perception of Hera Teleia and her husband Zeus Teleios as guarantors of marriage in Athens. We also know of an Attic festival known as *hieros gamos*, or Sacred Marriage or Wedding, which was dedicated to Hera Teleia and Zeus Teleios. The sources for this festival are fragmentary inscriptions, texts and lexicographers. Taken together, they allow us to draw some important conclusions about the festival and Hera's role.

The earliest evidence for the festival *hieros gamos* is in a calendar inscription, dating from around 440–430, from the deme of Thorikos in Attica. The calendar lists the sacrifices to be made to various deities in each month:[15] 'In the month of Gamelion, for Hera, for the Sacred Marriage . . .' The missing letters would have specified the sacrificial victim to be offered. The inscription makes it clear that the *hieros gamos* is a particular occasion, probably a festival. The name of the festival is likely to have been the origin for the name for the month, Gamelion, which suggests that it may have been the major cult occasion of the month.

A second sacred calendar dating from the first half of the fourth century from the Attic deme of Erchia lists sacrifices for Hera, Zeus Teleios, Poseidon and Kourotrophos on the same day.[16] The date for the sacrifices is the twenty-seventh day of the month, and all the sacrifices are to be performed in the shrine of Hera in the deme of Erchia. This inscription refers to the same month and goddess, Hera, as the Thorikos calendar; both inscriptions must relate to the same sacrifice and the same festival.

To these two inscriptions we may add a line from a fragmentary calendar from Athens, dating from the first half of the fifth century:[17] 'For Zeus Heraios, a pig.' The month in question is again the 'wedding' month of Gamelion. Much is missing from the inscription; the remaining part might have specified a date and place, or made a reference to Hera or to the *hieros gamos*. However, the cult title given to Zeus in this inscription is particularly interesting since it refers to 'Hera's Zeus'. Although Hera is not mentioned in the extant part of the inscription, the epithet Heraios strongly implies that Zeus was perceived as Hera's consort in this context, and was of secondary importance.

A fragment from a comedy of Menander supplies further evidence about how people may have celebrated the festival:[18]

> Chairephon, that most boastful of men, thwarted me, saying he was going to celebrate the *hieros gamos* on the twenty-ninth so that he could dine out on the twenty-seventh; the business of the goddess would go just as well.

Unfortunately we have no further information on the nature of the celebration. The point of the joke seems to be that Chairephon is a parasite who seizes every available opportunity to accept the hospitality of others, even if it means going out on the day of the *hieros gamos*. This suggests that it was normal to stay at home on the *hieros gamos*: it was probably a domestic celebration. It may have been comparable to a wedding anniversary celebration, for which married couples were expected to stay at home and celebrate together the institution of marriage.

From this combination of fragmentary and partial pieces of evidence about the *hieros gamos*, it is possible to draw some general conclusions about the festival. The principal deity was Hera, probably known under the cult title Hera Teleia, and Zeus Teleios or Heraios was also involved, though he was of secondary importance. The *hieros gamos* was celebrated in Athens itself, and in at least two demes on the same day, towards the end of the month of Gamelion, which corresponds to January. This suggests that it was a widespread festival in Attica, and was organised on a local basis, with sacrifices made in the demes. The Menander fragment implies that the *hieros gamos* usually involved staying at home to dine, perhaps because the festival was celebrated in part on a domestic basis. It is plausible to suppose that some aspects of the festival were for married people, and involved love-making between married couples. Perhaps unmarried men had no obligations to the deity, and were therefore free to dine out.

It has sometimes been suggested that the *gamos* of Zeus and Hera was enacted as part of the rituals of a *hieros gamos* festival, although there is no evidence for this. There is some evidence that a *gamos* of Zeus and Hera was imitated by worshippers at a place near Knossos in Crete, but the details remain obscure, and there is nothing to suggest that this was paralleled in Athens.[19] It has also been suggested that the wedding celebration at the end of Aristophanes' *The Birds*, in which Peisthetairos marries Basileia, is a parody of an Athenian *hieros gamos* ritual.[20] The bride and groom are not compared outright to Zeus and Hera, but a comparison is implied, since the procession of the gods mirrors the action of the wedding in the drama. In the procession the bride and groom are accompanied by the Moirai towards the bridal chamber. However, the wedding in the play need not correspond to an Attic ritual; it could be the dramatisation of the myth of the divine *gamos*.

Hera and Zeus seem to function in this festival as a paradigm for human marriage. The emphasis is on the positive aspects of their union, which serves as a guarantee for the institution of marriage on the mortal plane. Human couples celebrate marriage of the divine couple, men as well as women. This is striking, since evidence about marriage and cult largely concerns female participation. The participants in the Attic *hieros gamos* seem to have been those who were married, although the sacrifices appear to have been public ones which were made on behalf of the whole community of the deme and city. The festival may have corresponded in some way to a wedding anniversary, in that it provided an opportunity for couples to celebrate their marriages and affirm the importance of marriage within society and state.

II The Heraia at Olympia

The festival of Hera at Olympia may also be described as a celebration of marriage, though the form appears to have been very different from that of the Attic *hieros gamos*. The main festival at this site is that of Zeus; this was one of the major panhellenic festivals, celebrated with sacrifices and games and was as much a political as a religious occasion. Women were excluded from the celebration of the games of Zeus. However, there was a separate and autonomous festival for women, the Heraia.

The cult of Hera at Olympia was established relatively early, but seems to have remained less prominent than that of Zeus. However, the perception of Zeus and Hera as a couple seems to have been important at the site. Pausanias tells us that in the temple of Hera he saw an ancient group statue of Zeus and Hera together, which implies that the couple was significant in cultic terms.[21] The theme of marriage plays an important role in the foundation of the festival of Hera, and is linked in turn to the foundation myth of the games of Zeus. According to myth the king Oinomaus, ruler of Pisa, wished to preserve power by preventing his daughter Hippodameia from marrying. When suitors presented themselves, he proposed a chariot race for the hand of Hippodameia. Oinomaus had immortal chariot horses and always won, killing the suitors on the way. The thirteenth suitor was the hero Pelops, who won the race by substituting a wax pin for a wooden one in the king's chariot. He won, married Hippodameia, and gave his name to the Peloponnese; he also instituted chariot racing at the Olympic Games. The myth was prominent in the sanctuary. All visitors and worshippers must have been familiar with it, and it provided the subject for the sculptures of east pediment of the temple of Zeus at the sanctuary. Pelops and Hippodameia stand next to Zeus over the entrance to the temple, and Hippodameia wears a veil at which she plucks in a gesture which is a typical motif in bridal scenes.

The festival of Hera at Olympia is known from the account of Pausanias, who mentions various rituals which were performed by women at the festival. The games, which were its principal feature, are said to have been established by Hippodameia on the occasion of her marriage as a thank-offering to Hera. According to the myths, Hippodameia originally celebrated the Heraia with a group of sixteen *gynaikes*. From that time, a college of sixteen women cult officials took charge of the celebration of the women's games, and their duties included organising races for female competitors, who ran foot races in the stadium. The competitors were all *parthenoi,* and were divided into three age groups. The winner of each class received a crown of olive and a portion of the ox which had been sacrificed to Hera.

Races are often associated with initiation and transition ritual for children and adolescents, but are more commonly held for boys than girls. However, the division of the races into three age categories suggests that these games may have been significant in terms of the development of girls and their progress towards adulthood, which for *parthenoi* means marriage. We have a close parallel for girls' races and initiatory themes in the contests held at the festival of Artemis Brauronia in Attica. Painted pots show scenes of girls of various ages running races. There is iconographic and textual evidence to suggest that the age groups corresponded to well-defined stages in the biological and sexual development of the girls: the youngest are small children, the second group corresponds to those who have not yet attained the age of menarche, and the third group are *parthenoi* of marriageable age.[22] The three groups of girls at Olympia probably correspond more or less to the same categories as we find at Brauron. The girls participate in ritual races for Hera as part of the process of acculturation which leads them through the transitions from childhood through puberty to sexual and social maturity.

The college of women was also required to organise two ritual choruses for local heroines: Hippodameia, bride of Pelops, and Physkoa, who was associated with the foundation of the cult of Dionysus. Pausanias does not say who formed the two choruses, but since the links between Hippodameia and marriage are strong it is likely that the chorus was made up of *gynaikes*. A further duty of the sixteen women was to weave the new *peplos* offered to Hera every four years. It is unclear whether this *peplos* was specifically a wedding garment. It is tempting to suppose that it was part of a wedding costume, and there is a possible parallel for this in the cult of Persephone at Locri in South Italy.[23] However, the presentation of a new robe to a deity is a relatively common ritual, and we know of the presentation of such garments to Athena and Apollo, for whom there can be no nuptial overtones. What is worth noting is that weaving is an occupation particularly associated with women and the domestic sphere; the preparation and presentation of the *peplos* falls to women and is assigned to married women or to *parthenoi* of marriageable age.

The emphasis on marriage at the Heraia of Olympia is marked. The foundation of the festival derives from a mythical wedding, and married women played an important role in its organisation. The races for girls have the character of transition rituals, which mark the progress of the participants and their peer group through the various stages of becoming a marriageable *parthenos*. The festival is entirely female, with female participants and a female deity being honoured. Zeus is virtually absent from this ritual–myth complex, as are mortal men. The theme of marriage operates on the levels of both myth and cult: the deity Hera is divine bride and wife and patron of mortal brides. The heroine Hippodameia plays an important role, since it is her marriage which provides the *aition* for the whole festival. On the human level, it is married women who organise and participate in the festival, and who supervise rituals for young girls who will eventually become brides in their turn.

III The Daidala at Plataia

The third festival which I wish to consider is the Daidala at Plataia in Boiotia. We have relatively full accounts of the festival and of the associated myths.[24] These provide a good deal of material for commentators on the relationship between myth and ritual, and much has been written on this complex.[25]

The cult of Hera in Plataia appears to have been one of the major cults of the city. The city's temple of Hera, already a local landmark by the time of the battle of Plataia, housed two statues, one of which was made by the famous sculptor Praxiteles. The two statues were known as Hera Nympheuomene, 'Hera the Bride', and Hera Teleia, 'Married' or 'Fulfilling' Hera, or Hera the patron of brides, the same cult title as was known in Attica. Both cult titles are associated with marriage. Pausanias says that the statue of Hera the Bride is associated with a major local festival, the Daidala, which is more precisely known as two festivals, the Great Daidala and the Little Daidala. The Little Daidala was celebrated every four years, and the Great Daidala every sixty years.

We are fortunate in having two relatively good sources on the myth and festival, and can therefore reconstruct the rituals of the festival with some detail. The Little Daidala was celebrated by the Plataians every four or so years, though Pausanias' informant was a little uncertain on the precise periodicity. In the Little Daidala, the Plataians went to a sacred grove of oak trees and set out food for birds, and the tree to which the birds first flew was chosen for felling. The Plataians then made from the trunk a wooden statue (*xoanon*) of a female figure, to which they gave the name 'Daidale'.

After some fourteen cycles of the Little Daidala festival, the Great Daidala was celebrated. This was held on a much larger scale, and involved the participation of a number of other Boiotian cities. It seems therefore to have been a panboiotian affair and an event of some significance, even if it was not held very frequently. At the start of the Great Daidala, all the wooden figures which had been produced since the last Great Daidala were collected, and one was chosen by lot. The chosen figure was then designated as the bride, and underwent the wedding preparations typically observed by brides. First the figure was taken to the local River Asopos and was given the usual ritual bath in the stream. It is likely that the women of Plataia played a significant role in cleansing and preparing the *xoanon*, not least because of the assistance they give to Hera in the myth linked with the festival. Next the wooden bride was dressed up, probably in some form of bridal costume, though this is not specified. Then the figure was set in a waggon, and a local woman was designated as *nympheutria*, the bridal attendant. The waggon was conducted in a procession up to Mount Kithairon, and the participants of the festival joined in the procession, probably with music and singing to celebrate the wedding.

At the top of the mountain was a huge altar, constructed from blocks of wood. Here the final part of the festival took place. On the altar, each of the participating communities placed a cow as a sacrifice for Hera and a bull for Zeus. The wooden bride and all the other wooden figures from the Little Daidala celebrations were placed on the altar. The total number of wooden and animal victims for the participating towns was over forty, which gives some idea of the scale of the sacrifice. Wealthy individuals from the participating towns were also free to add private sacrificial victims to the altar, and the total number of victims may well have been over a hundred if we allow for all these private sacrifices. Finally, all the victims were burned in a huge and spectacular holocaust sacrifice, which could be seen for miles around.

According to the sources, the festival of the Great Daidala was a celebration of the reconciliation of Zeus and Hera after a quarrel. The accounts of Plutarch and Pausanias differ in detail, but confirm the general pattern of the myth and the ritual which it purports to explain. Plutarch gives two versions of a myth which connects Hera and Zeus with Mount Kithairon in Boiotia. The first concerns Zeus' seduction of Hera when she was a *parthenos*. The second story is presented as more frivolous, and provides the *aition* for the festival of the Daidala. According to this version, Hera and Zeus had a quarrel, and as a result, Hera withdrew from her husband. Zeus wished for a reconciliation, and was advised by the local Plataian hero Alalkomeneus to deceive Hera and make her jealous. Zeus took the advice and proceeded to pretend to marry a figure of a woman which was made from an oak tree. When she saw the false 'wedding' procession of Zeus and his wooden bride, Hera burst upon the scene with jealous fury and the women of Plataia joined her in rushing down from the mountains to interrupt the false wedding. The trick was revealed and Hera and the Plataian women then probably joined in the celebration. However, Hera was still angry at the false bride and burned it, although the figure was inanimate.

Pausanias' account of the myth is close to that of Plutarch and starts from the quarrel of the gods and Hera's withdrawal from Zeus. In this version, Zeus was advised by Kithairon to make a false bride called Daidale, and to say that she was the daughter of the River Asopos. When Hera discovered the trick she was reconciled with Zeus, and the festival of the Daidala is said to be a commemoration of that reconciliation. Pausanias goes further than Plutarch and provides the account of the rituals associated with the Daidala, but the essentials of the myth are the same. Hera withdraws from Zeus, Zeus tries to win her back through jealousy by pretending to marry a wooden bride, he succeeds in provoking his wife's jealousy and the pair are reconciled. The themes of this story are familiar from myths about the relationship of the divine couple: marital discord, the jealousy and withdrawal of Hera, the female rival for Zeus's affections, and the eventual reconciliation which is brought about by a cunning trick. It is clear that the myth functions as an *aition* for the festival, and this raises the question of the relationship between the ritual and the *logos* which is supposed to explain it.

This relationship raises a number of problems, which have received much attention. The main one stems from the relationship between the false bride and Hera. The Daidala is supposed to be a celebration of the marriage of Hera and Zeus, and the festival culminates in a huge sacrifice for the couple. However, the bride in the wedding ritual is explicitly identified as the rival of Hera, the false bride Daidale, and the wedding rituals are performed not for Hera but for her rival, the wooden bride Daidale. At the end of the festival, the bride is violently destroyed in the holocaust. It is difficult to account for all this emphasis on a false bride in a festival which is said to have been a celebration of the marriage of Zeus and Hera. The account of the festival as it stands gives far more prominence to the inanimate imposter who threatens Hera's marriage than to the deity herself. Nor does there appear to be any element in the ritual which corresponds to a reconciliation or to the re-establishment of the true couple.

No satisfactory solution has been proposed to the paradox of the Daidala and we can only speculate on possible answers to the problem. I suggest that there is a missing section in the ritual. At some point in the festival, the false bride Daidale was ousted, and her role as bride was taken over by Hera. When and how this happened is impossible to say, but this hypothesis would preserve the logic of the myth. The Daidale and the other wooden figures may have been destroyed as an act of propitiation for Hera. It is otherwise difficult to account for the destruction of so many valuable and sacred objects.

This festival, said to have been a celebration of the reconciliation of Hera with Zeus, has been described as a *hieros gamos* festival; however, it is a wedding celebration only in a certain sense. Although there are wedding preparations, there is no point which corresponds to a wedding, and no groom is present. The myth itself makes it clear that no wedding takes place because all the preparations are a trick to make Hera jealous. The festival plays upon wedding ritual and draws upon a number of themes from marriage rites, but is not a simple celebration of marriage.

The Great Daidala has a number of political and historical overtones. The participants in the Daidala are communities rather than individual brides and grooms; participation is on a communal, political rather than a personal level. There are several references in the myths to the early history of Boiotia and Plataia, since the false wedding is supposed to have taken place during the earliest history of Boiotia. The periodicity of the festival is another striking feature. Sixty years is an extraordinarily long time for the cycles of a festival, and there can have been few participants who witnessed two celebrations of the festival.

The Daidala festival celebrates Hera in her persona of marriage deity, as Hera Nympheuomene, yet it is not a celebration of marriage in the same way as the Attic *hieros gamos* can be said to be. Though the festival is said to have been founded to celebrate Hera's reconciliation to her husband, both the aitiological myth and the practices of the festival seem to focus on the quarrels of Zeus and Hera. Second, though the ritual itself is heavily dependent on themes from marriage and wedding ritual, the festival also brings together a number of communities to celebrate a deity who has regional importance as a political figure. The myth and ritual relate as much to the early history and identity of Plataia as they do to the wedding of Hera. The festival seems to be a celebration of Hera Nympheuomene, the principal deity of the *polis*, as well as a celebration of the political and cultural identity of Plataia and the cities of Boiotia.

My aim in this chapter has been to demonstrate the variety of ways in which the role of Hera as a marriage deity is articulated in different rituals and associated myths. The three festivals I have discussed are all associated with marriage, but the theme is articulated in different ways. In Attica, the *hieros gamos* is a celebration of Hera the divine bride and wife who is also patron of mortal brides and wives. The festival is set in a framework of civic cult calendars and appears to be a recognition of the importance of marriage within society. At Olympia, the Heraia is a festival exclusively for women and involves the celebration of what might be called 'wifely values'. It involves transition rituals for girls which are part of the preparation for wifehood. The participants are grouped according to their ages, which probably corresponded to distinct and well-defined stages in the progress towards adulthood and marriage. The third festival, the Daidala, draws upon myths about Hera as a bride and wife, and draws upon bridal ritual, but the festival itself seems rather to be a celebration of a poliadic and political Hera who is at the same time a bride.

The myths and rituals associated with Hera and marriage are not concerned only with Hera getting married, nor with mortal women getting married. Festivals which celebrate 'Hera, patron of marriage' do not follow a single pattern but vary considerably. They tend to focus on the characterisation of Hera as divine bride, or on the marital status of the participants, who are under the protection of the deity, or on both of these together. 'Marriage festival', like 'marriage deity', is not a clear and uncomplicated notion, and is a term which must be treated with caution.

NOTES

1 Brelich 1969; Calame 1977; Dowden 1989.
2 Sourvinou-Inwood 1987; Seaford 1987b.
3 Garland 1990: 217–25: Redfield 1982: 188–201.
4 Burkert 1985: 132.
5 Burkert 1983: 161–8 ; Avagianou 1991: 36–45.
6 Hom. *Il.* 14.330–60.
7 *Hom. Hymn to Pythian Apollo* 334–52.
8 Pötscher 1987: 95–110.
9 Avagianou 1991.
10 Salviat 1964: 647–54.
11 Aristoph. *Thesmo.* 973–6.
12 Zeitlin 1965: 463–508; Lebeck 1971: 68–73.
13 Aesch. *Eum.* 213–14.
14 Aesch. *Ag.* 973–4.
15 *SEG* XXVI 136.32; Daux 1983: 150–74.
16 *SEG* XXI 541, Erchia, Γ, 31–4
17 Sokolowski 1969: no.1.
18 Men. frag. 265.
19 Diod. Sic. 5.72; Verbruggen 1981: 53; Willetts 1962: 252–3.
20 Aristoph. *Birds* 1731–42; 1755–62.
21 Paus. 5.16.2–8.
22 Sourvinou-Inwood 1988.
23 Sourvinou-Inwood 1978: 113–14.
24 Paus. 9.2.5–4.3; Plut. frag. 157.
25 Nilsson 1906: 50–6; Frontisi-Ducroux 1975: 193–216; Pötscher 1989: 50–65; Furley 1981: 201–10; Schachter 1981: 242–50; Prandi 1983: 82–94; Avagianou 1991: 59–68.

3

DOMESTICATING ARTEMIS

Susan Guettel Cole

Artemis at the Borders of the *Polis*

Artemis, a goddess associated in particular with young women and biological maturation, was frequently worshipped at the physical margins of a *polis*, close to territorial frontiers. The rites of young women at these sites marked important transitions in the female life-cycle, but signified more than the individual female's safe passage across a personal biological boundary. The community as a whole depended on ritual activities undertaken in border areas. This chapter examines the cohesive links created between boundary and centre by women's festivals and processions and shows how the city recognised the importance of women's dedications to the goddess. Epigraphical evidence for these dedications, augmented by recently published material, demonstrates the centrality of women's religious role and the crucial part played by their offerings in securing the wellbeing and survival of the *polis*, most notably during periods of external challenge.

Sanctuaries of Artemis were often located some distance from inhabited settlements, at the extremities of a city's territory. Sacred space on a border defined the limits of a city's territory and protected the transitional area that divided one community from another. De Polignac describes such sanctuaries located on or near a border, like those of Artemis, or regional sanctuaries like that of Hera at Argos, as markers of territorial sovereignty. He concentrates on their role during the formative period of the *polis*, stressing the way in which they defined territorial solidarity and thereby marked the creation of new social and political communities during the late Geometric period (De Polignac 1994: 4–8; 1995: 32–81).

Legends about consolidation of territory during the period of early *polis* formation recognise these sanctuaries as both refuge and focus of conflict. Artemis was especially prominent in Lakonia, for instance, where her sanctuaries marked natural boundaries on both east and west. On the western border, the sanctuary of Artemis Limnatis on Mount Taygetos divided Spartan territory from Messenian. The sanctuary had a reputation as a neutral territory for shared festivals (Strabo 8.4.9), but such festivals could be a source of friction. In the earliest stages of Spartan history the Messenians were supposed to have provoked the First Messenian War by an attack on Laconian girls (*parthenoi*) celebrating a festival of Artemis here (Paus. 4.4.2).

On its eastern boundary Lakonia bordered on the territories of Argos and Tegea. The sanctuary of Artemis Karyatis, located at Karyai in Laconian territory, was nearby. It is said that under cover of a festival, enemy Messenians once kidnapped Laconian *parthenoi* from this place and held them for ransom (Paus. 4.16.9–10). These stories were told to recall Sparta's early history and to justify former defensive policies, but the concerns that originally created the border sanctuaries so prominent in myth and legend continued to require ritual attention and shape ritual practice during later periods. The civic space of the developed *polis* encompassed rural territory as well as town centres, and the gods were recognised at the outer margins of the political unit as well as at its centre. Artemis could appear in both locations, but her rituals at the margins had a special significance, and they were just as essential to the life of the *polis* as the more prominent spectacles and festivals for other divinities, performed in the central agora and acropolis of the city.[1]

When rituals of Artemis excluded males, females had no protection except that which the goddess herself could offer. Nevertheless, official festival calendars of Greek cities regularly required women and young girls to perform important public ceremonies at remote sanctuaries. These women were especially attractive targets for harassment, whether the sanctuaries were located in mountain areas, in the countryside, or where the land met the sea. Artemis was represented as protecting all three types of space (Schachter 1992: 50), and myths about her sanctuaries frequently stressed the vulnerability of her worshippers. These stories emphasised the negative consequences of interfering with the rites of the goddess, detailing horrific punishments for cities as well as for individuals. Such stories took many forms, with responsibility for incurring the goddess' wrath divided between males who molested celebrants and the females who were unable to control their own bodies.

A sanctuary of Artemis, like any sanctuary, could provide a place of refuge in time of stress or conflict (Sinn 1993), but the protection offered by Artemis to her female worshippers had a special meaning. There was a recognisable correspondence between the vulnerability of a city's women and the vulnerability of a city's borders. Challenges were considered provocative, and communities responded aggressively in retaliation. Successful celebration of female festivals at unprotected border sanctuaries was recognised as pleasing to the goddess and considered a sign of peace, security and territorial integrity. Violation of the safety of females at these sites was a sign of ritual failure and indicated that the security of the *polis* was threatened by a war with its neighbours.

Lack of respect for the boundaries of another community was expressed in myth by lack of respect for the integrity of its women. Such stories were told to justify retaliation. One story tells how Theseus abducted Helen from the sanctuary of Artemis Orthia on the Eurotas when she was still a young girl, before she reached the age of marriage. An invasion of Attika by the Spartan Tyndaridai was the result (Kearns 1989: 158).[2]

Another ancient story, one concerning a Lemnian incursion at Brauron, became part of the fifth-century rationalisation of Athenian activity at Lemnos. The sanctuary of Artemis at Brauron marked the site of an important harbour on the east coast of Attica, stepping-off place to Delos and Ionia and open to intrusion from the sea. Ancient Pelasgians from Lemnos, feuding with the Athenians, were said to have kidnapped Attic women from this sacred place and to have kept them as concubines (*pallakai*). Herodotus describes how the Lemnians had to kill the abducted women and their children in order to conceal their crime, and how consequently they themselves later suffered a three-fold disaster: blight in their crops, disease in their herds, and decline in their birthrate (Hdt. 6.137–40). Ritual transgression meant that the many could suffer from the mistakes of the few.

Females were often at risk while celebrating festivals at border or coastal sanctuaries, because sanctuaries of Artemis protected strategic, vulnerable areas. The sensitivity of these areas is measured by their frequent appearance in battle narratives or accounts of celebrated border skirmishes. To mention only the most famous, the Artemision on the straits to the north of Euboia and the sanctuary of Artemis on Salamis marked the sites of decisive naval battles in 480 BCE. Artemis' temple at Kalapodi, in the borderland between Lokris and Phokis, overlooked the pass that marked one of the most vulnerable points of entry from the north for the whole Greek mainland, the pass through which first the Thessalians, then the Persians and finally the Romans swept down into the territories of Phokis and Boiotia when they moved attacking armies into Greece (Ellinger 1987: 93).

Paradoxically, the risks of unprotected ritual were a necessary feature of the worship of Artemis. This paradox is usually explained as a consequence of initiation ritual, whereby an individual's transition to a new status is achieved by a temporary reversal of normal communal restraints and successful confrontation with the wilderness (Dowden 1989). The wilderness is symbolised in the case of Artemis by the nature of the goddess and by the location of her sanctuary (Vernant 1991). This sort of explanation, however, focusing on personal transformation, does not take into account the Greek *polis*, where ritual seems to have placed more emphasis on community than on the achievement of individual status. Unprotected ritual, performed by those who seemed most marginal to the society, was in fact part of a larger religious system, one that defined, sustained and protected the entire community. The Lacedaemonians who sent their daughters to perform the dances mentioned by Pausanias at Karyai tested Lacedaemonian strength and celebrated Laconian security by entrusting to Artemis the most vulnerable members of their community, whose safety, protected by the festival, signified and guaranteed their own.

THE ANGER OF ARTEMIS

Artemis could protect the borders of the *polis*, but she demanded a high price. The attack on the Laconian women at Karyai showed what could happen when the protection of the goddess was withdrawn. In myths associated with her sanctuaries, Artemis was apt to deny protection in situations where females demonstrated that they were not be trusted. Female unreliability was represented as a threat to the entire community, and punishment was particularly severe in cases involving ritual attendants. Young attendants, like the goddess herself, were expected to be still unmarried, *parthenoi*, and to remain sexually inexperienced for the term of office. Mythical narratives associated with particular sanctuaries, however, emphasise female duplicity and demonstrate how an entire community could suffer for one girl's carelessness. One legend describes how the *polis* of Patrai was punished with plague (*loimos*) and famine (*limos*) because a priestess of Artemis Triklaria entertained her lover in the sanctuary. The punishment was so severe because the young priestess had committed a triple violation: violation of the standards of purity for the sanctuary, violation of the requirements of sexual purity for service to Artemis, and, because the priestess represented all the young women in the community, violation of the social requirement that young women be kept from sexual experience until the time of marriage.

Pausanias describes the result of Artemis' rage and the consequent double calamity of disease and famine with, for him, unusually colourful language, echoing formulae in Herodotus' description of the punishment of the Lemnians: 'The earth no longer bore fruit and fatal diseases began to wear away the population' (Paus. 6.19.3). At Patrai, so the story goes, disease and blight could not be stopped until the Delphic oracle instructed the community to sacrifice the two lovers and to repeat the rite by sacrificing a young male and female every year. This narrative connects two issues: the failure of a *parthenos* in service to Artemis to maintain sexual purity, and the punishment of the entire community for one person's violation of a ritual requirement. In myths about Artemis these two issues are often kept separate. The Arcadian myth of Kallisto, for instance, concerned only with the first, shows the value Artemis placed on control of female sexuality. In this story, well known as early as the fifth century BCE, a young *parthenos* in service to Artemis was punished (in some versions she was turned into a bear) because she became pregnant. The fact that she was seduced is not considered relevant. She was punished because her pregnancy revealed sexual experience before marriage.[3]

The second pattern, where a story demonstrates how one person's disruption of a ritual requirement could affect the entire community, occurs in myths associated with rites of Artemis at the Attic sites of Brauron, Aulis, and Mounichia. In a version told about Brauron,[4] a young girl was supposed to have teased a bear sacred to Artemis. The bear scratched her in retaliation, and when her brothers responded by killing the bear, the whole community suffered from infectious disease (*loimodes nosos*). This plague was brought to an end only when the community established a regularly scheduled ritual, the *arkteia*, where young girls called *arktoi*, 'she-bears,' played the part of the bear and performed dances for Artemis. A variant, associated with Artemis at Mounychia, even required the girl's father to sacrifice her to the goddess (a deed he is said to have avoided by substituting a goat dressed as a girl). In these stories[5] the entire community suffered for the misbehaviour of a single member. The typical punishment in such stories is plague or pestilence (*loimos*), but one version attributed to Brauron mentions famine (*limos*; Schol. Leid. Ar. *Lys.* 645). Often mentioned together, both *loimos* and *limos* were considered serious punishments sent by the gods.[6] Artemis was more likely to be associated with disease (*loimos* or *nosos*), but disease inflicted by Artemis had specific consequences. Kallimachos makes this clear in his famous hymn to the goddess. He says that those on whom the goddess smiles have rich fields, healthy herds and long life. The unjust, however, on whom the goddess frowns, will suffer. Plague destroys their cattle, frost destroys their fields, and their women either die in childbirth or, if they do survive, give birth to infants unable to stand 'on upright ankle' (Call. *Hymn. Art.* 128).

Kallimachos draws on a tradition that associated deformed children and stillborn infants with insult to Artemis and communal failure. A similar pattern also occurs in an Arcadian narrative from Kaphyai, where Artemis Kondylea was said to have punished the local population for stoning a group of children because they had put a noose around her statue's neck (Paus. 8.23.6–7). The punishment took the form of a terrible disease that caused all infants to die in the womb. This disease was so severe that successful childbirth could not be restored until the community consulted Delphi, granted normal burial to the dead children, and honoured them with the sacrifice offered to special benefactors. The pattern of the story is familiar: a community's error offends a divinity, who sends punishment in the form of a plague or famine. Ruin is averted only when the community consults an oracle about the performance of appropriate ritual (here funeral honours for the dead children), in order to restore the normal life-cycle (Calame 1977: 281).

The story from Kaphyai explains an annual ritual in honour of the dead children and also offers a children's prank as the source for Artemis' curious epithet Apanchomene, 'Strangled'. Modern commentators have usually been satisfied to compare the epithet to rituals where images of a vegetation goddess were hung in trees (Jost 1985: 401–2, for a summary). Not satisfied with a generic explanation, however, Helen King has pointed out that the crucial element in this particular story is the medical meaning of the epithet

31

'strangled' (King 1983: 118–20), relevant here to the nature of the disease sent by the goddess. In Pausanias' account that disease had a very specific target and a very specific effect, namely, the interruption of the normal reproductive capacity of the community's women and the death of all infants before birth.

King explains the choking of the goddess in terms of Greek theories of female physiology. Hippocratic medical writers assumed a symmetry between lower and upper body entrances and exits, and they interpreted problems with breathing and swallowing as symptoms of reproductive distress. Strangulation or choking would have been an indication that menstrual bleeding was impeded. Female bleeding was considered a sign of health. Bleeding marked the important transitions in a woman's life: at menarche, at the first experience of sexual intercourse and at childbirth. Strangulation or choking would therefore have been a sign that an important female transition was incomplete. In the Hippocratic essay *Peri Parthenion*, strangulation and choking are interpreted as symptoms of impeded menstruation at the time of menarche. The Hippocratic author of this essay describes girls who suffered menstrual distress at menarche as subject to hallucinations – visions that were supposed to have driven them to attempt to hang themselves or to throw themselves down wells (*Peri Parthenion* 5–6). According to this diagnosis, strangulation or choking would indicate that a girl had not yet successfully experienced a major biological change.

At Kaphyai the descriptive epithet 'Hanged' or 'Strangled' (*Apanchomene*), when applied to Artemis herself, seems to have emphasised the asexuality of the goddess and the fact that she herself was untouched by biological change. For young girls, who had to pass through menarche and accept menstruation in order to fulfil biological and social roles, normal periodic bleeding was considered a sign of health. Artemis herself, however, could not bleed, and she could not pass through the stages of the maturation process that defined adult women. She had to be a permanent *parthenos* because she could protect girls, brides and adult women from the dangers of reproduction only if she herself was immune to its disabilities.

SERVING THE GODDESS

From Pausanias' story we are not able to reconstruct the details of the actual ritual events at Kaphyai, but the story he tells shows how successful ritual protected the women of the community from the anger of Artemis and encouraged the normal reproductive cycle. Service to the goddess represented the success of the community because success of the community was measured in terms of the reproductive capacity of its women and by the health of its children. Service to the goddess required a cycle of rituals celebrated at each stage of the female maturation process: before puberty, before marriage, between marriage and first pregnancy, during pregnancy, at time of childbirth, and for mothers, at important stages in their own children's developmental cycle. No single ceremony, however, stood out as more important than others. As Sourvinou-Inwood has said, a young girl's life was considered to be a 'series of gradual transitions based on the culturally mediated perception of biological events' (Sourvinou-Inwood 1988: 25). Artemis presided over each of these transitions. The critical series of transitions began even before the first signs of sexual development, was punctuated by the onset of menstruation, marked by the first experience of sexual intercourse, and lasted until the birth of the first child.[7] Age divisions were not precise. Hesiod divides a female's time of youth into four periods, assigning marriage to the fifth (*Works and Days* 698). At Olympia *parthenoi* were divided into three separate groups, according to age (Paus. 5.16.3). The precise age limits of each group, however, were not as important as the sequence of experience and the stages of sexual development. Greek terminology for the actual stages of the female life-cycle also indicates a certain ambiguity. *Parthenia* (usually translated 'virginity') was not necessarily coterminous with sexual inexperience, especially if that experience occurred outside of wedlock. A girl could be called *parthenos* until marriage, even if she had already borne a child (Sissa 1990: 342–43), and the status of bride, described by the Greek word *nymphe*, could last after the wedding, until the birth of the first child (Chantraine 1946–47: 228–31). Physical status and social status did not always coincide, but full adult status for a female, defined by the Greek word for woman (*gyne*), required childbirth and possibly even a living infant.

Young girls began to prepare for the event of first childbirth at an early age. Even before menarche young girls danced for Artemis, in some places playing the role of animals. At the Attic site of Brauron, in the rite called *arkteia*, girls representing the *polis* of Athens imitated she-bears, *arktoi* (Ar. *Lys.* 645). In Thessaly, girls performed a ritual where they played the part of fawns.[8] These roles were considered to be a preparation for the experience of pregnancy and childbirth.[9] At Athens, acting the she-bear for Artemis was said to be a prerequisite for sexual intercourse in marriage (Suda, s.v. ἄρκτος ἢ βραυρωνίοις), and, as Libanios says, girls were required to serve Artemis before proceeding to the service of Aphrodite (*Or.* 5; I 313, 10 Foerster).

Success at one stage of the maturation process had to be recognised in order to maintain the proper relationship with the goddess for the next stage. The anger of Artemis was always a risk. One commentator describes the girls celebrating the *arkteia* at Brauron as 'soothing' or 'appeasing' the goddess (ἀπομειλισσόμεναι τὴν θεάν; Suda, s.v. ἄρκτος ἢ βραυρωνίοις). Another says that girls had to 'placate the goddess for their virginity (*parthenia*), so that they would not be the object of revenge from her' (Schol. Theoc. 2.66).[10] The possibility of Artemis' revenge lasted until a woman had survived childbirth.

At Cyrene there were three separate stages of ritual for Artemis: the first before the age of marriage (the text is very problematic), the second as bride (*nymphe*), and the third during pregnancy (*SEG* 9.72).[11] These rituals were considered to be obligations. Females who did not perform the appropriate ceremonies had to perform propitiary sacrifices as a penalty (*zamia*). A similar obligation is implied in a dedicatory text from Thessaly. Here a husband's dedication to Artemis for the sake of his wife is described as redemption for a pledge, possibly made earlier when she served as a 'fawn' for the goddess (Clement 1934: 402).

The time of marriage was a time for looking both backwards and forwards. Girls on the eve of marriage recognised the protection of Artemis during childhood with dedications of the symbols of childhood.[12] At the same time they also sacrificed to Artemis in anticipation of their reproductive responsibility. Artemis as *Lysizonos*, 'she who loosens belts', presided over the sexual transition associated with marriage because a woman's belt was a visible sign of the invisible boundary by which she protected her body. The untying of a female's belt could represent both intercourse and childbirth. Recognition of Artemis at the time of the first breaking of this boundary was important for enlisting her support at the next (Schmitt 1977: 1063; King 1983: 121).

Childbirth itself was a crisis (Demand 1994: 70–86). Homer describes Artemis as a 'lion to women', because the goddess could strike a woman in labour with death (Hom, *Il.* 21.483). Ritual performed in advance could offer protection later. Gratitude for survival encouraged women to address Artemis as Lochia, Eulochia, Eileithyia and Genetaira, epithets stressing her role in aiding childbirth.[13] To relieve the pains of labour, women prayed to Artemis Soodina (*IG* VII 3407, Chaironeia) and to a 'twin' Artemis called Artemides Praiai ('The Double Tamed Artemises' *IG* VII 3101; Lebadeia). When delivered, women recognised her aid and performed sacrificial rituals called *Pausotokeia* (neuter plural, meaning something like 'rituals for ending childbirth'; Pingiatoglou 1983: 112).

Childbirth was the final test. Successful labour required a cooperative Artemis, a tamed Artemis, one who was not a lion. In the case of disasters like shipwreck or illness, people made dedications if saved or recovered (Van Straten 1981: 96–97), and surviving childbirth was likewise a well-known occasion for votive offerings. Describing the habits of Greek women, an ancient commentator remarks, 'When they bear children, they dedicate clothing to Artemis' (Schol. Call. *Hymn to Zeus* 77). The taming of Artemis was recognised by dedications representing domestic production. Women dedicated textiles made with their own hands. The goddess so often associated with the wilderness at the outer boundaries of the *polis* could be reached by products from the most intimate space of the family's home.

This contrast is well illustrated by a recently published relief from a sanctuary of Artemis at Echinos, a border town between Malis and Achaia Phthiotis, in northern Greece. The relief (Figure 3.1) shows a new mother formally presenting her young infant to Artemis (Dakoronia and Gounaropoulou

Figure 3.1 A mother (centre) presents her baby to Artemis (right). Votive relief from Echinos, late fifth century BCE.

1992: 219–23).[14] The mother offers sacrifice in thanks for her delivery and presents her daughter to the goddess in hopes of enlisting divine protection for the infant's upbringing. The infant, in her mother's arms, reaches out her own tiny hand to the goddess. The entire scene pivots around the baby's hand, the central object in the picture. Artemis herself is represented with a torch in her right hand and a quiver just barely visible behind her left shoulder, a reminder of the arrows in her arsenal, potentially fatal to women in childbirth (Hom. *Il.* 19.187; 21.103). A female servant carries a tray of offerings, apple, pomegranate, honey-cakes, myrtle branch and a bunch of grapes; the fruits are associated with fertility and sexuality. A male attendant leads in the sacrificial animal. An older woman, whose size, on a par with that of the goddess, indicates her status as donor (and probably also grandmother, perhaps the mother's mother-in-law), makes a gesture of prayer with her right hand held up, palm forward. Behind the figures, across the top of the relief, a clothesline is strung, and hanging on the line we see a pair of shoes, a shirt, two fringed garments, and a belted peplos.[15] Inscriptions elsewhere record the garments given in such situations, but this is the first known example of items actually pictured, an example especially important because it gives a context for an act of dedication. The scene marks the culmination of an important cycle for the mother, and as the baby reaches out to the goddess, a new cycle has begun.

I DEITIES AND THEIR WORSHIPPERS

Gifts for the Goddess

Dedications to Artemis, like the dedications to other kourotrophic divinities who nurtured the young, indicate a concern for female reproductive processes and the physical development of infants (Hadzisteliou Price 1978: 89, 137). Representations of female body parts occur often as votives in sanctuaries of Artemis. One of the earliest items from the temple of Artemis at Ephesos, from the foundation deposit of the original archaic temple, was a tiny gold object in the shape of a vulva.[16] Breasts and vulvae appear elsewhere (at Athens, Eleutherna on Crete,[17] Aivatlar, and Menge). Delian temple inventories record the dedication to Artemis of two silver wombs.[18]

Other items dedicated to Artemis are personal possessions whose relation to reproduction is not so obvious. These items include the tools women used in spinning and weaving and the products their work produced. Items found at Brauron include implements such as spindles, spindle whorls, loom weights and epinetra (thigh guards used for preparing wool for spinning). The textiles and garments actually donated survive only in the lists preserved on stone, but the place where the woven garments were displayed, hung on racks, has been located by excavation (Kondis 1967: 173–5 and pl. 106).

Dedications of textiles marked all stages of the female ritual cycle. The Hippocratic writer who wrote the short essay *Peri Parthenion* had little confidence in the efficacy of such offerings. When a girl suffering from the hallucinations associated with menstrual disorders attempted to strangle herself, he himself relied on physical therapies. His contempt for ritual nevertheless confirms its importance to his patients. He says that when girls recovered from the emotional trauma associated with first menstruation, women dedicated the most perfect examples of their own weaving to Artemis:

> And the virgins, those who are ripe for marriage, if they remain unmarried, suffer this more at the same time with the onslaught of their menstrual cycle . . . and when the girl comes to her senses, the women dedicate to Artemis many other things, but especially the most carefully finished of their female clothing, because the oracles demand it, but they are deceived.
>
> (*Peri Parthenion* 5–6)

This description of the women's dedications contains two important pieces of information. First, the writer stresses the role of oracles. Families consulted oracles in response to symptoms of reproductive failure, just as the communities in the myths associated with Artemis consulted oracles to avoid reproductive blight. The city and the family use the same procedures; both family and city look to ritual for remedies. Second, the samples of clothing dedicated by the women are described as *polutelestata*, 'expensive', or 'completely finished'. Adult females are described as responding to the recovery of their daughters with dedications of the finest examples of their own handiwork. The goddess deserved the best.

The most detailed evidence for such textiles survives on stone, in a series of inscribed inventories from Athens and Brauron. These inscriptions catalogue important dedications to Artemis Brauronia, whose major festival was organised and supervised by the *polis* (*Ath. Pol.* 54.7).[19] The lists from Athens,[20] inscribed on large stone stelai (slabs), record the year by year accounts of precious gifts once displayed at the sanctuary at Brauron. They are grouped according to material: gold, textiles, bronze and wood.[21] These inscriptions, found on or near the acropolis, were probably originally set up in the stoa of Artemis Brauronia on the acropolis. A typical sample lists textiles on display as they appeared at the time of inventory, organised in order of the date of accession. Individual items were tagged with the names of the women who made them; sometimes the letters of the woman's name were even woven into the fabric. The Athenian inventories are organised according to the year of dedication and under the year, by the dedicant. A sample follows:

> When Kallimachos was archon [349/8]: a little scalloped multi-coloured chiton, Kallippe; this has the letters woven in the pattern. Chairippe, Eukoline, a dotted garment in a wooden display box. Philoumene, a chiton made of linen from Amorgos. When Theophilos was archon [348/7]: Pythias, a long spotted robe. When Themistokles was archon [342/1]: a little variegated purple chiton in a display box, Thyaine and Malthake dedicated it. A variegated purple chiton in a display box, . . . and Eukoline dedicated it. Phile, a belt. Pheidylla, a white, woman's himation in a display box. Mneso, a frog-green garment. Nausis, a lady's himation with broad purple border in wave pattern around the edge. Kleo, a delicate shawl. Phile, bordered textile. Teisikrateia, a multi-coloured Persian-style shirt with sleeves. Melitta, a white himation and a little chiton, a rag. Glykera, wife of Xantippos, a little chiton with washed out purple border and two worn garments. Nikolea, chiton of linen from Amorgos, around the seated statue. Ivory mirror with handle, on the wall; Aristodamea dedicated it.
>
> When Archios was archon [346/5]: Archestrate, daughter of Mnesistratos of Paiania, chiton with tower pattern, in a display box. Mnesistrate, daughter of Xenophilos, a white himation edged with purple; this covers the stone seated statue. A little smooth chiton for a child, without a label. It has a border in tongs pattern. Xenophante, a little scalloped fringed chiton; this is on the basket. Nikoboule, a new multi-coloured coverlet; it has a figured design in the middle: Dionysus pouring a libation and a woman pouring wine.

Aristeia, a coverlet in a display box, in the middle it has figures with right hands joined. When Euboulos was archon [345/4]: a fine shawl, it is inscribed 'sacred to Artemis', around the old statue, Theano made it.

(*IG* II² 1514.7–38)

The inventories record the items handed over when the administrative office was transferred from one board to the next, and because each board was responsible for the items under its jurisdiction, care was taken to describe garments in some detail. The garments remained on display for many years; the same lists (with some variation) are therefore repeated from year to year. Dated lists survive from the middle of the fourth century BCE. No complete prescript survives, but explicit references to statues of Artemis and her possessions (e.g., 'sacred to Artemis'), indicate that Artemis was the principal recipient.

Clothing catalogues for other divinities are not uncommon, but in most cases, the clothing differs from that of the Attic texts. Clothing for other divinities tends to be given for dressing a particular cult statue and therefore is uniform in style and size (Romano 1988: 131–2). The Athenian inventories do indicate that some items were draped over a statue, but most of the Attic items, in a variety of sizes and styles, were clearly not made for the divinity. These garments were personal possessions, either belonging to the individual who gave the gift or the one on whose behalf the offering was made. Two other lists, however, one for Demeter at Tanagra and another from Miletos, are like the Attic texts. In all three places the clothing catalogued is primarily women's clothing. Most striking in all of these lists is the diversity. Belts, cloaks, tunics, headgear, veils and shawls, some made from fine materials, some in exotic styles, indicate that dedications were chosen from the best that individuals had to offer. Some items may have been clothing required for a specific ritual: *krokotoi* (yellow dresses), known to have been worn by the *arktoi* at Brauron (Ar. *Lys.* 644–45), appear several times in the Athenian lists. A *kalas(e)iris* at Miletos may have been the same type of ritual garment known from Andania (Günther 1988: 224). The variety of sizes indicates the possibility that the dedications pertained to life-cycle rituals. At Athens and Miletos there are a number of children's garments listed, and the list from Miletos also includes garments for ephebes. The four ephebic cloaks (*chlamydes ephebikai*) on the Milesian list could be dedications made by young men (or their mothers?) to mark service as ephebes. The only explicitly male item not easily associable with a life-cycle ritual is the 'man's cloak' (*himation andreion*), with no name attached, on an Athenian list, an item which could have been dedicated as a sample of a woman's work (*IG* II² 1514.47). The Milesian text, organised by condition and type of garment, lists only old, extremely frayed textiles:

a beautiful, old, useless eastern-style long garment, grey in the middle, with gold border; an old useless himation, bright in colour, with purple border; eight old useless purple garments, frayed; three old useless fine wool mantles, frayed; three purple-dyed himatia, useless and frayed; an old Karpasian linen garment; an old useless Sidonian garment; three old useless pieces of fine linen; two other linen napkins, frayed; four old useless ephebic capes; four old useless silken masks [veils?]; two other old useless pieces of wool; twelve old useless pieces of linen, an old linen head-dress, two other ones, useless; another one, half worn out, frayed; another useless silken one, frayed; another silken one, half worn to pieces, frayed; two light-green cut woollen ribbons, frayed; another old scarlet one, frayed; two old belts overlaid with gold, another old, bright red one with gold embroidered wave pattern; a woollen belt with gold overlaid, old and frayed; another of linen with a little clasp below, half worn out; ... Aianaios [?] dedicated [it?]; two old belts; two other old ones, larger; a small purple woollen mantle and one with a fine purple border, both for children, frayed; and other children's clothing, frayed.[22]

Both the beginning and end of the text are lost, but it is likely that this is a catalogue of garments dedicated to Artemis. Artemis Kithone (Artemis Clothed-in-a-Tunic)[23] was well known at Miletos.[24] The high proportion of belts on this list would therefore be another indication of Artemis' involvement in the transitional stages of a woman's life.[25]

The clothing at Miletos was savaged by age, not by use.[26] Age nevertheless did not obliterate its value. Once presented to the goddess, the garments could not be destroyed or thrown away. Made sacred by the act of dedication itself, they had to remain in the sanctuary, where they could eventually be disposed of only by burial within the sacred area. These were valuable items, representing the best clothing their donors possessed, given to the divinity to mark very special occasions. Their value for the city was reckoned not only by the value of the garment, but by the meaning of those occasions. In the case of Milesian ephebes, the occasion produced a new male citizen. In the case of the women who dedicated their belts, headgear and elaborate dresses, or the clothing of their children, the issue was not a single occasion but a full cycle of rituals to produce an adult woman. The clothing described by the Hippocratic writer as *polutelestata*, 'expensive', but also 'completely finished', dedicated by women on behalf of daughters recovered from menstrual difficulties, measured the woman a daughter would become.

The interest of the *polis* was the reproduction of the family, the basic unit of the *polis* itself.[27] A barren woman was a liability, but a woman who died too soon, as *parthenos*, as *nymphe*, or in childbirth itself, could be a greater potential liability to the community than a barren woman who lived out her life. Without children, females who died too soon were doomed to roam as *aoroi*, the untimely dead. Those who died as a result of reproductive crises would have been a threat to infants and mothers of other families, like the well-known frightening spirits Mormo, Gello and Lamia, believed responsible for the sudden death of new babies, little children and new mothers (Johnston 1995: 366–70).

The lists on stone of the elaborate clothing made by women's hands testify to the continuing concern of the classical *polis* for the rituals of Artemis. In the fifth century, perhaps during the years of the Peloponnesian Wars,[28] the Athenians expanded the Braunonion on the Acropolis, satellite to Artemis' sanctuary at Brauron. They did this in part because they had a political and economic interest in Brauron,[29] but they were also committed to the goddess because Artemis nurtured the children of the community. The little girls who took part in rituals like the *arkteia* were protecting their own productive lives ahead,[30] but the little girls who took part in the *arkteia* of the Athenian penteteric (quadrennial) Brauronia,[31] a select few chosen from the best families,[32] were representing the young female community of the entire city. Just as the entire community could suffer from one person's disruption of ritual, so too could the entire community benefit from one person's responsible and correct performance of ritual.

The females who danced for Artemis at the borders of the *polis* danced for the entire community. The part represented the whole. Successful performance of female rituals therefore reaffirmed the community's ability to protect its women and to protect, nourish and increase itself. As Kearns has made clear, in rituals concerned with the preservation of the city, groups that appear most marginal played a central role (Kearns 1990: 336–7). Precisely those characteristics that made females the most vulnerable members of the community also defined their importance. The females who walked unmolested from Athens to Brauron at the time of the Brauronia tested with their own bodies the security of the community. Processions and festivals that linked border territories with the heart of the city expressed the confidence and security of a community which was safe from incursion. They also served to identify a community which was secure and confident in its own future.

The traditional stories about intrusion on women's rites at remote sanctuaries recognised women's centrality. These stories were told not so much to record actual events as to rationalize policy. Theseus' abduction of Helen from the sanctuary of Artemis Orthia near Sparta set the stage for divine disapproval (mythographers stress that Theseus abducted the girl before she reached the right age for marriage), but it also provided a justification for later invasion of Attica by Lacedaemonians. For the same reasons, Herodotus tells the story about the Lemnian abduction of Athenian women from Brauron, demonstrating how it explains the Athenian military control of Lemnos in the fifth century BCE (Hdt. 6.137–40). Acknowledgement of the gods, appeals to precedents for divine support and political realities were always intertwined.

A series of partially published inscriptions from Brauron now gives us some idea of how a *polis* recognised Artemis during a real war. Brauron was still a strategic harbour in the mid-fifth century. The first inscription indicates that some time during that period the Athenians erected at the sanctuary an important decree, an inventory of the sacred funds of Artemis and Apollo (*SEG* 37.31). The same sanctuary also seems to have been a concern during the years of the Peloponnesian War (431–404 BCE), the period when the rural population of Attika withdrew within the walls of Athens for protection from annual Spartan invasions. A second inscription at Brauron, dated 416/15 BCE lists important dedications moved at that time to Athens for security, to be placed under the jurisdiction of the Treasurers of the Other Gods (*SEG* 37.30; Peppas-Delmousou 1988: 324–44). This decree includes a record of the loans repaid by the Athenians to Artemis Brauronia. The goddess was therefore deeply involved in the Athenian war effort, with her support acknowledged during the period of the lull in hostilities after the Peace of Nicias in 421 BCE. The fact that the text was set up at Brauron indicates that the Athenians were able to use the sanctuary during the temporary peace. When the Athenians found it necessary to move valuable dedications to Athens in 416/15 BCE, it is clear that they expected hostilities to be renewed. They therefore did not anticipate being able to maintain the quadrennial festival of the Brauronia, one that required a procession of young females to Brauron.[33] The inventories of the fourth century, however, as records of ritual for Artemis at Brauron, indicate that regular celebrations of the Brauronia were resumed after the war. Finally, in the third century, a third inscription describes how the Athenians appointed a special committee to confer about the maintenance of buildings and equipment in the sanctuary at Brauron (*SEG* 37.89). This inscription tells us that the catalogues of sacred offerings and the offerings themselves fell under the purview of this committee. Artemis is recognised in this inscription as having a special responsibility for the population of the city. The Athenians who directed the committee to evaluate and preserve these dedications described them as: 'all the other things which the city dedicated to the goddess for the sake of the health and security (*soteria*) of the *demos* of the Athenians'. This formula recognises the support of the goddess and acknowledges the gifts made to encourage that support.

The sacred inventories were more than records of administrative procedure. The textiles displayed in the sanctuary reminded the city of acts of individual piety, but when the garments for Artemis were inventoried and listed on public documents, the meaning of the display became greater than the accumulation of the details of the individual objects themselves. The inventories accomplished two things. As records of gratitude for the protection of the goddess, they reminded the community of the successful performance of public ritual. The stones on which the texts were inscribed, however, as gifts to the gods, stood to remind the gods of a history of collective ritual. Displayed by the city at both sanctuaries, sometimes even in duplicate, these inventories symbolised the city's achievement in promoting its rituals, supervising its women and producing its crop of healthy children.

NOTES

1 Pausanias mentions eighty-six shrines of Artemis (including places with only a statue or an altar) in seventy-one *poleis*; only fifteen are described as located in an agora. Pausanias does not always define the exact location of a sanctuary, but he does locate eighteen out of forty-nine Peloponnesian sanctuaries of Artemis on the road between two towns or at the borders between two territories. For a detailed catalogue of Peloponnesian sanctuaries of Artemis, see now Brulotte 1994.
2 The consequences of Helen's youth are important for the multiple versions of this story. See Lyons 1996: 138–9.
3 Sissa 1990: 358, for the necessity of a visible test for virginity; Henrichs 1987: 254–67, for analysis of the sources for Kallisto.
4 Suda s.v. ἄρκτος ἢ βραυρωνίοις, reading Φιλαιδῶν for the mss. Φλαυιδῶν. Philaidai is the deme where the sanctuary of Brauron was located; Sale 1975: 268.
5 The sources are conveniently quoted and analysed by Sale 1975: 265–84.
6 Considered as forms of suffering sent by the gods; see Delcourt 1938. For plague as a general issue in myths associated with Artemis, see Brulé 1987: 183–5, 201, 218–22.
7 King 1983: 122.
8 An inscription from Demetrias (Pagasai), in Thessaly, of the late second century BCE, states: 'Dynatis, daughter of Melanthios, (dedicates this), having served as fawn to Artemis of Pagasai'; *IG* IX.2 1123. Another dedication, found near Larisa mentions a woman who had served as a fawn to Artemis; Clement 1934: 402. Two new inscriptions from Atrax, near Larisa, record dedications of females who had 'played the fawn' for Artemis; see Tziafalias 1980: 276 (*SEG* 34.486) and 1988: 277.
9 For the tradition of bears as symbols of maternity, see Perlman 1989: 112–19; Osborne 1985: 163. Lyons 1996: 146–8 explains the theme of ritual substitution in narratives about Artemis and Iphigeneia.
10 For a fuller discussion, see Kearns 1989: 29.
11 For a convenient translation and helpful commentary, see Parker 1983: 344–6; for a summary, see Perlman 1989: 128–30.
12 A relief from Tyndaris (first century BCE) shows a young girl accompanied by parents making a sacrifice to Artemis Eupraxia; Deubner 1925: 210–12 and pl. 1.
13 For a catalogue of inscriptions where Artemis is named as a goddess of childbirth, see Pingiatoglou 1981: 163–9, E65–108; 107–112 (with many examples from Gonnoi). Artemis Eileithyia is more common epigraphically, where occasionally the epithet occurs as an independent name for another figure worshipped together with the goddess. Artemis Lochia is more common in literary sources.
14 For detailed discussion and enlarged views of individual figures, see Dakoronia and Gounaropoulou 1992.
15 Dakoronia and Gounaropoulou admit that it is difficult to identify these garments with the technical vocabulary of garments in inscriptions. My interpretation of the images differs from theirs in one respect. They identify the fringed garments as bedding; I prefer, from the size, to consider them clothing.
16 Van Straten 1981: 135; late eighth century or early seventh century BCE.

17 *ICrete* II XII no. 24, a relief plaque with two breasts, is inscribed: 'Soteria dedicated this relief according to her vow to Artemis Dynatera ('All-Powerful').' The preceding inscription, no. 23, describes Artemis as having saved a woman's life; see Van Straten 1981: 133.
18 *IDelos* 1442 A 55 (145/44 BCE).
19 For inventories as indication of public administration of a sanctuary, see Aleshire 1989: 14 n.5.
20 From the fragments published as *IG* II^2 1514–1531 Linders (1972) reconstructs six stelai. These stelai were inscribed with inventories of dedications to Artemis Brauronia made between years 355 and 336 BCE.
21 Linders 1972: 72. New inscriptions, found at Brauron, remain unpublished. The function of the building on the Athenian acropolis, a stoa, not a temple, is not known.
22 Found in 1912, the text has only recently been published; see Günther 1988: 221.
23 Artemis 'Clothed-in-a-Tunic' may be similar to Artemis Katagogis, which Perlman (1989: 127) translates as 'Artemis the Clothed'. Katagogis refers to an item of female apparel.
24 See Günther 1988: 234–35 for evidence (including a new inscription from the late archaic period) for Artemis Kithone at Miletos. For the traditions associated with her myths, see Burkert 1979: 131–2.
25 The diffusion of belts as dedications for Artemis is well summarised by Simon 1986: 204–5.
26 The Greek word I have translated by the English word 'frayed' is used by Aristophanes (describing Milesian wool) to mean 'gnawed' by moths; Ar. *Lys.* 728–30.
27 For representations on Attic grave reliefs of women dying in childbirth, see Vedder 1988: 161–91.
28 Little remains but the cuttings for the foundations. It is clear that there were at least two building periods on the site, but Rhodes and Dobbins (1979: 326–41) are able to distinguish three building phases. The shape of the Brauronion on the acropolis, an asymmetrical Pi-shape, with right wing longer than left, mirrors that of the stoa at Brauron, which remained unfinished after a flood in the fourth century BCE. Treheux, 1988: 354 n.31, argues that use of the singular (ἱερόν, *IG* II^2 1518, B col. II. 63–64) referring to both the sanctuary at Brauron and the building on the Athenian acropolis, indicates that they were thought of as a single sanctuary.
29 Not least because the harbour gave protected access to Delos from the east coast of Attica; the implications are worked out by Peppas-Delmousou (1988: 324–44), commenting on an unpublished inscription that mentions sacred funds of Apollo.
30 The diffusion of krateriskoi, the characteristic ritual vessel of the *arkteia*, in sanctuaries of Artemis throughout Attica (Cole 1984: 240 n.40 for references) indicates that the *arkteia* in some form may have been celebrated locally.
31 Lysistrata's boast may imply a complete penteteric cycle of ritual responsibilities for daughters of the elite (Ar. *Lys.* 642–47). Sourvinou-Inwood (1988: 113) argues persuasively that for the penteteric *arkteia* girls represented their deme and tribe. For *ergastinai* (women who wove the sacred *peplos* for Athena) chosen by tribe, she compares *IG* II^2 1034, 1036 (includes *parthenoi* who assisted), 1060, 1942, 1943.
32 Of 125 names on the Athenian lists, sixteen include a term indicating deme of origin (demotic). Seven of the sixteen husbands are known elsewhere (Osborne 1985: 158–59).
33 This festival was grouped with all other quadrennial festivals, all of which (except the Panathenaia) were under the jurisdiction of the ten hieropoioi; *Ath. Pol.* 54.7.

Part II

OBJECTS OF WORSHIP

4

MARRIAGE AND THE MAIDEN
Narratives on the Parthenon

Sue Blundell

In an essay entitled 'What is a goddess?', Nicole Loraux (1992: 13–14, 17) has outlined two hypotheses concerning the nature of female divinity in Greek thought. The first is that a goddess is simply 'a god in the feminine' – nothing more than the feminine form of the word 'god'. The second, alternative hypothesis is that a goddess's femininity is one of her essential characteristics, an interpretation which according to Loraux suggests two further possibilities. If it is essential, a goddess's femininity may either be the same as that found in ordinary mortal women or it may be of a different, more intense kind,[1] since a feminine trait, when projected from the world of humans onto that of the immortals, may become 'purified' and detached from the everyday feminine condition. In my analysis of the narratives that surrounded Athene on the Parthenon, I shall be arguing that the visual construction of the goddess's identity in these sculptures corresponded to the last of Loraux' formulations – that of an essential but more intense femininity. In spite of the mannish elements in her dress and her involvement in masculine activities, Athene's femininity was not being suppressed in the images which decorated the Parthenon; rather, it was being acknowledged as different from that of human females. At the core of this difference lay the fact that on a temple dedicated to a virgin goddess, marriage was being presented as the paradigm of an ordered civilization.

Acknowledgement of difference would have seemed to many Athenians of the fifth century BCE to be a crucial element in their representation of their patron deity. In myth, Athene was notable for her consistent refusal to marry, and hence for her repudiation of an institution which was seen as fundamental to the cohesion of the Athenian *polis*. Much of the social legislation introduced in Athens from the late seventh century BCE onwards had been aimed at protecting the integrity of the property-owning family, or *oikos*, whose maintenance as a viable economic unit was vital to the stability of the state as a whole. To this end, measures prescribing the regulation of marriage practices had been introduced, so that the framework for the organisation of relations between women and men was increasingly provided by the *polis* rather than the *oikos*. The dowry, though not in itself a legal requirement for a valid marriage, was subject to a number of statutory rules: for example, a husband was obliged to return its full amount to his wife's next-of-kin on the dissolution of their marriage, thus considerably increasing the woman's chances of a further union. Adultery – having sex with the wife of an Athenian citizen – became a public offence, for which the maximum penalty was death, while the wife involved in an adulterous relationship was punished by being barred from participation in state religious activities. To ensure the preservation of an *oikos* whose deceased male head had produced no sons, his daughter (termed the *epikleros*) was obliged by law to marry her father's next-of-kin; her son or sons eventually inherited their grandfather's property, and in this way filled the place of the missing heir. Divorce was not itself governed by any legal process, but an obligation to divorce was imposed in situations where a wife had either committed adultery, or had become an *epikleros* and had to be married to the next-of-kin. Legal regulations such as these, while helping to secure the provision of legitimate male heirs, at the same time maintained marriage as a flexible institution which could be made to accommodate the transfer of partners to new households should the reproduction of the existing social order require this.[2]

In 451 BCE, just four years before work on the Parthenon began, the political and social significance of marriage had been further underlined by the introduction of a new citizenship law drawn up by the statesman Pericles. This stipulated that, in order to qualify as an Athenian citizen, a man had to be of Athenian parentage on both sides and not just, as previously, on that of his father. The objectives underlying this law have been much discussed. One of its effects would certainly have been to deter Athenian citizens from marrying non-Athenian women, and hence to place much greater emphasis on marriage within the community. In this way, the kinship bonds uniting individual *oikoi* within the *polis* would have been significantly strengthened. The law would undoubtedly have generated a degree of controversy, since it excluded from citizenship the sons of those men already married to non-Athenians,[3] who would now be assigned the status of resident aliens.

At the same time, marriage was receiving a great deal of cultural attention. Most of the surviving Athenian tragedies deal with this topic to one degree or another. Among the most notable examples are the three plays which make up Aeschylus' *Oresteia* trilogy, produced in 457 BCE. In these, the story of King Agamemnon's murder at the hands of his wife Clytemnestra and the avenging of his death by their son Orestes is used as a vehicle for examining the relative significance of marriage and blood ties within the developing institutional framework of the democratic *polis*. The importance of marriage as a social bond was highlighted in the vase-paintings of the late sixth and fifth centuries BCE: artists representing the Athenian wedding frequently chose to depict, as its most distinctive ritual, the dynamic occasion of the wedding procession. The public transfer of the bride and her possessions from her father's to her husband's *oikos* was converted through the medium of the painting into a permanent spectacle, symbolising the ties that marriage created within the *polis*. On the *pyxis*, or cylindrical cosmetics jar, this notion was sometimes reinforced by the inclusion in the scene of a single door: the procession moves away from this door but also moves towards it, so that the two *oikoi*, the one which the bride is leaving and the one which she is going to join, are brought together in a single image.[4] In one *pyxis* in the British Museum, the body of the vessel shows a wedding procession with door (Figure 4.1), while its lid depicts another kind of orderly movement, that of the personified Sun, Moon and Night, with their horses: here marriage seems to be identified as an element of stability not just within the *polis*, but within the cosmos as a whole.[5]

When marriage was being accorded such a high cultural profile it is perhaps not surprising that its potency as a civilizing force should have been celebrated on the outstanding architectural monument of the period. The fact that the Athenian Acropolis was the site of many of the religious rituals performed by young Athenian women must surely in itself have ensured that some acknowledgment of the major social role attributed to women would be included in the decoration of the Parthenon. Just as warfare was seen as the determining activity of the young male, so marriage was regarded as the female's ultimate and definitive destination, and in the sculpture attached to the new temple of Athene these two themes were intertwined. The celebration of marriage on the Parthenon was certainly rendered paradoxical by the temple's association with a goddess who steadfastly rejected the role of wife, but this was not the first time that the paradox had been brought to the attention of the Athenians. In the *Eumenides*, the last play in Aeschylus' *Oresteia* trilogy, staged ten years before the Parthenon was commenced, Athene at the trial of Orestes affirms the importance of the marriage tie by agreeing that killing a husband (Clytemnestra's offence) is a more serious crime than killing a mother (Orestes' offence). In giving her casting vote in favour of Orestes' acquittal, she announces, 'I honour the male in all things, apart from marriage. With all my heart I am the child of the father.' (*Eumenides* 737–8). The Parthenon, I believe, was making a similar statement about Athene. In its sculptures, a discourse concerning marriage was being presented in structural opposition to the theme of the goddess's virginity.

Designed as a replacement for the temples which the Persians had destroyed when they sacked Athens in 480 and 479 BCE, the Parthenon was constructed between 447 and 432.[6] It was dedicated to Athene, and was probably linked to the main cult of the goddess on the Acropolis, that of Athene Polias, the protector of the city. However, although there is little evidence to suggest the existence at this stage of a separate cult of Athene Parthenos (or Virgin), the building soon became known as the Parthenon, while the colossal statue which it housed acquired the name of Parthenos.[7] In

Figure 4.1 A wedding procession, with door. Attic red-figure pyxis attributed to the Marlay Painter, c.440 BCE.

its overall design and most of its detailing, the Parthenon was a conventional Doric temple; but in terms of both its size and the richness of its sculptural decoration it was exceptionally impressive, and incorporated a number of unusual features. Sculpture was applied to three principal external elements: the pediments (the low-pitched gables at either end of the building); the metopes (separate rectangular slabs above the outer columns on all four sides); and the frieze, a continuous band of low relief in the Ionic style – an innovation in a basically Doric structure – which extended above the porches and along the external walls of the cella, or inner chamber (Figure 4.2). Forming a backdrop to rituals performed on behalf of the community in Athens' most prominent sanctuary, the building as a whole would undoubtedly have had a religious impact, and would have been seen as making statements about divinity in general and about the goddess Athene in particular. But the Parthenon was also a major monument erected by the state to celebrate both its current eminence and its earlier victories in the epic struggle against the Persians[8] and as such it would have given expression to some of the fundamental tenets of Athens' civic and military ideology. The Athenians themselves would not have perceived any contradiction here. Athene the patron deity of Athens was both a divine being and the symbol of the *polis*. Where the Parthenon sculptures were concerned, construction of meaning would have occurred in the context of a complex interweaving of political and religious motifs.

An elaborate work of art like the Parthenon and its sculptures was many layered in its significance. In highlighting just one of these layers of meaning I am not attempting to attribute to it any kind of priority, but rather to draw attention to an underlying sculptural theme which was intimately bound up with the goddess's identity. Responsibility for the creation of the Parthenon's thematic programme probably lay with a number of official personnel, although it is impossible now for us to identify these people with any certainty. The sculptor Pheidias, the creator of the Parthenos statue, was also the general overseer of works on the Acropolis, and as such he may have been given the task of producing an overall design for the Parthenon sculptures. But he may also have had to secure the approval of one of the committees of Athenian citizens which operated as part of the democratic constitution, as was the case with the artists who prepared designs for the *peplos* or robe presented to Athene at the Panathenaia festival.[9] In making their choice of themes, both the sculptor and the committee would have been constrained to some extent by artistic conventions and by earlier decisions about the values to be promoted in major public monuments. But, at this time of rapid social change and burgeoning self-confidence, elaborations and innovations were also to be expected. When the Parthenon was being constructed Athens was at the height of her power and prosperity, and the designers of the Parthenon sculptures could probably rely on appealing to a shared set of assumptions about the merit of Athens' political and cultural achievements, while at the same

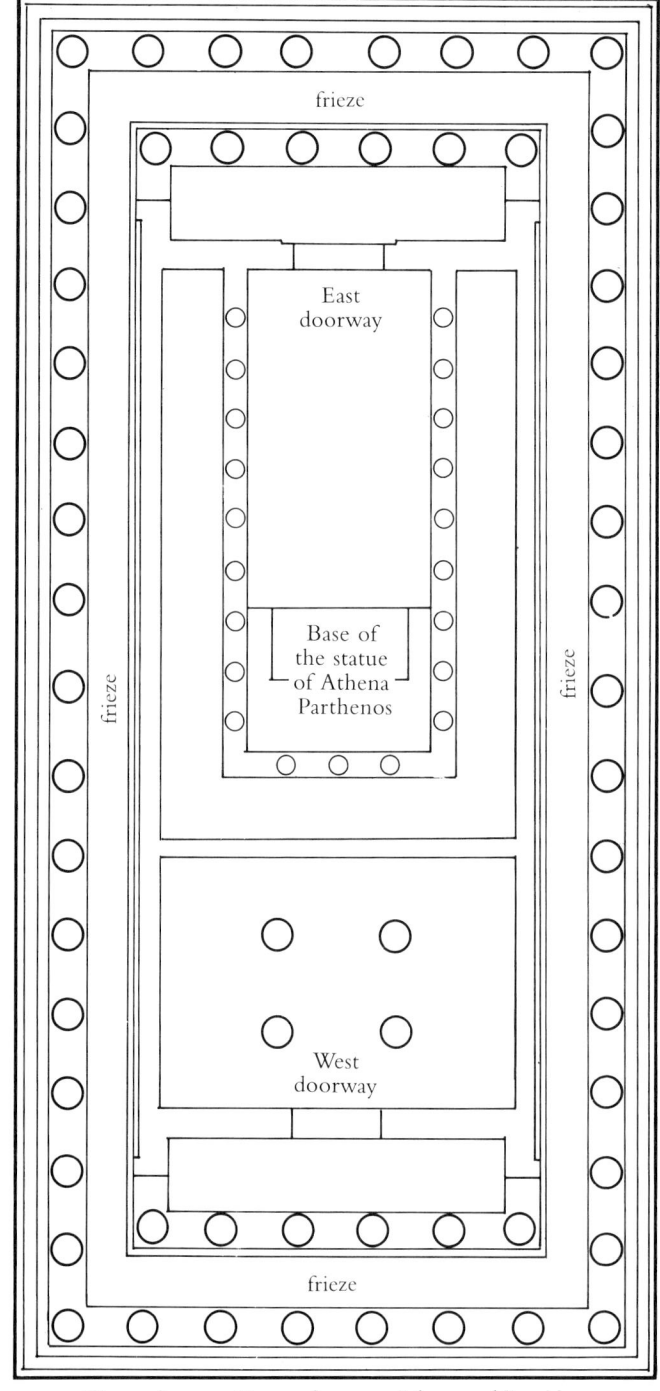

Figure 4.2 Plan of the Parthenon, showing the position of the pediment sculptures, the metopes, and the frieze.

time feeling free to introduce references of a more controversial character. As we have seen, marriage was not a new theme for the Athenians but, during the period when the consequences of the Periclean citizenship law were still being assimilated, the topic may have acquired a new relevance. At this juncture the Parthenon's designers may well have considered that a restatement of the cohesive power of this vital social institution would constitute a worthwhile subtext. The majority of Athenian citizens would probably not have dissented radically from the general tenor of the values being presented in the sculptures, but even among these viewers the subject of marriage may have provoked a degree of tension; while other visitors, particularly women and resident aliens, are likely to have contemplated official pronouncements on this issue from a more critical perspective.

The Parthenon sculptures could not be viewed statically; to see them the spectator had to move around the building, so that interpretation became a dynamic and physically participative process.[10] A fifth-century visitor to the Acropolis (Figure 4.3) approached the temple at its western end, and saw, in the west pediment, a set of sculptures which told the story of Athene's successful bid to become patron deity of the city when she defeated the god of the sea, Poseidon, in a contest.[11] The historian Herodotus (8.55) makes a brief reference to this confrontation but unfortunately none of the more detailed accounts of the event which survive is contemporary with the Parthenon. According to Apollodorus (3.14.1), who may have been writing as late as the second century AD, the contest took place during the reign of Kekrops, the legendary first king of Athens. Poseidon, arriving on the Acropolis in advance of his rival, laid claim to the city as his special place of worship by striking the rock with his trident and producing a 'sea'; but Athene soon put in an appearance, and planted an olive tree. When fighting broke out between the two contestants, Zeus parted them, and appointed the twelve Olympian deities as arbiters. The decision went in Athene's favour, and Poseidon in retaliation flooded Attica. The first-century BCE writer Varro produced a rather different version, preserved by St Augustine (*City of God* 18.9), in which the sudden appearance of an olive tree and a spring of water was interpreted by the god Apollo as a manifestation of signs sent by Athene and Poseidon. Apollo told Kekrops that the citizens of Athens should decide from which of the two deities they wanted their city to take its name; once again, Athene was the victor, and Poseidon responded angrily by masterminding a flood. Hyginus (*Fab.* 164), whose handbook of myths was probably compiled between 45 and 200 AD, provides a third variant, in which Zeus alone was the judge of the contest.[12]

This story of how Athene acquired her pre-eminent position in the city may well have evoked a complex response among the Parthenon's original spectators. It was also the story of a female deity's victory over a male deity, a victory greatly resented by the loser. The anomaly implicit in a patriarchal society's worship of a powerful and independent goddess may not have been

II OBJECTS OF WORSHIP

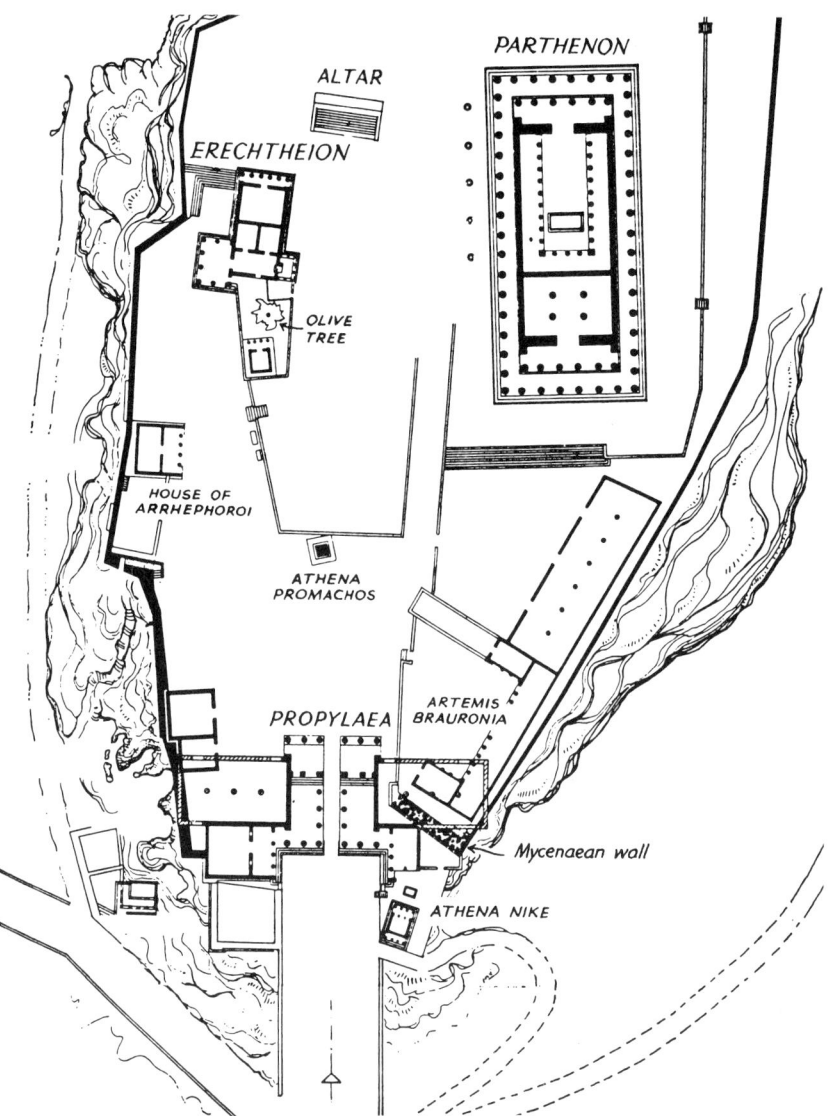

Figure 4.3 Plan of the Athenian Acropolis.

ever-present in the minds of Athenian citizens, but there were occasions when it was given conscious expression. In Aristophanes' comedy *The Birds*, produced in 414 BCE, one of the characters involved in the founding of *Cloudcuckooland*, a utopian republic in the sky, asks who the new city's patron deity will be. 'Why not Athena Polias?' his compatriot suggests. 'How could a state be well organised when a deity who was born a woman stands there in full armour . . . ?' is the prompt rejoinder (*The Birds* 826–30).

In the Parthenon, the anomaly of the goddess in full armour was being confronted and negotiated: the west pediment's visual account of Athene's ascendancy over Poseidon has to be viewed within its overall sculptural context, and in particular in relation to the narrative with which it was juxtaposed, carved on the west metopes below the pediment. This was the story of the battle between the Greeks and the Amazons, the mythical warrior women who lived apart from men, and won many famous victories, but eventually met their match when they invaded Attica, set siege to the Acropolis, and were defeated by Athens' legendary king Theseus.[13] By the 440's the Greeks versus Amazons conflict had acquired an established place in the official iconography of Athens. There can be little doubt that this episode, like the ones represented in the other metopes of the Parthenon (Greeks versus Trojans, Lapiths versus Centaurs, and Gods versus Giants), was being seen as a mythical analogue of the struggle against the Persians; and that collectively the metopes celebrated the values of order and self-control which had enabled the Greeks to withstand the onslaught of foreign invaders notorious for their arrogance and excessive behaviour. The parallel between Amazons and Persians was a particularly close one: in myth, the Amazons were most frequently located in the north-east of Asia Minor, an area which by the fifth century was part of the Persian Empire and, like the Persians, they were responsible for an incursion into Greece which was directed in particular at Athens. The identification seems to be confirmed by the fact that in vase-paintings of the second half of the fifth century the Amazons are regularly furnished with oriental dress and weaponry – leggings, leather caps, curved bows, axes and hide-covered shields.[14] In a speech composed by the orator Lysias in the early fourth century BCE, the historical implications of the Amazon invasion were given verbal expression: the defeat of the warrior women, who 'made the memory of our city's valour imperishable, and rendered their own country nameless on account of the disaster which they suffered in our land' (2.6), is paraded as the first in a long line of legendary exploits which preceded the victories won against the Persians at Marathon, Salamis and Plataea.

The Amazons then, like the other mythical opponents of the metopes, can be seen on one level as an example of the 'defeated barbarian' type. By the time that the Parthenon sculptures were being designed, the struggle against them had been adopted as one item in a patriotic recital of achievements disseminated in particular through the media of oratory and the visual arts. But when well-established narratives were brought together in a new combination within the framework of the Parthenon, they could take on fresh levels of meaning. They could make statements about the character of the civilization whose values had been so ably defended, and about its relationship to the female deity who protected it. In the case of the Amazons, these statements were likely to revolve around the one fundamental and visible characteristic which distinguished them from the Persians – their femininity. As women who practised the quintessentially masculine activity of warfare, and rejected the female's definitive role as wife, the Amazons represented a subversion of Athenian social norms. Such transgressive behaviour might flourish unchecked in barbarian territory, but when the Amazons encountered the Greeks its inherent weaknesses were bound to be displayed. Although the battle depicted in the west metopes of the Parthenon was apparently evenly-matched, with no obvious winners or losers, every Greek who contemplated this scene would have known what its outcome would be. He (or possibly she) would have been able to enjoy the spectacle of an ongoing struggle against a set of assertive and athletic female opponents, secure in the knowledge that eventually the Amazons would be defeated.

On this basis the Amazons could be represented as vigorous and sexy while still retaining their function as a negative role model. The message of their story was that women who assumed the masculine role and tried to take control of events were doomed to failure. This validation of the personal and political dominance of the human male was tellingly linked to the sculptural depiction of Athene's victory over Poseidon in the Parthenon's west pediment. At the beginning of their tour of the temple, fifth-century spectators were invited to contemplate two scenes which addressed the paradox of Athene's pre-eminence in terms of both likeness and difference. As a female warrior who repudiated the institution of marriage, Athena was dangerously like the Amazons. But she was different because in her personal confrontation with a male opponent she emerged victorious. Athene had won, but the Amazons would lose; female dominance in the divine sphere, displayed in the pediment, would be counterbalanced by the suppression of female aggrandisement in the human sphere, outlined in the metopes below.

If we take into account some of the details of the electoral arrangements described in Varro's version of the Athene versus Poseidon contest, then we can elaborate on the construction of difference being presented to the spectator at the western end of the building. The subordination of the human female may have been pictured not just as a counterweight to the goddess's supremacy, but as a direct consequence of it. The assembly of citizens which, in the Varro story, was given the task of deciding between the two deities included the female inhabitants of Athens, who at the time possessed full political rights. All the men voted for Poseidon, and all the women for Athene; and as the women outnumbered the men by one, Athene won. When Poseidon retaliated with his flood, the Athenians appeased him by imposing a three-fold penalty on the female population: women were deprived of the vote, of their ability to pass on their names to their children, and of their right to be addressed as 'Athenian women' (*Athenaiai*). In real life, women in fifth-century Athens did indeed suffer from all three disabilities, including the last: they were generally referred to not as Athenians, but as Atticans (*Attikai*).¹⁵ Unfortunately, we cannot be sure that the Varro version of the myth was current in the fifth century, and the surviving sculptures from the west pediment are so fragmentary that they give us very few clues as to narrative detail. There are, however, some indications that the designers of the pediment scene may have had this particular rendering of the story in mind. Jacques Carrey produced a drawing of the sculptures in 1674, shortly before the Venetians managed to blow the Parthenon up and inflict considerable damage at its western end,¹⁶ and in this drawing the assembled throng which witnesses the confrontation seems to include more females than males. Moreover, they all appear to be ordinary mortals: they have none of the attributes of the Olympian deities, who are the judges of the contest in Apollodorus' narrative, the main surviving alternative.

Some literary support for the existence of a Varro-type version which was contemporary with the Parthenon can be derived, tentatively, from Xenophon (*Mem.* 3.5.10), who puts into the mouth of Socrates the remark that 'Kekrops' people gave judgement in the contest'. Myths about women's rule and its overthrow by men were certainly promoted in fifth-century Athens – witness the Amazons – and it would not be surprising if a similar charter for male control had been incorporated into the story of Athene's triumph. Varro's account of female disempowerment within the family during the reign of Kekrops is matched by a piece of information relayed by Athenaeus (555D), in a section where he is quoting from the work of Clearchus of Soli, a pupil of Aristotle: 'Kekrops was the first to join one woman to one man; before, unions were loose and promiscuity was general . . . earlier, men did not know their own father, on account of the great number'. Kekrops' reign, it would seem, was recognised as a watershed in the development of a civilization in which the establishment of orderly patriarchal government was intrinsically linked to the institution of marriage.¹⁷

If we assume that the Varro version of the story was current in the fifth century and was being alluded to in the west pediment sculptures, then the narrative can be interpreted as one which explains the origins of difference. There is a causal link between Athene's pre-eminence and the political and social subordination of the human female: you cannot, in other words, have a top goddess without also having inferior mortal women. In this context, the paradox of Athene's difference was being exploited in order to elevate rather than downgrade the role of the human male. The scene in the pediment provided spectators with an account of the establishment of male dominance within Athens; when their eyes travelled downwards to the metopes they learned that Athenian men could then go on to overcome the external threat posed by women who lived by an inverse code – posed, that is, by the Amazons.

Having viewed the sculptures at the western end, the spectator walked along either the north or the south side of the building.¹⁸ The north metopes told the story of the sack of Troy; those on the south side depicted the battle between the Lapiths and the Centaurs. Both narratives served to reinforce the notion of difference constructed by the scenes at the western end, since both described the successful defence of marriage, the institution rejected by Athene. Marriage could be seen here as the model of the male-dominated system of order whose values were being proclaimed, and the assimilation of women into this system was underlined. In the Trojan War, marriage was being defended against the machinations of Paris, a non-Greek who had subverted civilised marriage exchange practices and flouted the laws of hospitality by stealing a wife from his Greek host Menelaos. The north metopes are badly damaged, but among those that survive in a reasonably decipherable condition there are two, from the western half of the series, whose subject-matter is fairly clear.[19] Menelaos is shown with his sword in his hand approaching Helen, who has taken refuge at the cult statue of a deity; Aphrodite stands between them, interceding with the deserted husband on her protégée's behalf. So as the spectator moved along the north side of the Parthenon, he or she saw at an early stage a representation of the prelude to the reinstatement of the marriage whose disruption had precipitated the clash between Greeks and Trojans.

In the battle depicted in the south metopes, the objective was the defence of marriage against bestial and promiscuous sexual activity. The Centaurs, part-horse, part-human creatures notorious for their propensity towards drunkenness and lechery, had been invited to the wedding-feast of the Lapith king Peirithoos. True to form, they imbibed too much, and tried to rape the bride and the other Lapith women present, but were vanquished by the Lapith males. A number of scholars have pointed out that, up until the end of the sixth century, the wedding and the fight had been viewed as two separate though causally linked events, with Lapiths and Centaurs meeting after the wedding in a pitched battle out in the countryside. It was only in visual representations of the fifth century that they were shown fighting it out at the wedding itself. It seems, then, that by this time the marriage theme was being emphasised and, as in the Trojan War narrative, was being intertwined with a message about the sanctity of the laws of hospitality: these two institutions were emblematic of the societal order which was being threatened by the uncontrolled and impious behaviour typical of barbarians. In the south metopes of the Parthenon, the idea of a fight precipitated by an attempted rape at a wedding banquet was conveyed by the inclusion of women in six of the scenes (Figure 4.4), and by the presence in three scenes of wine-jars, the debris of the wedding feast.[20]

All the metopes which have been discussed so far served as a frame for the Parthenon frieze: as the latter was positioned 40 feet (approx. 12 metres) above ground level, it would have been viewed most comfortably through the building's outer columns, and hence would have been bounded on its uppermost edge by the outer architrave, topped by the metope scenes (Figure 4.2).[21] Most scholars are satisfied that the procession represented in the frieze

MARRIAGE AND THE MAIDEN

Figure 4.4 A centaur carries off a Lapith woman. Metope from the south side of the Parthenon.

is the one that was staged every four years in Athene's honour as the culminating event of the Panathenaia festival. The most significant display of this kind ever mounted in historical Athens, the procession made its way from the main gate of the city to the Acropolis, where sacrifices were performed, and a newly woven *peplos*, or robe, was presented to the goddess.[22] Although it is difficult to believe that any other procession would have been depicted on the Parthenon, it has to be admitted that as a descriptive account of the event, the frieze leaves quite a lot to be desired.[23] One particular difficulty is that roughly half of it is occupied by horsemen, and no foot soldiers are depicted, although at the time the bulk of the Athenian army consisted of infantry rather than cavalry, and its representatives would undoubtedly have played a dominant role in the real-life procession. One solution to this problem has been offered by Osborne (1987: 103–4), who argues that in the frieze the spectator was being presented with an official view of the Athenian *polis*, and that this involved the application of an aristocratic image, represented by the horsemen, to the general body of Athenian citizens.[24] According to this interpretation, the heroic values which in epic poetry were attributed to the individual aristocratic warrior were in the frieze being transferred to the *polis* as a whole, of which the procession was a visual embodiment. Osborne also points out (99–100) that the frieze would have been viewed in snatches created by the outer columns, and that the frame would have been continually changing as parts of the frieze were obscured and others came into view. In this context, he suggests, the spectator was encouraged to move with the flow of the sculpted figures and hence, as it were, to join the procession and identify with the aspirations which it represented. To this analysis I would like to add a couple of points. First, the transfer of heroic values to the *polis* was made visible, in that the spectator's eye passed from the individualised scenes of legendary conflict depicted in the metopes to the image of the collective displayed in the frieze: in the layering of the Parthenon sculptures, the *polis* was wrapped around with the heroic tradition. And second, the heroic values which were seen as sustaining and uniting the *polis* included a belief in marriage as a civilizing and cohesive force.

The contradiction created by the west pediment's demonstration of Athene's pre-eminence in close proximity to scenes underlining the importance of marriage was resolved when the visitor approached the eastern end of the building. At the culmination of his or her tour around the Parthenon, the spectator came to realise that Athene's difference – the elements in her identity which distinguished her from ordinary mortal women – involved not a rejection but an intensification of her femininity. At the temple's east end, four separate images of the goddess were presented – in the pediment, in the metopes, in the frieze and, when the door of the temple was open, in the colossal statue of the Parthenos which glimmered inside. It was extremely unusual for a deity to be represented so many times on his or her own temple, so it is difficult to avoid the conclusion that the designers of the sculptures were intending to make some kind of statement about the goddess, whatever its precise significance.

The east pediment told the story of Athene's birth from the head of her father Zeus. The relevant central sculptures are missing, but a reference in Pausanias (1.24.5) helps us to identify the scene. It is one that is represented frequently in Athenian vase-paintings, although it is generally assumed that in the pediment a fully grown and not a diminutive goddess was depicted (Figure 4.5).[25] The most familiar literary account of this miraculous event was provided by Hesiod in the *Theogony* (886–900, 924–26). Soon after Zeus had established himself as sovereign among the Olympians, he received from his grandparents a prophecy that his wife Metis would one day bear a son who would rule over gods and mortals. He responded by swallowing the pregnant Metis whole, and some time later he produced Athene out of his own head. The birth of the goddess therefore helped to confirm Zeus in his pre-eminent position by forestalling a threatened takeover of his powers by a

Figure 4.5 The birth of Athene. Side A of an Attic black-figure amphora, attributed to Group E. Mid-sixth century BCE.

hypothetical son. In the east pediment of the Parthenon, the event was seen as central to an orderly universe: the birth scene was framed by an assembly of deities to whom tidings of the new arrival were being transmitted, and ultimately by a representation of the planetary system, with the chariot of the sun-god Helios rising from the waves in the south angle of the pediment, and the chariot of the moon-goddess Selene sinking down in the opposite angle. The metopes below the pediment, which depicted the battle between the Gods and the Giants, illustrated Athene's subsequent defence of her father's regime. When monstrous creatures born from the earth made an assault on Mount Olympus in an attempt to dislodge Zeus and his associates, the warrior goddess fought at her father's side and personally disposed of two of their adversaries.[26] The central positioning of the figure of Zeus in both the pediment and the metopes would have ensured that on Athene's temple the father was viewed as a dominant presence.

In interpreting these episodes, we can make use of the analysis which Vernant (1983 [1971]: 127–75) has applied to Hestia, another of the virgin goddesses. On the human level, fathers had to give their daughters away in marriage, and other men's daughters had to be imported into the *oikos* in order to reproduce it. As we have seen, the significance of this orderly exchange of womenfolk as a civilizing force had been graphically advertised in the metopes on the north and south sides of the Parthenon. But, as Vernant points out, this element of mobility in a woman's life — the fact that she and not the male made a transition from one household to another — meant that there was a fundamental ambiguity in the female's symbolic association with the fixity and permanence of the home. On the level of religious representation, however, this contradiction could be resolved in the persona of the virgin goddess, who was able to exercise her function of fertility without marrying and leaving the paternal home. Although Hestia, as goddess of the hearth, offers a more obvious example of domestic stability and fruitfulness than the extrovert warrior maiden, in her relationship with her father Athene admirably fulfilled the role which has been outlined by Vernant. She demonstrated that among the gods the relationship between father and daughter need not be fractured, because at the end of the day the divine household was self-sufficient. If he put his mind to it, Zeus could give birth all by himself. In the Parthenon sculptures, the progression from the earthly domain of Athens pictured at the west end to the vision of cosmic order in the east pediment was accompanied by a declaration about Athene which linked the two spheres of operation. The goddess's virginity made her different, but ultimately it served the same end as marriage among the humans — the maintenance of masculine control. To quote Beatrix Campbell's comment about Margaret Thatcher, another female who achieved prominence in a male-dominated society, 'She has not feminised politics ... but she has offered feminine endorsement to patriarchal power and principles.' (1987: 246). At the eastern end of the building the spectator discovered that the Parthenon's celebration of marriage did not involve any fundamental contradiction: the virgin goddess who had triumphed over her rival Poseidon was nevertheless unswervingly loyal to the male establishment.

In these narratives the goddess was seen to embody in her relationship with her father a feminine trait which was exhibited by the human female in her role as wife. When projected onto Athene, loyalty to the male became purer and less compromised, because it was no longer subject to a transfer from father's to husband's household. Once the goddess's difference — her 'more intense' femininity — had been recognised in this way, her involvement in the activities of the young women who led the Panathenaic procession in the eastern section of the frieze could be acknowledged (Figure 4.6). As the procession approaches the east porch and the entrance to the cella, its pace slackens and it eventually comes to a halt. This creates a marked contrast between the frenetic activity of the horsemen who dominate its earlier stages and the calm dignity and immobility of the women who stand at its head, the only female participants to appear in the whole length of the frieze. Six of the twenty-nine women are empty-handed, the rest are carrying ritual objects and vessels used for pouring libations to the gods. At least sixteen of

Figure 4.6 Women in the Panathenaic procession, from the east section of the Parthenon frieze: slab VIII, c. 440 BCE.

them are represented as unmarried women, distinguished from their married companions by their long hair and possibly also by their style of dress.[27] The exact identity of these women is uncertain, but some at least may be representatives of the *ergastinai*, the women responsible for the weaving of the *peplos*, or robe, presented to Athene at the culmination of the Panthenaia festival.[28] Two more young women, denoted as adolescents by their shorter stature, appear in the central scene of the frieze's eastern section, between two groups of Olympian deities: both are carrying stools on their heads, and they are met by an older, full-grown woman who is probably a priestess; to the right, a priest and a younger child are holding a folded cloth which is usually identified as the *peplos* (Figure 4.7). The girls with stools are often seen as *arrhephoroi*, young women who in conjunction with the priestess of Athene set up the loom for the weaving of the *peplos*.[29]

Just as the young men in the frieze are presented in their definitive role as warriors, so in its eastern section there are references to the definitive destination of these young unmarried women – their transition to new households and the responsibilities of a wife.[30] Whatever their precise identity, the women are either nearing puberty or have just passed it. As *arrhephoroi* or

II OBJECTS OF WORSHIP

Figure 4.7 Left to right: female attendant carrying stool; priestess; priest and child, with the *peplos*; Athene; Hephaistos. East section of the Parthenon frieze: slab V, c.440 BCE.

ergastinai, they would have been initiated into the art of wool-working, seen by Greek men as the quintessential activity of the married woman in the home. The *arrhephoroi*, who also performed secret rites for Aphrodite in a sanctuary which stood at the foot of the Acropolis, would in addition have undergone a form of initiation into the sexual duties of a wife.[31] Moreover, their presence would have carried an allusion to the reign of Kekrops, that mythical era when the establishment of the institution of marriage was associated with the incorporation of women into a patriarchal system. The rituals performed by the *arrhephoroi* dramatised the story of Kekrops' daughters who, as the producers of the first woollen garment, had links with the shaping of a distinctive culture, presided over by Athene, their city's new guardian and the patron deity of spinning and weaving.[32] Ritual and mythological references to marriage may have been underscored by a visual parallel. The positioning of the young women at the head of the Panathenaic procession could have been viewed as a foreshadowing of their next appearance as objects of public display; like the brides depicted in Athenian vase-paintings, the women were seen walking in procession away from and towards a door. In the Parthenon, the doors were real, not represented: the one which they were moving away from (at the western end of the building) led into a back room which probably housed the Athenian treasury, while the one which they were approaching (the main entrance to the temple) was situated just beyond this section of the frieze, inside the eastern porch.

In the frieze, the two strands of the procession which the young women are leading converge, in the centre of the eastern section, on two groups of deities – the twelve Olympians. Here, the seating arrangements have produced some quasi-marital pairings.[33] Hera, a genuine wife and the goddess of marriage, is shown sitting next to her husband Zeus, making the veil-lifting

64

Figure 4.8 Nike, Hera and Zeus, from the east section of the Parthenon frieze: slab V, c.440 BCE.

gesture (*anakalupteria*) which in Greek art is symbolic of both a bride and a married woman (Figure 4.8). Athene herself, though not a wife, is seen to share in the concerns of these young women. Shown in the frieze without her helmet and shield, she appears in a predominantly feminine guise, bringing her closer to the females who approach her (Figure 4.7). Her position next to the *peplos* of the central scene would have reminded the spectator, not just of the ritual which formed the climax of the procession, but also of the goddess's supervision of the wifely art of wool-working. The blacksmith god Hephaistos sits on Athene's left hand, and turns towards her: his presence would have called to mind the joint association of these two deities with technology and the crafts, and also their pseudo-sexual relationship. Hephaistos had once tried to rape Athene, and when she repulsed him he ejaculated onto her leg; the wool which she used to wipe away his semen was thrown onto the ground, and as a result a child, Erichthonios, was born from the earth. The infant, who in some versions of his story had a torso which terminated in a snake, was then adopted by Athene as her foster-child and entrusted to the care of the daughters of Kekrops. According to Pausanias (1.24.7), he was symbolised by the great snake curled up inside the shield of the Parthenos statue, while some modern scholars believe that in the frieze the child standing next to

Figure 4.9 The 'Varvakeion' Athene: a Roman copy of the Athene Parthenos statue.

Athene and Hephaistos and handling the robe in some way represents Erichthonios, who in later life became the founder of the Panathenaic festival.[34] But these signs of the goddess's closeness, in some aspects of her biography, to the mortal woman's role as sexual partner and mother are accompanied in her image on the frieze by a small reminder of her difference: as Hephaistos turns towards her she holds her aegis, whose centrepiece the Gorgon's head turned men into stone, defensively over her genitals.[35]

The spectator's reading of the Parthenon sculptures ended, inside the temple, in an encounter with an overwhelming image of difference. Pheidias' colossal Parthenos statue (Figure 4.9), 40 feet (approx. 12 metres) high and covered in leaves of gold and ivory, presented the viewer with a recapitulation of the discourses introduced in the external metopes. Greeks versus Amazons were depicted on the outside of the goddess's shield, and Gods versus Giants on the inside; while Lapiths and Centaurs waged war around the rim of her enormous sandals. The Gorgon's head, symbol of her power to keep masculine foes at bay, was prominently displayed on her breast. In this final epiphany Athene appeared, not as a female who shared some of the roles and activities of ordinary mortal women, but as the Virgin Warrior, the loyal daughter who in the idealised world of the gods could resist all pressures to marry. The need for marriage had been displaced downwards, onto an imperfect human world. The relief on the statue's base represented the creation of Pandora, the first woman and, of course, the first wife. As in the east pediment of the temple, an assembly of deities witnessed the new arrival, and the scene was framed by a depiction of Helios on the left and Selene on the right.[36] In this way Pandora was exhibited as Athene's earthly surrogate, the human female who had been awarded the task of reproduction repudiated by the goddess.[37] In Hesiod's *Works and Days* (60–105), Athene gives Pandora instruction in the wifely art of weaving almost as soon as she appears on the scene; and she also provides her with the beautiful robes which help to convert her into an alluring but deceptive gift, accepted by the race of men along with her infamous jar of evils. In Hesiod's view, the first woman and her descendants are a bitter necessity without whom men are condemned to a miserable and childless existence (*Theogony* 590–607). But on the level of the divine this disturbing male dependence could be safely abolished, and the female reconstructed on an altogether grander yet less threatening scale. In Athene, the deity who towered above Pandora in the Parthenon, the dangerous femininity of Pandora's daughters had been purified and elevated. The goddess who presided over Athens from her eminence on the Acropolis was nurturing and protective, but at the same time powerful and virginal. Her duality was such that she could honour the male in all things, but at the same time resist the bonds of marriage.

II OBJECTS OF WORSHIP

NOTES

1. In the French version of the essay in Loraux 1991, the word translated here as 'intense' is 'exacerbé' (p.33).
2. For a discussion of the social significance of marriage, see Vernant 1980 [1974]: 45–70.
3. For a summary of the main suggestions concerning the objectives of the law, see Humphreys 1974: 93–4, Patterson 1981: 3, 97–107, and Blundell 1995: 120–1, 205, n.18. Patterson (1981: 95–6) thinks that the law was probably not retroactive, in that it probably did not disfranchise those men with a non-Athenian mother who had attained citizenship before 451 BCE; but that it may have disqualified men born before 451 who came of age after that date. Humphreys (1974: 92) shares this opinion.
4. See, for example, a red-figure pyxis in the Louvre (L55) dating to c.460 BCE.
5. See Walters 1921: 145 and pl. VI for a discussion of the lid; and Lissarrague 1992: 147–50 for wedding processions and doors.
6. The Parthenos statue housed in the temple was dedicated in 438 BCE. The roof of the temple must have been in place by then, and therefore the metope sculptures below the roof must have been in position. But it is likely that the pediment sculptures, and possibly the frieze, were carved after 438.
7. See Herington 1955: 6–15, 43–7 for the view that in the fifth century BCE there was no separate cult of Athene Parthenos; Herington believes, however, that Parthenos and Polias represented two distinct aspects of the goddess, her war-like and her civic personae respectively. Mansfield (1985: 232, n.19) and Ridgway (1992: 135) are inclined to believe in a separate cult. The earliest surviving reference to the temple as the Parthenon occurs in Demosthenes (22.13 and 76); Pausanias (5.11.10 and 10.34.8) is the earliest known writer who calls the statue the Parthenos.
8. See Spivey 1996: 138–40 for the general significance of the Athenian relationship to the Persians in the creation of the Parthenon and its sculptures. Spivey takes up the suggestion made by Root 1985 that the Parthenon frieze both reflects and challenges the themes of the reliefs of the Apadana, the great audience chamber at the Persian ceremonial centre of Persepolis, but believes that the differences are more striking than the similarities.
9. Aristotle *(Ath.pol.* 49.3) tells us that at one time the designs for the robe had been judged by the *Boule* or Council, but that in his own day this was done by the *dikasterion* or jury-court.
10. See Fehl 1961: 9 – 'In the contemplation of the frieze the source of "animation" is the locomotion of the spectator' – and Osborne 1987. Osborne's account of the process of viewing is outlined below. The sequence in which the sculptures were viewed was to a large extent determined by the restricted nature of the route around the building (see Jenkins 1994: 18); but the pace of the viewing and the order in which superimposed sculptural elements were contemplated was within the control of the spectator.
11. The west pediment sculptures are the earliest surviving visual account of the contest. The story may only have been invented after the Persian Wars, when Athens' emergence as a naval power was beginning to demand that the sea god Poseidon be given some kind of role in the city. See Morris 1992: 324–5.
12. For other references to the contest, see Ovid *Met.* 6.70–82; Pausanias 1.24.5 and 1.26.5; and Plutarch *Life of Themistocles* 19.
13. Brommer 1979: 21–2 points out that in the west metopes, which are badly eroded, the figures in oriental dress are not, in their present condition, incontrovertibly female. He suggests that this could be a Greeks versus Persians confrontation. However, most scholars accept that the figures are indeed Amazons. Boardman 1982: 18, for example, believes that the large number of riders among the orientals, and the difficulty of accepting that a historical as opposed to a mythological episode could have been included in this position, make the battle against the Amazons the more likely subject.

14 For the conflicts in the metope sculptures as mythical analogues for the struggles against the Persians, see Castriota 1992: 134–83. At the time when the Parthenon was being constructed, juxtaposed scenes showing battles against Amazons and against Centaurs were already in existence in the paintings of the Theseion, dating probably to the late 470s or early 460s. The Stoa Poikile, which probably dated to the late 460's, had paintings representing battles against Amazons and the sack of Troy. As far as we know, the battle between the Gods and the Giants had not previously been depicted in Athens in combination with the other mythical conflicts of the Parthenon metopes. However, as the subject of the scenes woven into the *peplos*, or robe, presented to Athene at the Panathenaia festival, it may have appeared a natural choice for the Parthenon sculptures: it had already been represented in the pediment sculptures of the old temple of Athene destroyed by the Persians; and the *peplos* itself was to be depicted in the eastern section of the frieze (perhaps with a small painted scene of the battle against the Giants added to it), on the same side of the temple as the Gods versus Giants metopes. For the perceived links between Amazons and Persians, and their impact on Athenian iconography, see Boardman 1982: 13–28. Boardman suggests that the story of the Amazon attack on Athens may only have been invented after the Persian invasions of Greece, a view which is shared by Morris (1992: 345–6).
15 For the last disability, see Patterson 1987.
16 See Brommer 1979: 49, fig. 23.
17 For a discussion of the possible sources for the narrative represented in the west pediment, see Castriota 1992: 145–50. For the promotion of myths of matriarchy in the fifth century BCE, see Pembroke 1967.
18 The northern route was the more likely, since this was on the shady side of the temple, and was followed by festival processions.
19 See Boardman 1985: 234, metopes 24 and 25.
20 For the changes which took place in the setting of the Lapiths versus Centaurs struggle, see for example Cohen 1983, especially pp.172–5. The central metopes on the south side, 13–20, appear to represent a different story, the identification of which has been the subject of considerable debate. Simon's suggestion 1975: 106–16, that they contain a depiction of the story of Ixion, the father of Peirithoos, preserves the thematic unity of the south metopes. As Castriota 1992: 158–63 has pointed out, the inclusion of this narrative would have meant that the motif of the violation of marriage was being repeated.
21 For the viewing of the frieze through the outer columns, see Stillwell 1969 and Osborne 1987: 98–9.
22 See Jenkins 1994: 24–26 for a résumé of the most prominent theories about the nature of the Panathenaia festival being represented. Concerning the identification of the procession as that of the Panathenaia, the most significant dissenting voice is that of Connelly (1996), whose interpretation has been disputed by a number of scholars.
23 See Jenkins 1994: 25, for a summary of the discrepancies between the frieze and the literary accounts of the procession.
24 Osborne's view can be compared with Boardman's assertion (1984: 211) that the presence of the horsemen demonstrates 'the heroic character of the participants'. Elsewhere (1977), Boardman has argued more specifically that the frieze celebrated the heroisation of the 192 Athenians who died at the battle of Marathon: though these were infantry soldiers, they were shown on horseback because this was indicative of their heroic status. Spivey (1996: 147–8) supports Boardman's view, and refers to an 'ethos of heroisation'. There are a number of objections to the Marathon theory; but its rejection does not fundamentally detract from the general argument that the horsemen inject a heroic character into the frieze. Rhodes (1995: 90) believes that in the frieze 'the lack of specificity . . . elevates these humans . . . to the realm of the heroic'.
25 See Harrison 1967: 30 and pl.16, fig.10 for one suggestion as to the arrangement of the missing central sculptures.

II OBJECTS OF WORSHIP

26 See Apollodorus 1.6.1–2.
27 For the overall distinction between two groups of women on the frieze, see Mansfield 1985: 294, who refers to the second group as 'perhaps consisting of married women'; and Roccos (1995), who argues in favour of the unmarried/married distinction. For the distinction in hairstyles, see Harrison 1989: 53 and Simon 1982: 131. In the cases where both hairstyle and clothing are still recognisable, the women with long hair wear *peploi* and shoulder-mantles, the women with chignons wear chitons and *himatia*; however, it is not always possible to distinguish the *peplos* from the chiton. For discussions of the clothing worn by unmarried women, see Clairmont 1993: 32–3 and Roccos 1995. Roccos believes that the distinctive garb of the unmarried women in the Parthenon frieze identifies them as *kanephoroi* or basket-bearers in the procession.
28 See the inscriptional evidence cited by Mansfield (1985: 296). Mansfield believes, however, that the participation in the procession of the women who wove the robe may have been an innovation of the third or second century BCE.
29 For the identification of the girls with the stools as *arrhephoroi*, see Simon 1983: 67, and Jenkins 1994: 35–9. Jenkins (1994: 45, note on Chap. 5, *Myth or cult?*) gives a useful list of references for the various interpretations of the central scene of the east frieze.
30 Compare Jenkins 1994: 33, who believes that both the young women at the head of the procession and the young men in its earlier stages are past puberty but, in the case of the women, are not yet married, and, in the case of the men, are not yet full citizens (that is, they are *ephebes*). Thus both are socially marginal, and they also 'mark the boundaries of the frieze, and, at the same time, define the physical limits of the path traversed by the procession'.
31 See Gould 1980: 51 and Jenkins 1994: 38.
32 For the daughters of Kekrops and their place in the rites of the *arrhephoroi*, see Burkert 1966.
33 Compare Mark 1984: esp. 289–312 and Harrison 1994. Harrison believes that the theme of marriage is alluded to not just in the grouping of the Olympian deities, but also in the figures of the central '*peplos*' scene, where the priest can be identified as the Archon Basileus and the priestess as his wife, the Basilinna.
34 See Jenkins 1994: 25 and 35–7. Jenkins himself believes that the child is a temple servant; but because of the close links between the ritual of the *peplos* and the myth of Kekrops' daughters he suggests that the child can be said to be impersonating Erichthonios. There is in fact some doubt about the sex of the child – see the references cited by Jenkins on p.45 – but the theory that it is in fact a girl has not been generally accepted.
35 Athene's closeness to young women is also indicated by the fact that in Greece as a whole, out of all the female deities she received by far the greatest number of consecrated statues of girls: over half of the archaic *korai* have been found in her sanctuaries. See De Polignac 1995 [1984]: 44, n.22. These statues can be seen as symbolising the consecration of the community's young women to the goddess.
36 See Leipen 1971: 24–7.
37 Hurwit (1995: see esp. 182–6) points out that the scene of dressing and gift-giving in which Pandora is involved on the statue base could have been seen as a parallel to the activities which took place before a contemporary Athenian wedding. He also points to a number of parallels between the Pandora story and other elements in Athene's biography. Much has been written on Pandora. For a definitive account, see Vernant 1980 [1974]: 168–85, and for a recent view, see Zeitlin 1996.

5

BORN OLD OR NEVER YOUNG?

Femininity, childhood and the goddesses of ancient Greece[1]

Lesley Beaumont

Students and scholars of the classical world, when leafing through books on the mythology and art of ancient Greece, do not have to turn the pages very far before meeting stories and pictures which tell of the birth of many of the Greek gods and, more rarely, of the goddesses.[2] Dionysos, Athene, Hermes, Aphrodite, Zeus, Artemis, Apollo and Asklepios each emerge into being at their own, often extraordinary, nativity. On closer examination and reflection, however, a peculiar dichotomy becomes apparent between the presentation of the male and female figures within this group. For while the gods are born as infants and subsequently experience a phase of childhood, the goddesses Athene and Aphrodite begin their lives as adults. Further, though Artemis does very occasionally in the fourth century appear as an infant, her experience of childhood has, as we shall see, little or no innate significance and, according to one version of the myth, she matures with sufficient rapidity to assist Leto at the birth of her twin brother Apollo.

It is with this dichotomy between male and female divine birth, and in particular with its implications for our understanding of the sacred and the feminine in ancient Greece, that this chapter is concerned. First, the ancient evidence under consideration, both literary and iconographical, and dating mostly to the fifth and fourth centuries BCE, will be reviewed. Subsequently, in seeking to illuminate any factors underlying the male/female dichotomy, we shall consider two complementary lines of thought. The first of these involves consideration of the way in which the ancient Greeks characterised their female deities, as compared and contrasted with the male gods. Second, the dichotomy is discussed as, at least in part, a possible reflection of the socio-historical context in which the mythographers and artists were rooted. Finally, the chronological significance of changes in the presentation of female divine birth and childhood in the fourth century and the hellenistic period will be examined.

11 OBJECTS OF WORSHIP

THE EVIDENCE

Birth and childhood of the gods

Perhaps the divine child most popular with classical Greek artists and mythographers was Dionysos. The ancient literary sources tell how Zeus' union with the mortal woman Semele incited the anger of jealous Hera. The goddess therefore tricked the pregnant woman into requesting Zeus to appear to her in his full godhead; but, being a mere mortal, Semele could not withstand such a revelation and was consumed by Zeus' lightning. Zeus, however, snatching the unborn child from Semele's womb, sewed him into his own thigh, until the time should be ripe for the child's birth. The literary sources tell variously that after the birth the infant Dionysos was entrusted to Hermes, to the nymphs of Nysa, or to Athamas and Ino.[3]

Representations of this story appear frequently in Greek art, in both vase-painting and sculpture. For the archaic period, Pausanias (iii.18.11) provides us with a description of a scene on the Amyklaian throne (Pipili 1991: 143–8), showing Hermes bearing the child Dionysos to heaven. In the fifth and fourth centuries the infant Dionysos becomes a popular theme with Attic red-figure vase-painters: he appears in a variety of contexts which range from his first birth from Semele or his second birth from Zeus' thigh to his delivery by Zeus into the care of the nymphs of Nysa, or by Hermes into the care of the nymphs, a satyr or silen,[4] Papposilenos, or Athamas and Ino.[5] This last subject of the child brought to Athamas and Ino is also taken up in the fourth century on a Faliscan red-figure stamnos.[6] Attic red-figure vase-painting also provides evidence of the divine child entertained by nymphs/maenads and silenoi/satyrs, and two further categories of associated representations treat the birth and childhood of Dionysos in his manifestations as Dionysos-Zagreus and Dionysos-Iakchos.[7] Classical sculpture, too, also favours the child-god, the most famous of such sculpture groups which has come down to our own day being that of Praxiteles, depicting the babe on the arm of Hermes (Figure 5.1). Both this group and that of another fourth-century sculptor, Kephisodotos, had earlier been foreshadowed in the fifth century by Polykleitos' and Kresilas' respective sculpture groups of Hermes with the infant Dionysos (Loeb 1979: 47–9, 294–5 D27, D28 and D32; Rizzo 1932-40). Indeed, the group established in the fifth century of Hermes or Papposilenos with the child Dionysos becomes, in its various permutations, the enduring iconographic motif employed for the representation of the infancy of Dionysos during the fourth century and the Hellenistic period, whether in sculpture, on painted or plastic vases, or on coins (*LIMC* iii, Dionysos IXA).

Though not appearing as frequently as the infant Dionysos, the gods Hermes, Apollo and Asklepios are also to be found as children in Greek art and myth. Even Zeus, the great father of men and of gods, was once himself a

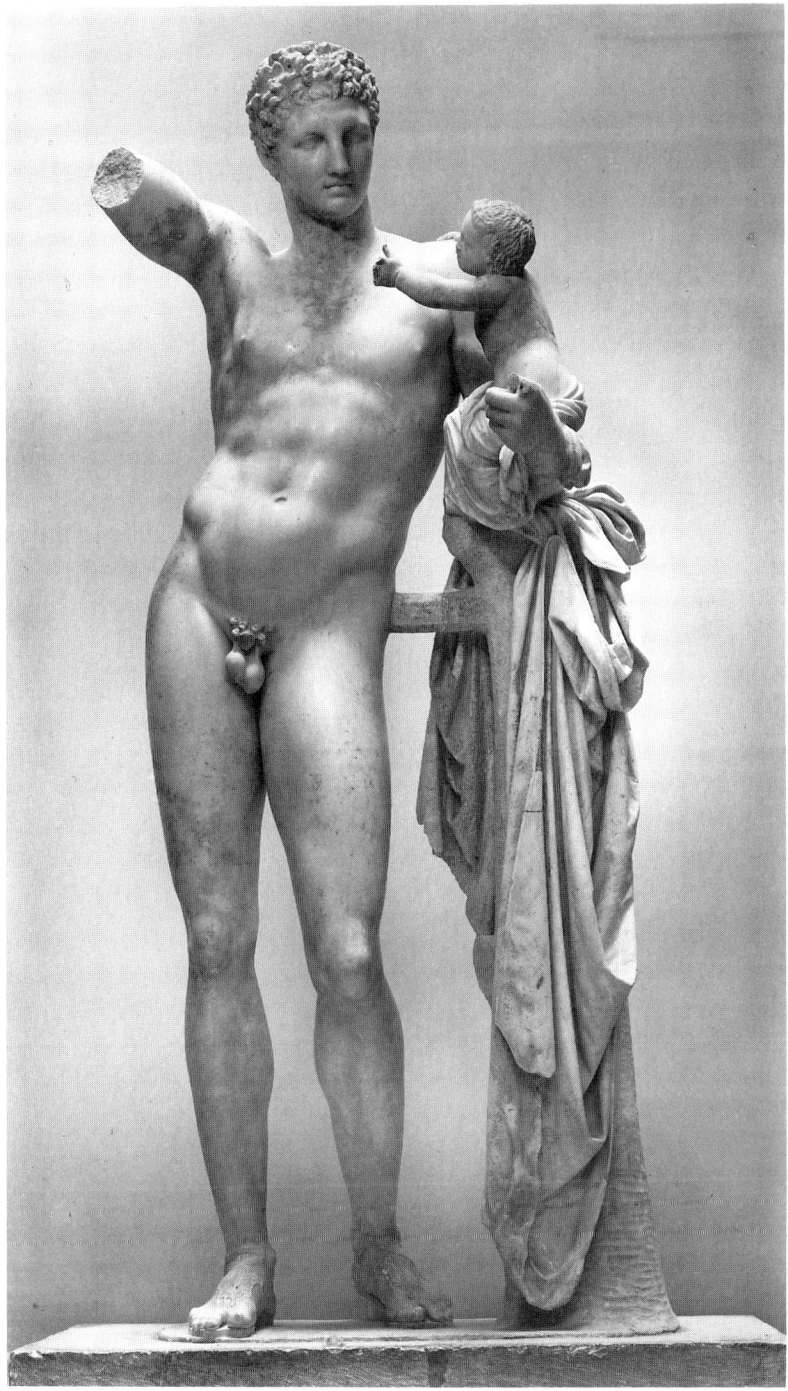

Figure 5.1 Marble group of Hermes with the baby Dionysos. Perhaps an original work by Praxiteles, third quarter of the fourth century BCE.

defenceless baby. Our major literary source for the story is Hesiod's *Theogony* (453–506), and Kallimachos later wrote a *Hymn to Zeus* on the theme of the god's nativity and childhood. According to Hesiod the birth took place in Crete, whither Rhea had fled in order to protect her offspring from Zeus' father, Kronos. But Kronos, forewarned that his powerful son would overthrow him, was intent on destroying the child by swallowing him, just as he had previously swallowed his earlier progeny. Rhea responded to this by hiding the infant Zeus in a cave on Cretan Mount Aigion and, as a substitute, swaddled a stone which she gave to Kronos, who duly swallowed it down.[8] The story finds artistic expression both in classical sculpture and in vase-painting; it should, however, be added that what the vase-painters depict is not the baby himself, but rather a swaddled bundle masquerading as the infant.[9] Nevertheless, the child Zeus did appear 'in the flesh' in contemporary sculpture. Pausanias (vii.47.3), for example, tells us of an altar, probably classical, of Athena Alea in Tegea, which was decorated with figures of Rhea and the nymph Oenoe with the baby Zeus. Elsewhere (ii.17.3), he writes about the sculptures of the fifth-century temple of Hera at the Argive Heraion, where a birth of Zeus scene decorated most probably the east pediment of the temple. He also reports (vii.24.4) that a bronze statue of the boy Zeus, made by the late archaic or early classical sculptor Ageladas of Argos, could be seen at Aigion in Achaia.

A handful of Attic red-figure vases present us with the figure of the infant Hermes, either in the arms of the messenger goddess Iris or taking refuge in his cradle after stealing the cattle of Apollo (Figure 5.2).[10] This second theme also appears on a somewhat earlier black-figure Caeretan hydria of circa 530 BCE.[11] Both the Attic and Caeretan vases depicting the infant cattle thief agree closely with the fourth *Homeric Hymn*, which tells of the birth of Hermes. There, in order to win himself a place among the gods, the newborn child is immediately up and about performing various cunning deeds, one of which is the theft of the cattle of Apollo. After sacrificing two of the cattle, he returns to his cradle in the cave of his mother, Maia, to await the arrival of the enraged Apollo. It is perhaps surprising that the subject of the infant Hermes with Apollo's cattle did not have a greater appeal for the ancient painters and their clients, since the myth must have been a popular and well-known one in the late seventh, sixth and fifth centuries BCE. Alkaios, who is said to have flourished in the forty-second Olympiad (612–609 BCE), wrote a *Hymn* to Hermes on this theme, while the *Homeric Hymn* to Hermes probably dates to the earlier part of the sixth century. And in the fifth century Sophokles wrote the *Ichneutae*, a satyr play which also treated the theft of Apollo's cattle by the little Hermes, but which gave its own twists to the tale.[12]

Pindar and Hesiod furnish us with the birth story of yet another divine male child, Asklepios.[13] Koronis, daughter of King Phlegyas of Thessaly, was already pregnant by Apollo with the child Asklepios when she very unwisely

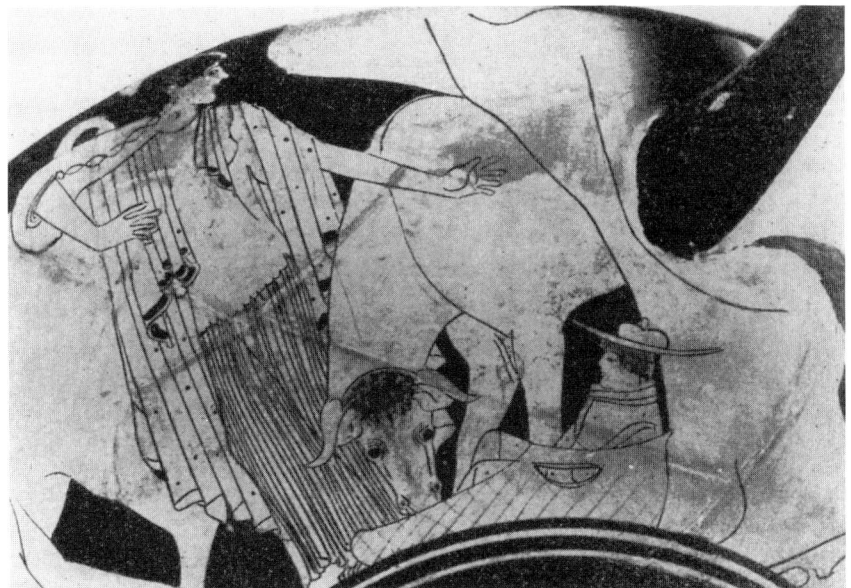

Figure 5.2 The infant Hermes nestles in his cradle while his mother Maia and the cattle of Apollo look on. Attic red-figure cup by the Brygos Painter, c.490 BCE.

chose to consort also with Ischys. This, naturally, roused the anger of the god, who sent Artemis to slay her. But, taking pity on his unborn child, Apollo rescued the little Asklepios from his mother's corpse, even as it was licked by the flames of the funeral pyre – a fate reminiscent of that of the infant Dionysos. However, although the birth of Asklepios is well attested in the ancient literary sources, it finds only a single extant and securely identified representation in classical Greek art: this appears on a fine Attic red-figure plate decorated by the Meidias Painter shortly after 420 BCE.[14] Here the infant's nurse is the place nymph Epidauros, and the presence of a tripod atop a column suggests that the picture may celebrate a victorious dithyramb, most likely written on the Asklepios theme. Although we have no other surviving depictions of the little Asklepios, Pausanias (viii.25.11, viii.32.5) does, however, make reference to the cult of the Child Asklepios in Arkadia, and describes a cult statue of the boy-god at Megalopolis. It is, furthermore, interesting that in producing one of the earliest extant representations of Asklepios in the whole of ancient Greek art, the Meidias Painter on his plate presents him in his infant, rather than his adult, form.

Finally, we come to the birth and childhood of the god Apollo. Euripides in the *Iphigeneia in Tauris* (1239–51) relates that after giving birth to Apollo on Delos, Leto carried the baby to Delphi where the divine child slew the dragon Python from the safety of his mother's arms.[15] During the fifth and fourth centuries BCE this story of the infant dragon-slayer also appears in sculpture and vase-painting,[16] a subject to which we shall presently return in our search for the child Artemis in classical art and myth.

This brief survey of the birth and childhood stories of several of the gods thus presents clear proof that the divine male infant is no stranger in Greek art and myth. Let us now turn to the evidence for the birth of the goddesses, in order to compare the figure of the divine newborn female with that of her male counterpart.

Birth and childhood of the goddesses

Greek art and mythology, while plentiful in their references to the birth and infancy of the male gods are, by contrast, remarkably empty of references to the birth and childhood of almost all of the goddesses. Notable exceptions are Aphrodite and Athene, whose respective births are popular subjects in classical literature, sculpture and vase-painting alike. However, whereas the gods are depicted as infants at their birth, the two newly born goddesses are presented as adult and fully formed. According to Hesiod, Homer, Pindar and others,[17] Athene was conceived by Metis when she lay with Zeus. But Zeus, forewarned that Metis would eventually bear him a child more powerful than he, responded by swallowing her whole. As a result, Zeus developed an almighty headache which Hephaistos offered to relieve by applying his double-axe to the god's throbbing head: thereupon out leapt Athene in her fully developed form as goddess of war, arrayed with magnificent golden arms and armour.

Greek art of the archaic and classical periods depicts the birth many times, employing one of three alternate iconographic formulae.[18] The miniature figure of the adult Athene emerging fully armed from the head of Zeus at the moment of her birth is a schema particularly popular in the archaic period:[19] it appears in painted form on Attic and Corinthian black-figure vases, in relief on bronze shield bands from Olympia and on a relief pithos from Tinos and, according to Pausanias (i.24.2, iii.17.3), in now lost pieces of freestanding sculpture which once stood on the Akropolis at Athens and in the temple of Athene Chalkioikos at Sparta (*LIMC* ii: Athena B1.II). A second schema, found in Attic vase-painting of the sixth and early fifth centuries BCE, presents the miniature, adult and armed goddess standing on the knee of her father Zeus, in a quieter moment following her birth (*LIMC* ii: Athena B1.III) (Figure 5.3). Alternatively, the newborn Athene, adult, full-size and armed stands before her divine parent: such scenes were painted on Attic vases by black-figure painters in the sixth century BCE, and such also seems to have been the iconographic schema employed in Pheidias' presentation of the scene in the east pediment of the Parthenon (*LIMC* ii: Athena B1.IV).

The birth of Aphrodite, recounted by Hesiod in the *Theogony* (188–202) and attested in the sixth *Homeric Hymn* to Aphrodite, follows the castration of

Figure 5.3 The newborn Athene stands on the knee of her father Zeus, and is greeted by Eileithyia. Attic red-figure pelike by the Geras Painter, c.480 BCE.

Ouranos by Kronos, and the casting of the severed genitalia into the sea. There in the foam that gathers around them is created Aphrodite, who emerges from the ocean at her birth onto the dry land of Cyprus as a full-grown, fully developed and sexually alluring goddess. Birth of Aphrodite scenes first appear in Greek art in the fifth century BCE and can also be divided into three main iconographic types.[20] The goddess may, for example, rise from the sea as an adult female figure, a schema employed not only by red-figure vase-painters but also apparently by Pheidias on the base of the cult statue of Zeus at Olympia, and further seen on the mid-fifth-century, south Italian sculpture relief now commonly known as the 'Ludovisi Throne' (Figure 5.4). On red-figure vases and in terracotta figurines of the fourth century BCE she may, alternatively, be seen to emerge from a shell at her birth, and in fifth- and fourth-century Attic and south Italian red-figure

II OBJECTS OF WORSHIP

Figure 5.4 Aphrodite rising from the sea at her birth on the so-called 'Ludovisi Throne', a South Italian sculpture relief of c.460 BCE.

vase-painting may ascend from the depths of the earth at her 'anodos' ('rising'). Further, in the fourth century she may ride in an opening scallop shell. In each case, however, Aphrodite, like Athene, is represented not as a babe but as an adult woman.

The number of goddesses whose birth or first days of life are attested in classical art and myth is, as we have noted, remarkably few, and the only other divine female whose birth or childhood is presented by the ancient sources is Artemis. Until the third century BCE, however, Artemis as a child seems to appear only in association with her brother, almost as an afterthought tacked on to Apollo's childhood adventures. The ancient literary sources indeed tell us little about the birth of Artemis: the *Homeric Hymn* to Delian Apollo (14–16) and Pindar's processional song *On Delos* reveal little more than that her mother was Leto, her brother Apollo, and that she was born on Ortygia or Delos. It is interesting, then, that in the third century BCE Kallimachos pays a little more attention to the character and activities of the child Artemis, describing her sitting on the knee of Zeus (*Hymn to Artemis*, 4–5) and relating how at the age of three she showed signs already of her prodigious strength by tearing out handfuls of hair from the chest of the Cyclops Brontes (*Hymn to Artemis*, 72–9). On the other hand, he elsewhere implies that Artemis after her birth matured so rapidly as to assist Leto at the birth of her twin brother, Apollo (*Diegesis* on *Aetia*, frag. 79).

In Greek art of the classical period Artemis seems never to be represented

Figure 5.5 Leto, carrying the infant Apollo (left) and Artemis (right), flees from Python. Attic or Apulian red-figure neck-amphora, first half of the fourth century BCE.

at the moment of her birth, either as an adult or as a child figure. Indeed, evidence for the presentation of any scenes of her early life is not to be found until the fourth century BCE, when she takes on a passive role as a child spectator witnessing the slaughter of Python by her infant brother, Apollo. This scene, showing both children nestled safely in the arms of their mother, Leto, appears very occasionally in fourth century vase-painting and sculpture.[21] A red-figure neck-amphora, of either Athenian or Apulian manufacture, and showing Leto fleeing with her children in order to escape Python (Figure 5.5),[22] may reflect a statue group by Euphranor: this piece, itself no longer extant, is attested by Pliny (*NH* xxxiv. 77) as a bronze group of Leto carrying the infant Apollo and Artemis and standing, in Pliny's day, in the temple of Concord at Rome (Palagia 1980: 36–9). Strabo (xiv. 1. 20) also records at Ephesos a statue group by Skopas which depicted a standing Leto holding a sceptre and accompanied by Ortygia, the place-nymph or personification of Delos, who carried Leto's children.

Assured, extant representations of the infant Artemis in Greek myth and art of the fifth and fourth centuries BCE are thus highly elusive. It does, however, seem that, unlike Aphrodite and Athene, Artemis did on rare occasions appear as a child in fourth-century Greek art and in third-century Greek literary sources. I do, however, believe it to be of significance that the child Artemis apparently does not make her appearance before the fourth century, and to this point of chronology I shall presently return.

*

This brief review of the evidence for divine birth and childhood in classical Greek art and literature bears out my opening assertion of a dichotomy in the presentation of the newborn male and female gods. For while the male gods are frequently represented as children, infant and child goddesses are virtually non-existent: Aphrodite and Athene, at their respective births, appear as adult women and although the child Artemis, it is true, does occur in the fourth and third centuries BCE, this seems to be only on very rare occasions and usually on the pretext of accompanying her infant brother on his adventures.

How then might we account for this divergence in the presentation of male and female divine birth and childhood? Although, on the whole, this is a subject little observed or discussed by modern scholarship, Susan Woodford does briefly address the puzzle of infant gods and newborn adult goddesses, suggesting that this might be 'evidence of male myth-makers recalling their own helpless infancy and the adult competency of their mothers': a reflection in art, that is to say, of the 'male experience of a childhood in which a young boy was very much under the control of full-grown women'(Woodford 1981: 221–2).[23] We might also suggest that the near-total absence of artistic and literary representation of the goddesses as child figures may perhaps reflect an inability on the part of the classical Greek (male) artist or poet to visualise the female body as anything other than sexual or maternal. Yet this can hardly be the case, since if we turn to representations in classical Greek art of the mortal female figure, girls, both as infants and as older children, are common enough. These female offspring appear on late fifth- and fourth-century painted choes[24] as crawling babies, distinguished from their male counterparts by a different coiffure (often a topknot), and the absence of male genitalia (Figure 5.6).[25] A series of late fifth-century black- and red-figure krateriskoi (small pedestalled bowls) from Brauron and other sites in Attica, showing the young initiates of Artemis known as the 'bears', are also now well known: here, girls of apparently diverse ages, some naked and others clothed, perform a variety of activities in honour of Artemis Brauronia (Sourvinou-Inwood 1988; Kahil 1965, 1977, 1981). Mortal female children are also depicted in fifth- and fourth-century Greek sculpture, both as freestanding figures such as those that again come from Brauron and elsewhere (Figure 5.7), or more commonly in relief on grave stelai. For example, on the early fourth-century stele of Mynnia we see a little girl named Artemisias kneeling on the ground, while a stele illustrated here (Figure 5.8) shows a little girl who, standing at the knee of a seated woman, probably her mother, reaches out her arms beseechingly to her.[26] The female child figure *per se* was not therefore considered by classical artists to be unsuitable subject material for representation. In view of this, what other factors might we then explore in our attempt to understand the puzzling absence of an infant birth and childhood phase in the case of the Greek goddesses?

Figure 5.6 Attic red-figure chous depicting a mortal baby girl. She is naked except for a string of amulets, and plays with a ball which she throws towards a chous. c.410–400 BCE.

CHARACTERISATION OF THE GODDESSES

Let us turn first to a consideration of the way in which the ancient Greeks characterised their female deities, as compared and contrasted with the male gods. As scholars from Sarah Pomeroy onwards have pointed out (Pomeroy 1975: 4–13), the goddesses of classical Greece tend to be more closely defined than the gods by a particular sexual status: the virgin in the persons of Athene, Artemis and Hestia, the sex symbol in the shape of Aphrodite, the wife in the form of Hera, and the mother or matron in the figure of Demeter. Accordingly, their mythological adventures and the roles allotted to them in myth are, on the whole – though with the exceptions of Athene and Artemis

Figure 5.7 Marble figure of a mortal female child, seated on the ground and holding a bird in her right hand. From Athens, c.340–30 BCE.

Figure 5.8 Attic grave stele depicting a little girl at the knee of a woman, probably her mother. A third female figure, perhaps an older daughter, stands to the left. c.380 BCE.

with whom we shall deal shortly – appropriately focused and defined within the boundaries of these respective *female* characterisations. The gods, on the other hand, are not in the same way prescribed or defined primarily by a particular sexual status or even by their gender: the mythology of Zeus and Apollo, for example, presents them variously as sexual partners in both homosexual and heterosexual affairs, as fathers and, in the case of Zeus, as actual birth parent to Dionysos and Athene.

It is therefore of significance for our present enquiry to note that the characterisation of the goddesses as virgin, sex symbol, wife or mother, in each case necessitates a state of sexual maturity; for, in order to assume these roles, the female must have passed beyond the childhood stage. What, for example, could the representation of Aphrodite as an infant add to her well-defined mythological identity as the goddess embodying the powerful forces of sexual love and beauty? Surely, Aphrodite is born in her lovely, developed and voluptuous form precisely because this underscores her particular, closely defined character: to have represented her at her birth as an infant could only have undermined this. As the purified and concentrated form of sexual love and feminine beauty, she simply *is*: that is to say, she never develops into her state of sexual potency from a lesser phase of sexual immaturity. Even in the case of the virgin goddesses Hestia, Athene and Artemis, their central identity as chaste virgins requires their sexual maturity: for their virginal status has significance only through their rejection of their developed capacity to enter into relations with males. Where the virgin goddesses are concerned, however, it is not perhaps unthinkable to envisage them experiencing a phase as pre-pubescent *parthenoi*, and we might possibly understand the very occasional presentation of Artemis as a child in Greek myth and art along these lines. And yet Artemis, as the only Greek goddess to be represented as a child, gains precious little by her appearance in infant form; for, as we have noted, until the hellenistic period she takes only a passive role as a bystander in her brother Apollo's adventures, and displays no independent identity as a divine child in her own right. This contrasts strongly with the use of the childhood phase in the mythology of the gods as a means of exploring the dynamic character of the divine male: the baby Apollo, for example, is not only the infant son of Leto, but also fierce dragon-slayer and ruler of Delphi. Hermes, too, as well as being the day-old child of Maia, is inventor of the lyre, and both cattle thief and cunning acquisitor of the divine role he seeks for himself as lord of the herds.

So far, so good: our comparison of the characterisation of the goddesses with that of the gods seems to indicate that while the latter can accommodate a childhood phase and, further, can utilise childhood in order to display aspects of the divine male character, the childhood state, conversely, does not apparently find an appropriate niche in the more 'exclusive' and focused character of the goddesses. However, as the *sole* factor underlying and determining the divergent presentation of the newborn male and female gods, our discussion of characterisation falters when we reach the case of Athene.

As we noted earlier, the characterisation of the Greek goddesses is both gender-specific and defined by a particular sexual status. This gendered identity thus excludes the incorporation of dynamic male aspects within the character and activities of the goddesses: aspects, for example, such as the intellectual or the warlike. In the case of Athene, and also of Artemis, however, this does not altogether hold true, for in them we are able to identify many aspects of characterisation that they share with the gods, characteristics which transcend their identity as female and as virgin. This is not to say that Athene and Artemis do not manifest the clearly defined sexual identity required of a goddess: they are both, first and foremost, virgins, and exhibit none of the sexual ambivalence or promiscuity that is so common to the gods. Virginity is, nevertheless, only one facet of the identity of Athene and of Artemis, for their mythology in addition presents them as dynamic figures who juggle a wide range of roles, several of which belong to the male sphere of activity, and certainly not to the virgin state as it is usually elsewhere defined. Thus Athene is, amongst other things, warrior, foster mother, intellectual, platonic friend and helper of male heroes, judge, ruler, and so on. At her birth she clearly appears in one of these roles, and a male role at that, as an armed figure resplendent in her golden armour. And like, for example, the gods Apollo and Hermes, Athene derives glory and divine status and position from her birth and her newborn character as a dynamic figure, ready to challenge anyone who might stand in her way or call her power into question. But why then at her birth is she, without exception, presented as an *adult* warrior, and not as an infant or child figure, brandishing her weapons? That representation as a valiant infant combatant was acceptable in the case of the similarly multi-faceted gods we have, for example, already seen in the person of Apollo. Artemis, meanwhile, in her manifestations as huntress, shooter of the bow and arrow and ruler of wild things, particularly animals, also reaches beyond accepted roles normally associated not only with the virgin figure but also with the female gender: for these dynamic and aggressive characteristics belong to the male sphere. It perhaps, then, seems appropriate that Artemis, as a goddess who shares various features with the male deities also, like them, appears in Greek art and myth as a child figure, and we might therefore expect to find her childhood utilised as a means to explore and display her wide-ranging divine character. And yet, as we have noted before, this, prior to the hellenistic period, is clearly not the case.

Analysis of the way in which the ancient Greeks characterised their goddesses, as compared and contrasted with the gods, does in part help to illuminate the observed dichotomy in divine birth scenes. But our discussion of the character and birth of Athene demonstrates that this factor cannot, alone, completely account for the absence of infant female divine birth. What other contributory factors might we then explore in order to more fully comprehend the dichotomy?

It is, I think, worth noting that the only two goddesses with well-developed birth stories share not only a common presentation as adult newborns, but are also both born of male deities and without mothers: Athene of Zeus, and Aphrodite of Ouranos (Demand 1994: 134–40). By contrast, Artemis, who *is* born of a mother, finds occasional presentation as a child figure in the fourth and third centuries BCE. Might we possibly detect here an underlying idea that a divine father, having usurped the female capacity for childbirth, is able alone to produce superior offspring: that is to say, offspring who are fully developed and potent from the moment of their birth? One can, however, counter this with the argument that Zeus alone also gives birth to Dionysos, and that Dionysos *is* born as an infant. Nevertheless, it may be worth considering whether for a divine father to give birth to an infant female would, in the classical Greek mind, constitute a comic idea, and as such present a scenario which could only threaten the parent's divinity. But I am leaping ahead too far and too quickly. The avenues of thought into which we are now venturing concern not only discussion of the characterisation of the classical Greek male and female deities, but also require examination of the socio-historical context in which were rooted the mythographers and artists who provide us with our source material for this study.

CLASSICAL GREECE: THE SOCIO-HISTORICAL CONTEXT

No work of art, whether visual, literary or oral, is created free of its social context: a society's attitudes inevitably affect, and are reflected in, the public and popular art produced for and consumed by that society. This is not to say that artistic conventions lack their own dynamic and independent existence; but it does mean that modes of visualisation, and their artistic expression, are related to, among other things, a society's perception of the several discrete groups it comprises. The particular subjects on which our discussion is centred are the child and the female in the divine sphere. Although, of course, the divine children and female deities of classical Greece were certainly different from, and other to, their mortal counterparts, nevertheless, mortal children and mortal women inevitably provided the artists and mythographers of classical Greece with the tangible templates and starting point for the representation of the infant and the female in the divine sphere. An examination, therefore, of particular aspects of classical Greek attitudes to children and to women, and a consideration of displacements in these attitudes as applied to children and females in the divine sphere, may illuminate our understanding of contemporary modes of visualisation and artistic realisation.

Of necessity, our consideration of the socio-historical context must be Athenocentric, since for the classical period it is from Athens that most of our evidence, both literary and archaeological, is derived. We begin then with Athenian social attitudes to children. In brief, children were considered to be physically, morally, and intellectually weak and incomplete. Plato in the fourth century describes them as lacking in knowledge and reason, gullible, simple, foolish, and holding insignificant values and opinions.[27] Aristotle further classes them as incomplete beings, and denigrates childhood as a stage of life to which no one in his right senses would wish to return.[28] Though these sources essentially post-date the fifth century, there is evidence that similar attitudes to children did pertain then. Sophokles in his *Oidipous Tyrannos* (1511–12) makes reference to children's immature intellect, while Aischylos in the *Eumenides* (38) assigns to the same unfavourable category a child and an alarmed old woman, both of them fearful and powerless. He also refers to children's mindlessness and lack of understanding and of sense in his *Prometheus Bound* (987–8) and his *Agamemnon* (277, 479).

Mark Golden has, furthermore, drawn convincing parallels between the social status of children and that of slaves in classical Athens (Golden 1985).[29] He notes that, at least from the time of Aischylos, the word *pais* was used to denote both a child and a slave. It is interesting, too, that in fifth-century iconography the artistic convention which often used to depict both slaves and children is that of a diminutive figure, suggesting that diminution of size often signifies inferiority (Kästner 1981: 307; Himmelmann 1971). Plato too several times classifies children and slaves together, stating that they suffer from many of the same undesirable natural characteristics and tendencies, such as unruly appetites and pleasures (e.g. *Rep*. iv. 431 c). Aristotle goes even further, claiming that children can be grouped together with the sick, the bad and brutish, the drunk, and the lunatic.[30]

Children, therefore, while doubtless loved and valued by their parents and wider family, seem only to have occupied the lowliest position in the Athenian social order. Plato further places women in the same category as children and slaves,[31] and that this view of women's lowly social status also prevailed in fifth-century Athens has been well illustrated by much recent research, which does not require repetition here (Blundell 1995; Demand 1994: 147–54; Cohen 1989; Hunter 1989; Just 1989; Cantarella 1987; Peradotto and Sullivan 1984; Gould 1980; Pomeroy 1975; Gomme 1925). A comparison of the status of mortal women and of the goddesses as perceived by a fifth-century Athenian Greek therefore makes it self-evident that a 'goddess . . . is not a woman' (Loraux 1992: 20), but is something greater and other. In revering powerful goddesses, such as the Olympians Athene, Aphrodite, Artemis, Hestia, Hera and Demeter, the classical Greeks were not worshipping *women* deities: they were, rather, venerating divine beings who, in Loraux's words, happened 'to be marked by a feminine sign' (Loraux 1992:16). As we have already noted, the goddesses of classical Greece in some of their manifestations embodied the gender-specific characteristics which belonged to mortal women defined by a particular sexual status: virgin, sex symbol, wife, mother. But at the same time, the goddesses represented a state of existence to which no mortal woman could aspire, namely independence and non-reliance on males. However, in order to achieve this, they needed either to deny or to exploit their femininity and sexuality. It is, therefore, possible for a Greek divinity to exhibit a female identity, as long as the goddess in question both comprises and yet transcends mortal feminine characteristics and attributes: what Loraux calls 'a displaced form of femininity' (Loraux 1992: 43).

In similar fashion, the literary and archaeological evidence also seems to imply that it is possible for a male deity to exhibit an infant or child identity, as long as the god in question both embraces and yet transcends the nature of childhood: what we might call a displaced form of infancy or childhood. The most obvious illustration of this is provided by the infant adventures of Hermes and Apollo: the newborn Hermes steals the cattle of Apollo and then returns to snuggle down in his cradle, while the infant Apollo performs the slaughter of Python while nestled in his mother's arms. Childhood for the gods, then, is not the same as childhood for mortal men. This is further demonstrated in the ancient literary sources by the assertion that it was the gift of the gods, fed on nectar and ambrosia, to grow and develop at an abnormally rapid rate and pass quickly through childhood.[32] This is also confirmed by the evidence of vase-painting since, although mortal children may be represented at all stages of their development, from babyhood through to the verge of adulthood, divine children almost without exception are depicted as infants, and nearly always as babes in arms.

Consider, however, the difficulties involved in presenting a goddess as a child. In both practical and, more importantly, social terms the female child constituted a completely dependent figure on the grounds of both sex- and age-related status (Demand 1994: 5–11). Here, two quotes from Aristotle are particularly illuminating:

> There is a difference of character between the rule of the free over the slave and that of the male over the female and that of the man over the child. In all of these the elements of the mind are present, but they are present in different ways. For the slave does not possess the faculty of deliberation at all. The female possesses it but in an indecisive form. The child possesses it but in an imperfect form.
> (*Politics* i. 1254 b 22–3)

> Further, a boy actually resembles a woman in physique, and a woman is as it were an infertile male; the female, in fact, is female on account of inability of a sort, viz., it lacks the power to concoct semen . . . because of the coldness of its nature.
> (*Generation of Animals* 728 a 17–21)

In both cases the observation seems to be that the male child and the adult woman are equivalent on account of their incompleteness. The boy, however, has the potential to develop into a complete being. The female child, on the other hand, possesses no innate significance because she embodies impotency and the inability ever to attain completeness. The adult goddesses, as we have noted, both comprise mortal feminine characteristics and yet transcend the limitations of the human female condition. Given, however, the state of utter powerlessness represented by the mortal female child, it seems well-nigh impossible to envisage ways in which an infant goddess might transcend, as well as embrace, her limitations. Could this, then, account for the discrepancy between the infant birth of the gods and the adult manifestation of the goddesses? For while, on the one hand, the former possess the capacity to develop their full divine power, the *essential* nature of the female child conversely, in its very inability ever to attain completeness, personifies and embodies a state of existence incompatible with the nature of divinity.

If we accept that the nature of the divine effects a transformation in the feminine condition as it is expressed in the person of the goddess, and equally effects a transformation in the character of childhood as it is manifested in the male god, it therefore follows that the state of childhood in the feminine case would require a double transformation or displacement in order to achieve incorporation into the divine sphere. The fact that this double transformation or displacement does not occur, with the result that the goddesses experience birth in an adult state does, I think, lend weight to the suggestion that, at least down to the end of the fifth century BCE, the (Athenian) Greek perception of the female child and of the divine was that they were states of being so polarised as to be irreconcilable.

This also leads us back to the observation made earlier that divine fathers, alone and without female assistance, give birth to *infant male* offspring (Zeus as lone parent of Dionysos) but to *adult female* offspring (Zeus and Ouranos as lone parent of, respectively, Athene and Aphrodite). This, I suggest, implies further that the supernatural father's own divinity would have risked dilution and compromise as a result of such intimate association with, and as sole begetter of, a female infant.

TIME AND CHANGE: FEMININITY, CHILDHOOD AND THE GODDESSES IN THE FOURTH CENTURY AND THE HELLENISTIC PERIOD

Finally, I return to a discussion of the chronological significance of the first rare appearances of the infant goddess in the fourth century, and subsequently in the hellenistic period. In the fourth century, Artemis appears as a child both in pictorial and in plastic art, namely, as we have seen, on a red-figure vase and in sculpture groups by Euphranor and Skopas: in the third century she is further found in the literary descriptions of Kallimachos. The mythological corpus in the hellenistic period also starts to provide us with tales about the childhood of Athene. Apollodoros (*Bibl.* iii. 12. 3) relates that Athene was brought up by Triton, together with his own daughter, Pallas: one day while at play the girls fell out and, during an ensuing fight between the two, Athene unintentionally killed her playmate. Here, then, the childhood of Athene is explored as a means of establishing the warlike nature of the goddess as an essential feature of her character from her earliest days: this utilisation of the childhood stage to display and explore aspects of the divine character is a phenomenon already commonly found much earlier in the case of the male deities.

That a goddess could be presented as infant or child in the fourth century and the Hellenistic period, though this certainly never becomes commonplace, should not, I think, surprise us if we consider the parallel and gradual liberalisation taking place in Greek social attitudes towards children and women, and in ideas about the nature of the mortal's relationship to the divine.[33] Though restrictions of space do not permit an in-depth discussion of the growing status and significance of the child in fourth century and in hellenistic society, we can at least note the reflection of this change in the rise of the child figure in art (Deissmann-Merten 1984: 276–81; Rühfel 1984: 185–310; Zahn 1970). This, in fact, begins as early as the late fifth century in the minor art of vase-painting, when an increasing number of Athenian red-figure vases present the viewer with scenes of everyday life which include, amongst other subjects, infant and child figures by now convincingly naturalistic both in attitude and in physical form. In addition, in the late fifth or early fourth century the famous monumental painter, Zeuxis, seems to have been interested in the portrayal of infancy (Pliny *NH* xxxv. 63; Lucian *Zeuxis or Antiochus* 3–4). By the early and mid-fourth century, infant and child figures depicted in naturalistic fashion have also entered the major art of stone sculpture, notably in the Brauron child statues: significantly, these also display a degree of pathos or feeling for the childhood condition. In this, they are forerunners of the popular hellenistic genre of sculpted child figures which are sentimental, and perhaps even nostalgic, in their form and content: the well-known group of chubby boys struggling with a goose is a good example of this (Smith 1991: 136–7, Fig. 170).

At the same time, the changes in the position and perception of women which are so striking a feature of the hellenistic period (Fantham *et al.* 1994: 136–82) represent the culmination of a process which can be traced back to the closing years of the fifth century. At that time at Athens, there was a marked increase in the production of red-figure vases depicting genre scenes not only of children but also of women, many of the latter decorating vase shapes such as the *pyxis* (cosmetics or trinkets box) which were made specifically for the use of women and suggesting that this section of society, in the potter's quarter at least, was now established as a market force. Nevertheless, at Athens the development of new economic and legal rights for women seems to have lagged far behind much of the wider Greek world in the fourth century and the hellenistic period (Sealey 1990: 89–95; Schuller 1985: 106–26; Schaps 1979). Further evidence that the lives of women came to attract greater interest can be found in Middle and New Comedy, which is amply peopled with female characters drawn from real life rather than from mythology (Fantham 1975). It is notable, furthermore, that the exposure of a newborn child was now presented as a dramatic theme worthy of attention and debate. There is evidence, too, that from the fourth century onwards more female children began to obtain a formal education, and also that it became more acceptable for 'respectable' Greek women to pursue jobs outside the home in the intellectual, artistic and scientific spheres (Pomeroy 1977). The process whereby the 'ideal of female seclusion was coming under growing pressure in the fourth century' has been discussed recently by, among others, Sue Blundell (1995: 195–200). This can be seen as one result of the gradual debasement of the *polis* system which, with its rigid social distinction between the male-populated public domain and the private female sphere of existence, had hitherto circumscribed the lives of women and children and had shaped social perception of these discrete groups.

Changing attitudes not only to the feminine but also to the divine in the fourth century and the hellenistic period are perhaps most strikingly manifested in Praxiteles' ground-breaking depiction of the nude Aphrodite. Here we have the loosening, though never dissolution, of the taboo concerning the female body, for the goddess, though naked, is nevertheless divine and, as a cult statue, deserving of honour and worship (Osborne 1994: 81–96; Smith 1991: 79–83). In statues such as this and also, for example, in Praxiteles' Hermes with the infant Dionysos, the mortal worshipper is now permitted closer access to the divine, to witness intimate and private moments in the lives of the gods and goddesses. It has often been argued that this, along with the rationalistic approach to myth and religion adopted by the Sophists and dramatists of the late fifth century BCE, is symptomatic of a degeneration in Greek religious thought and practice (Nilsson 1948: 66–78, 116; 1940: 94, 115, 122). As Mikalson, however, has argued, this is almost certainly an over-simplification of historical reality (Mikalson 1983: 110–18). Nevertheless, that the mortal worshipper could now draw closer to the divine certainly signals a change in the perceived relationship of the mortal with the gods; and that change surely was that 'a personal rather than a collective relationship' with the gods now seemed possible (Blundell 1995: 195). Indeed, this 'personal' relationship may have been of a more intense nature than that experienced via the collective religious practices that lay at the heart of the *polis* system: the increasing popularity in the late fifth and fourth centuries of the various mystery cults would seem to bear this out. Inseparable from this change in the nature of the mortal's relationship and interaction with the divine was undoubtedly the growing concept of the significance of the individual, a development which can be seen throughout Greek society from the late fifth century on.

Given this gradual liberalisation in attitudes towards, and the developing status of, women and children, and therefore also by inference of the female child, it seems plausible to suggest that by the fourth century and the hellenistic period the previously insurmountable contradiction between the nature of divinity and the state of being represented by the female child had been diluted sufficiently to permit the representation of a goddess in her infant form. The shift in the nature of the mortal's relationship with the gods, which now permitted somewhat greater openness of approach and access to the divine, also very likely contributed to this process. Nevertheless, for all these changes, the infant goddess never becomes a common figure in the ancient Greek literary and artistic sources. The distinction between infant male birth and childhood, and adult female manifestation in the divine sphere had, by the fourth century, certainly undergone a degree of moderation; but the basic, culturally determined factors governing gender roles and religious belief in Greek society had only been modified and not overturned. Cultural continuity therefore ensured a blending of new attitudes and social codes with a large measure of the old and the established. It is interesting, therefore, when the figure of the female deity begins to appear in infant form in the fourth century that, as far as we can tell from the extant body of archaeological material, it is the goddess Artemis who first appears in this guise. This, it would seem, was change and innovation which developed in line with cultic associations already long established: for it was Artemis, of all the Olympian goddesses, who not only functioned as a goddess of childbirth but who also claimed a special relationship and cultic identification with young girls. The latter association can be seen, for example, in the ritual dedication of childhood toys to the goddess by girls before their marriage, and also in their celebration of the cult of Artemis Brauronia.

Summary

Analysis of the way in which the ancient Greeks characterised their goddesses, as compared and contrasted with the gods does, in part, help to illuminate the divergence in male and female divine birth scenes. For the goddesses, in tending to be more closely identified than the gods with a particular sexual status must, therefore, exhibit sexual maturity – possession of which very capacity distinguishes the adult female from the child. The gods, on the other hand, who are not restricted in this way, are able to accommodate a phase of childhood and, further, utilise the childhood stage to display and explore aspects of the divine male. However, a discussion of the character of Athene who, though female, exhibits many parallels with the male deities, demonstrates that the peculiarities of divine characterisation, as manifested essentially in the masculine and the feminine, cannot alone account for the discrepancy in the presentation of male and female divine birth and childhood. For Athene, a multi-dimensional mythological figure who juggles a wide range of roles, several of which belong to the male sphere of activity, is nevertheless presented as an adult figure at her birth.

In an attempt to understand this discrepancy it has therefore proved fruitful to supplement this discussion of the characterisation of male and female divinity with an examination of ancient Greek social attitudes to children and to women, and to consider how these attitudes may have affected contemporary perception and visualisation of the divine. It must here be stressed that no direct relationship is assumed between art – whether visual, literary or oral – and social consciousness: that is to say, Greek art and myth does not *illustrate* Greek social attitudes or values. Nevertheless, art is the externalised expression of modes of visualisation at an individual and/or collective level, and it is these modes of visualisation that are strongly influenced by the social context in which they develop. For fifth-century Athens, our consideration of the ancient sources indicates that the female child occupied, on the grounds of both sex- and age-related status, only the lowliest position in the social order. Contemporary religious sensibilities, meanwhile, seem to have required that the gods in their infancy demonstrate that their divinity was not limited by the dependency of the childhood state. Such perception of the nature and manifestation of divinity was, it is suggested, incompatible with the totally dependent and powerless female child figure: for the essential nature of the female child, in its very inability ever to attain completeness, personified and embodied a state of being irreconcilable with the divine. As a result, I therefore suggest that Greek artists and mythographers devised for the goddesses the concept of adult birth.

Social and religious attitudes are not, however, static: they are, rather, dynamic and are forever undergoing modification and change, to a greater or a lesser degree. In examining the first, though still rare, appearances of Greek female deities in the guise of infant and child figures in the fourth century, and subsequently in the hellenistic period, I have therefore argued that this can be explained in terms of the liberalisation and modification over time of Greek social attitudes towards children and women, and of the changing perception of the nature of the mortal's relationship with the gods. As a result of these changes, it seems likely that the previously insurmountable contradiction between the nature of divinity and the state of being represented by the female child figure had been diluted sufficiently to permit the representation of a goddess in her infant form.

It is a complex picture which finally emerges, involving the consideration of many interrelated factors, such as religious perception, social attitudes, modes of visualisation, and chronological change. Nevertheless, it is, I suggest, only through the assimilation, contextualisation and synthesis of such factors that we may approach some degree of understanding of particular aspects of ancient society. Society has never been a simple construct, and there is certainly no reason to expect otherwise in the case of ancient Greece.

ACKNOWLEDGEMENT

The author's thanks go to Sue Blundell and Margaret Williamson for their many stimulating ideas and suggestions for the improvement of this chapter. Its shortcomings, of course, belong to the author alone.

II OBJECTS OF WORSHIP

NOTES

1. This chapter develops a discussion begun by the present author in Beaumont 1995. The reader is referred to pp.340–41 of this article for methodological criteria for the identification of a child figure in the pictorial and plastic arts of classical Greece.
2. Throughout this chapter the term 'god(s)' refers only to male deities, while 'goddess(es)' denotes female deities.
3. Homer *Il.* xiv. 325; *Hymn. Hom. Dionysos* i. 6–7; vii. 56–7; xxvi. 1–6; Hesiod *Theog.* 940–2; Pindar *Ol.* ii. 25–7; Euripides *The Bacchae* 1–9, 88–98, 288–97; Apollodoros *Bibl.* iii. 4. 3; Diodorus Siculus iv. 2. 2–3, v. 52. 1–2. On the ancient literary sources for the birth and childhood of Dionysos see further *LIMC* iii, Dionysos p.417; Arafat 1990: 39–50; Loeb 1979: 28–59, 286–300; Laager 1957: 112–50.
4. Satyrs and silenoi are the companions of Dionysos: partly human in appearance, they have the addition of pointed ears, snub noses and, variously, horse or goat tails. Papposilenos is the aged leader of the silenoi.
5. For a list of red-figure vases depicting the infant Dionysos, and for further references concerning the iconography of the young Dionysos, see Beaumont 1995: 341, ns7–17 inclusive.
6. Faliscan red-figure stamnos, Rome, Villa Giulia 2350. *LIMC* ii, Athamas 3.
7. Dionysos-Zagreus, offspring of Zeus and Persephone, was torn to pieces and devoured by the Titans. Athene, however, rescued the child's heart and gave it to Zeus, who refashioned it into the second Dionysos whom he begat on Semele. Iakchos was a minor Eleusinian deity who, from the fifth century onwards, seems to have been closely assimilated with Dionysos.
8. On the ancient literary sources for the myth, see further Laager 1957: 156–94.
9. For a list of Attic red-figure vases depicting the infant Zeus story, and for further references concerning the iconography of the young Zeus, see Beaumont 1995: 342, n.18, n.19.
10. For a list of Attic red-figure vases depicting the infant Hermes, and for further references concerning the iconography of the child Hermes, see Beaumont 1995: 342, n.20.
11. Caeretan black-figure hydria, Paris, Louvre E702. *LIMC* v, Hermes 241.
12. On the ancient literary sources for the infant Hermes, see *LIMC* v, Hermes p.286; Laager 1957: 151–5; Pearson 1917: 224–70.
13. Pindar *Pyth.* iii. 1–46. Hesiod *Catalogues of Women and Ehoiai*, Evelyn-White 1954, frag. 63, 88–9; Merkelbach and West 1967: frag. 50, 59–60. The *Homeric Hymn* to Asklepios also makes reference to the parentage and birth of Asklepios, and we know of a dithyramb on the Asklepios theme by Telestes of Selinus at the beginning of the fourth century BCE. See further *LIMC* ii, Asklepios on the ancient literary sources for the birth and childhood of Asklepios.
14. For details of this red-figure vase, and for further references concerning the iconography of the infant Asklepios, see Beaumont 1995: 342, n.22.
15. On the ancient literary sources for the myth, see further Fontenrose 1959: 13–22; Laager 1957: 54–111. In some literary accounts, as in some representations in art, it is the adult Apollo who slays Python.
16. For a list of black- and red-figure vases depicting the child Apollo, and for further references concerning the iconography of the infant god, see Beaumont 1995: 343, n.23, n.24, n.25. For the sculptural representations see Figure 5.5.
17. Hesiod *Theog.* 887, 924–9; Homer *Il.* v. 875–80; *Hymn. Hom. Athena* 28; Pindar *Ol.* vii. 35–7. On the ancient literary sources for the birth of Athene, see *LIMC* ii, Athena p.985.
18. On the iconography of the birth of Athene, and for lists of representations, see Arafat 1990: 32–9; *LIMC* ii, Athena p.985–90; Schefold 1981: 19–23, 1978: 12–20; Brommer 1980: 10; Loeb 1979: 14–27; Aebli 1971: 83–8.
19. On the miniaturisation of Athene in many of the representations of her birth in art, see Beaumont 1995: 349–51.

20 On the iconography of the birth of Aphrodite, and for lists of representations, see Arafat 1990: 30–2; *LIMC* ii, Aphrodite 1158–1188; Schefold 1981: 75–85; Brommer 1980: 1–2; Loeb 1979: 60–105; Bérard 1974: 153–60; Aebli 1971: 130–3; Devereux 1970: 1229–48; Simon 1959.
21 For a list of representations of the child Artemis, and for further references concerning the iconography of the infant Artemis, see Beaumont 1995: 351 n.53, 352. For additional representations in which the child Apollo appears without Artemis, see Beaumont 1995: 343, n.23, n.24.
22 Athenian or Apulian red-figure neck-amphora, once Naples, Second Hamilton Collection, now lost. *LIMC* ii, Apollon 995.
23 I am grateful here for the generous help and stimulating comments of Susan Woodford, received via a personal communication of 15 December 1994.
24 Choes: wine jugs used during the celebration of the children's 'choes' day at the festival of the Anthesteria.
25 See e.g. Athens Nat. Mus. 1739 (here Figure 5.6) and 14532. Van Hoorn 1951: figs 278–9.
26 Freestanding marble figure of seated girl illustrated in Figure 5.7: Athens Nat. Mus. 695. See Vorster 1983 for further examples of freestanding sculpted figures of mortal female children. Stele illustrated in Figure 5.8: Athens Nat. Mus. 3289, Clairmont 1993: ii, 846b. Stele of Mynnia: Malibu, J. Paul Getty Museum 71.AA.121, Clairmont 1993: ii, 718. See Hirsch-Dyczek 1983 for further examples of grave stelai depicting mortal female children.
27 See e.g. *Tht.* 197 e; *Rep.* 441 a--b; *Gorg.* 464 d and 502 e; *Soph.* 234 b--c; *Euthd.* 299 d; *Phlb.* 14 d.
28 See e.g. *EE* i. 1215 b 23–4; ii. 1219 b 5a.
29 See further on the social status of and attitudes towards children, Golden 1990, esp. 1–12.
30 See e.g. *EE* i. 1214 b 30; vii. 1238 a 33; *NE* vii. 1154 b 10; *Pol.* vii. 1323 a 33; *Probl.* xxx. 14. 957 a 43.
31 See e.g. *Ep.* viii. 355 c; *Rep.* iv. 431 c.
32 *Hymn. Hom. Del. Ap.* 123–5; Hesiod *Theog.* 492–3; Sophokles *Ichneutae* 271–2.
33 I wish here to reassure the reader that having used the evidence of Plato and Aristotle in an attempt to understand Athenian social attitudes to children, and to a lesser degree to women, in the classical period, my argument for a change and modification of these attitudes in the fourth century does not, as may first appear, constitute a circular debate. In the first place, the very fact that philosophers in the fourth century were now focusing on children and on gender issues as subjects worthy of discussion implies, regardless of the particular views being expressed, that for the first time children and women had taken on a more visible social profile and prominence than heretofore. Indeed, it seems likely that, in part at least, it was in reaction to such changes that Aristotle's writings attempted, amongst other things, to reinforce traditional social views of and roles for children and women. The Athenocentric nature of the written evidence for the classical period, down to and including the fourth century BCE, when compared and contrasted with the archaeological evidence from the wider Greek world during the same period, also makes it imperative for us to remember that Athens seems to have retained a greater degree of social conservatism than elsewhere. Furthermore, it is only when the archaeological and the literary evidence is taken together that something approaching a realistic picture of ancient society can be formed. For while the written evidence of the philosophers articulates a particular view of society that is educated, generally idealistic in principle, and usually aristocratic and male in perspective, the archaeological evidence is better suited as a mirror of wider social realities, in which changes and modifications are reflected, often unconsciously, at a much earlier stage than they appear in the conscious medium of literature.

6

THE NATURE OF HEROINES

Emily Kearns

That superhuman beings, recipients of worship, bear a resemblance to those who worship them, is an old perception: 'The Ethiopians say that their Gods are snub-nosed and black, the Thracians that theirs are blue-eyed and red-haired' was Xenophanes' way of putting it in the sixth or early fifth century BCE,[1] and with many modifications the idea has continued to be influential in more modern studies of religion, notably in the Durkheimian tradition. Even after it has been formulated, Xenophanes' own preferred model of 'one God who is greatest among Gods and men, not like mortals in form or in thought'[2] is not an easy one to work with. The mind tends to slip back to images and concepts more clearly within its grasp, to patterns of thought which derive largely from its own direct experience, social and psychological. And yet such patterns are not always and not only a simple projection of day-to-day experience onto a more than human plane. If the divine has always been perceived in at least partly anthropomorphic terms, it has also and simultaneously been constructed as 'the other'.

One obvious field in which this paradox holds is the predication of gender onto the divine. The existence of a narrative dimension within a religious tradition seems to demand that some sort of sex (physical or quasi-physical) and 'socially-defined' gender be assigned to the divine participants, and yet it is often the case that gender roles, in particular, do not completely follow the lines laid down by the society which has formulated the tradition. And since it is the female which is the 'marked' gender, the one which is perceived as somehow different (we seldom speak of 'the position of men in antiquity'), it is the female roles among the divine which are more likely to differ from those of their human counterparts. In the Greek tradition, a male, in the shape of Zeus, gives birth, to be sure; but with this important exception, where the male gods differ from their human counterparts is not in respect of their roles *as males*, whereas the positions and functions of, say, Athena, Artemis and Aphrodite differ quite considerably from those ordinarily assigned to human women *as females*. 'War will be the concern of men' says Hector to Andromache,[3] but Athena seems not to have heard this. The prolonged virginity of Athena, Artemis and Hestia was not a choice that Greek women could make, or have made for them. And the free and easy sexual choices of Aphrodite, as indeed her status as a married woman, were surely in reality available to very few prostitutes or *hetairai*. We need then to be cautious about interpretations which explicate the goddesses of the Greek pantheon in terms of supposed male perceptions of the fragmented roles of women.[4] If this is a valid viewpoint at all, goddesses represent a refraction, not a reflection, of the way men view women, a kind of subconscious exercise on a 'what if' theme.[5] We might also suppose that women's perceptions of their own roles – and of what was not possible for them – would have some relevance to the concept of a goddess. Is it plausible that men were the only makers of myths?

Goddesses, then, are poised between possible and impossible roles for women, and also have affinities both with women and with male gods – their divine status, as Nicole Loraux (1992) points out, usually taking precedence over their sex where relations with humans are concerned. But goddesses and gods are not the only objects of worship in the archaic and classical Greek world: apart from 'gods' and 'humans', the Greeks spoke of a category 'heroes', generally thought of as individual dead people who had acquired exceptional powers, approximating to those of gods, and whom it was proper to worship in ways analogous to, if not identical with, the modes of divine worship. We may also think of mythical characters, especially those conforming to common story-patterns, as 'honorary heroes', since it was normal for cult heroes to be identified with such figures, and even our surviving evidence shows how very widespread the cult of the protagonists of myth and epic was. Included among the heroes, as goddesses among gods (*theoi*) are some female specimens of the type, who may be called by their own feminine form, *heroinai* or *heroissai*. The potential affinities of these beings are quite complex. Whereas the position of goddesses can be shown in a simple diagram:

Goddesses Gods
Women   Men

the three-step sequence gives another pattern:

Goddesses Gods
Heroines   Heroes
Women   Men

in which the heroine may resemble her neighbour in three directions, the goddess, the hero, and the woman. Does she in fact stand at a point equidistant between them? Does her human past make her resemble an ordinary woman more than a goddess, or does her status as an object of worship approximate her more closely to the divine – and how do her relations with gender roles let us see the answers? Are all the functions of a male hero open also to heroines, or (and) do heroines have roles distinct from their male counterparts? Finally, is it ever possible to guess whether the 'meaning' of a heroine was more relevant to men or women?

Heroic beings were, as we have said, generally thought to have been human before their deaths. The degree of importance attached to this human life would vary in individual cases, and it was sometimes less essential in the case of heroines than of heroes: significantly, heroines can merge into the theoretically non-human nymphs, and on occasion the same figure may be classified as either.[6] But probably more often than not there was a story, or several competing stories, about the hero(ine)'s life, which would account for the heroic status after death. Only in a very few cases, however (Herakles, Theseus, the Iliadic heroes) could this story be compared to a biography. More usually, the story related to one moment, perhaps the hero's institution of a divine cult, or typically in the case of a heroine, her death.[7] Such heroes do not, perhaps, seem like 'real' people, as they exist for only a short moment in mythical time, but the actions which they perform, though usually in some way outstanding, are strongly coloured by the heroes' humanity. The hero has a two-phase existence, a human lifetime and a more-than-human afterlife, corresponding very roughly to myth and cult. We might expect then that while the human lives of heroines show them, naturally enough, as human women, in cult they would be little constricted by human gender roles and show a pattern much closer to that of the goddess. But we do not need to probe very far to see that this is not always so.

Our information about the cult of heroines is unlikely to be a typical sample, because much of it is related by sources interested in literary connections and in the picturesque and unusual. But the evidence of inscriptions supplies us with some incidental information which is valuable precisely because to describe the worship of heroines is not the main purpose of the documents. The picture of the heroine's place which emerges from the sacrifice calendars of the Attic *demes* is a remarkably unexciting one, with the heroine apparently acting as adjunct to a male hero. In the fourth-century calendar of the Marathonian Tetrapolis, for example (IG II^2 1358), several sacrifices to heroes, usually named or at least given an epithet, are prescribed, and each is followed by a sacrifice of lesser value[8] to an anonymous heroine. The sacrifice to the heroine is necessary, from the human point of view, but her subordinate position in regard to the hero is also clear.

We get a similar impression from the so-called 'Totenmahl' reliefs, a type of picture set up as a votive originally in honour of heroes and later for the ordinary dead.[9] Here, typically, the male hero reclines on a couch, enjoying a banquet or symposium, while a female attendant is seated beside him (sitting being the less relaxed and honorific position), offering him food and drink. The female figure does not seem to be a worshipper (they appear in quite a different style, sometimes on the same stone) – rather a personage of essentially the same type as the hero but of lesser status. This supposition is confirmed by the inscriptions which exist in many examples, recording a dedication to a male and a female name. The two figures must be identified as hero and heroine, both objects of cult, yet with the heroine occupying a subordinate position and playing the role of a woman of the hero's household. It is tempting to say 'the role of the hero's wife', and in fact in some of the sacrifice groups, where a mythological identification has been made, the relationship of the two figures is unambiguously that of a married couple. In other cases, the nature of the grouping is not so clear. In the calendar of the deme Thorikos, for example,[10] a hero is several times accompanied by 'heroines' in the plural – not several wives, presumably. Two possibilities suggest themselves: the heroines might have been thought of as the hero's wife and daughters (one might compare here well-known mythological groups such as the daughters of Kekrops or of Erechtheus), or else the relationship was not strongly conceptualised in terms of human society. Whichever is closer to the truth, it is still the case that the heroines are secondary to 'their' hero: the heroines of the deme's eponym Thorikos, for instance, receive not a sacrifice but a table-offering, a much lesser gift, when Thorikos himself receives sacrifice of a selected sheep or ox. Just so among human beings: women often received smaller portions of food than men,[11] explicitly because they were thought to need less nourishment, but no doubt also confirming their lesser status. The heroines of Attic cult, then, seem to know their place, analogously to mortal women. From this angle they both reflect the preferred relation of the sexes and provide an unconsciously applied model for it.

Mythology, however, complicates the issue. The same Thorikos calendar includes offerings to Kephalos and Prokris, the famous pair of hunters whose myths centre on their stormy marital relations. As with the hero–heroines groupings more typical of this calendar, Kephalos receives a sacrificial victim while his female associate gets a mere table-offering, so that in cult the pair follow the normal, paradigmatic relation of a man and his wife or womenfolk. But Prokris' story makes of her a character very different from the ideal submissive wife. To start with, a married woman as huntress is itself an anomaly: mythical huntresses should be virgins, just as for males hunting is associated with the period of passage to full manhood, not with maturity itself.[12] As one of those rare heroines with something approaching a life-story, Prokris further offends against views of how a wife should behave by falling for a 'Cosi fan tutte' trick with her disguised husband, by associating suspiciously closely with Minos in Crete, and by spying on her husband when she suspects him of infidelity. The outlines of the story were demonstrably known in the fifth century. It is of course quite uncertain to what degree such stories were present in people's minds as they attended the sacrifice to Kephalos and Prokris, but it seems clear that myth and cult are pulling in different directions here. Like a goddess, the mythological Prokris behaves with a degree of freedom which is both unrealistic, in the context of the women of classical Athens, and undesirable in terms of accepted morality. I shall have more to say about 'disreputable' aspects of mythology later; for the moment we may note that this case shows a complete reversal of the expected pattern of a 'human', rather constrained, lifetime and a 'divine', freer afterlife.

The type of cult we have been considering, where heroines are neatly subordinate to heroes and so mirror normal human society, can be considered to speak equally to both sexes, confirming their view of proper relations. But heroines are also worshipped apart from heroes, in a variety of circumstances. A conspicuous group among them is formed by those heroines whose cult is performed largely or exclusively by women, often but not always by young girls before their marriage. The subject of 'girls' transitions', rites with a broadly initiatory character which appear to prepare a girl for marriage and maturity, or mark her readiness to make the change, is one that has received much attention in recent years.[13] With the exception of rites performed directly before marriage, these rituals were performed at regularly recurring festivals and by groups, not individuals, and so it is likely that the initiatory element was less clear to the participants than it is to modern students of religion; all the same, we can fairly suppose that a girl taking part would have in mind not only the deity in whose honour the festival was held, but also the fact that she herself was now old enough to participate. Not all of these rites are connected with heroines but a large number of them are, through cult or myth or both, and as Dowden has shown, where a heroine is involved, the initiatory element is that much clearer and more explicit because 'the heroine is the necessary prototype for the maiden'.[14]

To take some examples. On Delos, young girls took part in the island's major festival by singing hymns for Apollo, Artemis and Leto, at the same time as other cities also sent choruses. Callimachus (*Hymn* 4. 278–99) links the custom with the original arrival of the daughters of Boreas, elsewhere said to be Hyperboreans ('from beyond the north wind'), for whom the maidens of Delos also cut their hair before marriage.[15] In Sparta, a passage in Theocritus' 'Wedding-song of Helen' (*Idyll* 18) allows us to see that young girls honoured Helen by hanging garlands and pouring libations of oil on a certain plane-tree said to be hers. This is put into the mythical context of the Helen who has just left her friends and their typically adolescent occupation of running races, and married Menelaos. In Athens, four or, more likely, two girls between seven and eleven were appointed as *arrhephoroi* for a year, a custom plainly initiatory in origin though confined to so few participants. Their occupations were mirrored in myth by those of the daughters of Kekrops: thus they took part in the weaving of the *peplos* ceremonially presented to Athena, where the daughters of Kekrops were claimed as the inventors of weaving, and the ritual which concluded their service, from which they got their name, has clear affinities with the story of Athena's entrusting the child Erichthonios to the sisters.[16] The connection is confirmed by dedicatory inscriptions in which the *arrhephoroi*, or their families, record their service 'to Athena and Pandrosos' – in the myth, the 'good' sister who obeys Athena's instructions.[17] It is not too much of a leap to suggest that the girls understood that they performed their action in honour of Pandrosos and her sisters. Slightly less perspicuous is the much-discussed *arkteia* or bear-ritual of Brauron, on the coast of Attica, a custom in which many more girls took part. Though a heroine, Iphigeneia, was undoubtedly worshipped alongside Artemis in this cult complex, the tie-in between the myth in which she is sacrificed, or nearly sacrificed but saved to become Artemis' priestess, and the ritual, in which girls in some way imitate bears, is to say the least oblique. We are helped out to some extent by the *aition* of the closely related cult of Artemis at Mounichia, which relates that the bear imitation was imposed by an oracle as remedy for a plague which came about when two boys had killed a tame bear in Artemis' sanctuary after it had scratched their sister. It can be shown that the girl in this story is partly parallel to Iphigeneia at Brauron, but a gap still remains between what girls did at Brauron and what they heard about the local heroine.

While it is possible that in all such ceremonies heroic beings were involved, at least as an *aition*, in many it was a goddess, often Artemis, who was the dominant figure. As a virgin goddess, who also presides over the chief danger of the married state, namely childbirth, Artemis is relevant enough to a girl's present and future experience and to the moment of transition between the two. But mythical background and everyday events are widely divergent: as we have seen, no human female remains unmarried indefinitely as Artemis does, and so Artemis can only be the model for the first stage of the process, before the transition is made. Heroines are a little more like women in this respect. During their life they too are assumed to have grown up with marriage as destiny; for them as for their human worshippers, the transition was a necessity, and yet as heroines they retain a connection with the virginal state by not in fact making that transition, or making it in an irregular way.[18] Thus there is still a gap between heroine and woman. The mythical experience is either implausible in terms of 'real life', or not what a girl would wish for herself. Iphigeneia is sacrificed, or else saved by the goddess's personal intervention to become her virgin priestess, perhaps in a distant, barbarian land. Disaster comes to Pandrosos and her sisters when they carry out the task Athena gives them. Helen marries normally, it is true, but her history after her marriage was scarcely one to be imitated, even if we discount the story of her earlier abduction by Theseus. The Hyperborean maidens died on Delos, before they could return to their homeland. And there are many other heroines whom we know or can infer to have received special cult from unmarried girls, who either died before they could be married – often in some dramatic way – or who, like Kallisto in Arcadia, died as a result of premature sexual experience.[19] For all of these, the change from girl to married woman, from child to adult, is crucially relevant in a way it is not to the virgin goddesses Artemis and Athena, but either it is attended with danger and/or disgrace, or it is substituted with a transition from life to death, from human to heroic status. The heroine's destiny, often tragic, always different from the expected norm, sets her apart from the ordinary and differentiates her from the merely human. Heroines of this type, then, are significantly different from both goddesses and women. Paradoxically for a group with such female concerns, they are perhaps more comparable with their male counterparts in this respect, for boys too experience rituals with strong initiatory elements, which dramatise their status as nearly-but-not-yet adults, and which sometimes include the heroic cult of boys like themselves. Some rites involve a fixed number of boys and girls together, possibly pairing hero and heroine.[20] Occasionally, figures even cross the gender boundary in terms of worship: before marriage – a clearer rite of passage for the individual than any regular festival – the girls of Troizen, we are told by Euripides, used to dedicate their hair to the young unmarried hero Hippolytos (*Hippolytus* 1424–7). Conversely in Attica, as we shall see later on, the *ephebes* – adolescent boys in training for full citizenship – worshipped Pandrosos' sister Aglauros. Patterns of sex reversal like this are not uncommonly connected with liminal or transitional states such as those of adolescence. But in general the patterns for girls and boys remain along parallel lines, comparable, but not meeting. We can see, for instance, that figures like Hyakinthos at Sparta stand in a similar relation towards boys: like so many of our heroines, he dies on the verge of maturity and never succeeds in making the transition to adulthood, yet is worshipped by those who hope to do so. Heroine and hero stand in an analogous relation to the humans who pay them cult.

But heroines, of course, do not all die young and virginal. Those whose myths have them proceed to the next stage of life often become participants in an event quite definitely not open to males: motherhood. The role of paramour – or rape victim – of a god and mother of a hero is one of the oldest attested manifestations of the heroine, being the stated subject of the Hesiodic *Eoiai* or *Catalogue of Women*. The whole idea has an obvious genealogical function: through a local (male) hero or ancestor an area or people is supplied with divine antecedents, while the hero's own glory is enhanced by his more than mortal father. The mother need be no more than an inevitable biological link. But the fragmentary Hesiodic poem already shows much more than this and, as well as genealogy and the deeds of the heroes, it is clearly interested in the women themselves. Epic, too, refers in passing to the circumstances of conception of the sons of the gods, often in some detail: the minor fighter Eudoros, for instance, was conceived when Hermes spotted his mother Polymele at a maidens' dance for Artemis (transitional rites once more!) and went with her secretly to an upper chamber.[21] More conspicuously, Odysseus in the underworld sees the heroines, the mothers of heroes, before he encounters the heroes themselves.[22] Obviously there is interest in such women as a class: what sort of women could thus catch the attention of the gods?

Not all of the participants in this very common mythical pattern can be shown to be heroines in the cult sense, although we know that some among them did receive cult. Occasionally, they were worshipped together with the god who was their lover,[23] sometimes with their son,[24] but most often there was no obvious cult grouping. Certainly their mythology scarcely permitted them to appear as the wifely adjunct of a male hero. Viewed from the standpoint of ordinary women, their position is anomalous. Clearly, most women would have hoped to bear sons, and illustrious sons if possible; equally clearly, pregnancy without marriage was a disaster. These heroines, then, combine the conventional and approved with the abnormal and condemned, although in broad terms both parts of the equation remain possible for ordinary women. Where the heroine differs from the ordinary woman is in the nature of her lover and her state of closeness to the divine. The *Catalogue of Women* in fact explicitly puts sex with a god into the context of a former time when gods and mortals sat together and shared banquets (fr 1.6–7), a privileged age far better than the present. And because such heroines are remembered for glory rather than for shame, it might seem that the pluses outweigh the minuses – very different from the situation of the ordinary unmarried mother, who can only recover something of her good name if the father of her child will agree to marry her. However, the position of the heroine has enough resemblance to a potential real-life scenario for the typical myth to show her difficulties.[25] Occasionally, the girl's family is kind to her, and her father brings up the child as his own son, as in the case of Polymele (above). More often, she is driven in fear to expose her child (Psamathe, the Attic Chione), nearly killed by her father (Danae, whose father admittedly had special reasons[26]), or actually killed by him (Alope, subject of lost tragedies by Sophocles and Euripides), or by her brother (Apemosyne, the ironically named 'Carefreeness', whose child unusually was never born). If her partner is Zeus, the unfortunate heroine is likely to suffer from the jealousy of Hera (Io, Semele), which again may not implausibly be taken as reflecting human circumstances. Refusing or escaping the god's advances has also its drawbacks (Daphne, Kassandra) so, altogether, catching the eye of a deity would seem to carry a high risk. Euripides' memorable portrayal in *Ion* of the sufferings of Kreousa, raped by Apollo and driven to expose her child, though a psychological *tour de force*, is really only an exploration of what is already a major strand in the mythical pattern. There is then usually a split between the heroine's experience of these events 'in her lifetime' – in the myth itself – and afterwards, when she is worshipped as a cult heroine or remembered as one of the beautiful, privileged women of an older and better age. Unlike some of the cases we looked at earlier, such a split corresponds very neatly to the heroine's classic position between goddess and woman and her double life, 'then' as mortal woman and 'now' as something more. For goddesses of course, like Aphrodite and Demeter, may bear children outside marriage without incurring any reproach.[27]

So far we have been examining heroines primarily in connection with sexuality, in a broad sense: with virginity (and its loss), with the role of the wife, with motherhood. This fits in both with the tendency of Greek men to see women largely in a sexual and reproductive light and, very likely, with women's own perceptions of these states and roles as articulating their lives. But although gender was of central importance in determining what a woman did and how she did it, her concerns could never be exclusively gynaecological. We have already seen how, in the mythical sphere, Pandrosos and her sisters were the first to practise women's typical work of weaving (following the prevalent pattern of the πρῶτος εὑρετής, the first inventor), as well as being concerned with childcare. And while it is on the whole true to say that women's activities take place inside the home, there are cases where they are required to go out, notably for religious celebrations. The extreme example here is the priestess, who not only fulfils her duties physically outside the home, but who occupies a public position in the *polis*. The role of priestess is one very frequently taken by the heroine, and as she is usually the first priestess of a particular cult she is also an inventor-institutor figure, receiving her instructions from the deity in person and acting as model for her successors. As we might expect from the parallelism between female and male priesthoods, this is a pattern found with male heroes too. The chosen one becomes priest(ess), and after death a hero(ine) who is worshipped in the sanctuary (s)he served. This is illustrated very clearly at the end of Euripides' *Iphigeneia among the Taurians*, where Athena first tells Orestes to institute a temple and a particular sacrificial ritual for Artemis, then turning to Iphigeneia says (1462–7):

> 'And you, Iphigeneia, must be priestess [κληδουχεῖν] of this goddess at the holy meadows[28] of Brauron. When you die, you will be buried there, and people will dedicate to you the beautifully woven dresses that women in life-destroying labour leave behind in their houses.'

Once more we see a split between lifetime and after-life, but here the heroine is poised even more clearly between goddess and woman; as a priestess, she is like a woman, specifically like her successors, but she receives cult which, if not identical to divine cult, at least brings her much closer to goddess than to mortal.[29] The location of her activities in the sacerdotal sphere both reflects human realities (what was possible for women) and places the pattern in the same area as male priestly heroes.

Authority in the limited religious sphere of a particular priesthood was in the classical period the only public authority a woman might have, and participation in religious events was normally women's most conspicuous appearance in the visible, public life of the *polis*. Politics, in the modern sense, was properly the concern of men. Obviously, we would expect to find male heroes mirroring the concern of Greek men with the affairs of the *polis*, and indeed it seems that there is often a particularly close and characteristic link between the hero and the city. A cursory inspection makes it equally clear that – moving up a notch – goddesses are not constrained by the embargo on their sex in politics which applies at the mortal level. The goddesses who side so passionately with the Achaeans in the Iliad – Athena and Hera – are precisely those who appear most often as patron city-goddesses, actively concerned in the welfare of the *polis*. What then of heroines? The picture, as we might predict, is not quite straightforward.

One obvious way in which heroes are linked with political units (cities, territories, groups within the city) is through a sort of patronage expressed by a similarity of name. The eponymous hero is then believed to have given his name to the group: thus an ancestor Lakedaimon named the area around Sparta so called,[30] the sons of Ion gave their names to the four Ionian tribes, and so on. Sometimes such connections were no more than speculative fiction, but in other cases it is clear that such heroes had a real identity, and plausible that they were felt to be both the prototype and the protector of the community. 'The community' in this sense, of course, is primarily a male community, because it expresses itself in the public, political field. An eponymous heroine would seem to be an anomaly, therefore, and indeed there are fewer female than male eponyms. But women are far from unknown in the role. According to Strabo, famous Asian cities like Ephesos, Smyrna, Kyme and Myrina were named after their Amazon founders.[31] Amazons, of course, exist in order to do things which are normally done by men; as far as *Greek* heroines go, the picture is a different one. The pages of Pausanias show how on the narrative level their role was a passive one, and hence normal: typically they were the wives or mothers of the founders, who named their new city after a female relative.[32] A partial exception is formed by the Arcadian city of Mantineia, whose 'second founder', the originator of the city's site in historical times, was a woman, Antinoe, who in typical founder style was buried at the city's common hearth.[33] In one other case, Pausanias' language suggests that a heroine had a hand in the foundation, but there the schema is the stereotype of the ambitious wife urging her husband to political activity.[34] But where the eponym had an actual existence in cult, her importance might well seem greater than that of a passive honorand. The heroine Triteia was worshipped alongside Ares, her mythical lover, in the small Achaian city of that name, probably receiving divine rather than heroic honours. Plataia, eponym of the Boiotian city, was identified as the daughter of the river-god Asopos, so put firmly under male control, but in her sanctuary, near the altar of Zeus Eleutherios, she was apparently her own mistress.[35] Here, cult gives the heroine an importance which is lacking in the narrative dimension, for genealogical and 'historical' myth sticks to the realities of life, which exclude women from politics.

With a very few exceptions. The eponym of Lampsakos in the Troad was the heroine Lampsake, who like Triteia came to receive divine honours. She was said to have been the daughter of a barbarian king, who revealed to the Greek colonists the existence of a plot against them, hence enabling them to exterminate their enemies and consolidate their foundation. When she died of an illness, in gratitude they named their city after her.[36] The story is a picturesque and exciting one, giving the eponym a crucial importance. Without her, the city would not exist, yet she does not go beyond the woman's role by actually founding or ruling it. She has a close affinity with a group I have discussed elsewhere, those young girls who die or are sacrificed to save their city, and who subsequently become heroines.[37] City saviours of this type step out from their usual place, carefully guarded within the home, and intervene in what is usually a life-and-death matter for the whole community, yet they could not be said to be participating in public affairs in anything like the normal ways open to men. Lampsake herself, a non-Greek, is an appropriate patron for a city of mixed racial composition; it is interesting that the figure thus expressing the city's special identity is female, and prompts comparisons with the Amazon founders of other Asian cities.

Returning to eponymous heroines, we find far fewer examples among the city's subgroups than we do among cities or territories. These subgroups were divisions of the citizen body, and so their composition was primarily or exclusively male; normally this is reflected in their eponyms. An interesting counter-example, perhaps the only one, is the heroine Hyrnetho (Doric Hyrnatho), eponym of a tribe at Argos. Here, as in other Doric-speaking cities much of the population was divided into three tribes supposed to be named after the sons of Herakles, while a fourth group, believed to be of non-Dorian origin, was placed in a group of its own. The name of the non-Dorian tribe varied from city to city; the Argive Hyrnathioi were believed to take their name from the daughter of King Temenos (himself a Heraklid and so Dorian), who was a heroine real enough to have cult at both Argos and Epidauros. Why was this? It is hard to imagine that a group of men within the city would actively wish to take their name from a woman, when parallel groups were named from men. Perhaps the tradition could have begun as a put-down for the non-Dorian element in Argos. But if so, the Hyrnathioi managed to manipulate the tradition to their own advantage, by producing the story which became known: Hyrnetho was Dorian by birth, and the wife of Deiphontes, whom her father Temenos favoured above her brothers. The brothers then showed their true nature by killing their father, and in some versions they accidentally kill Hyrnetho too, in trying to separate her from her husband; in others, Hyrnetho and Deiphontes succeed to the rule of Temenos. In either case, she is necessary to the succession of the (presumably) non-Dorian Deiphontes, so both providing the link with the present day and joining the two sections of the population. This of course reflects one kind of importance which ordinary mortal women could have in the world of politics: as brides, they forged links between families and created new loyalties. For all that, Hyrnetho as cult-figure and eponym had an importance which Deiphontes did not.

Of course, the mere fact of being the object of cult or the subject of myth placed the heroine in a public arena which few living women could occupy. But with a few exceptions,[38] they do not reach this heroic status by stepping into what is seen as men's territory during their 'lifetime'. Their actions or destiny may be outstanding and unusual – they would not be heroines if that were not so – but they remain within the range of what is defined as feminine. This is much more clearly the case for heroines than it is for goddesses who may, for instance, remain virgin without dying and who may participate directly in war and politics. Male heroes also typically perform acts defined as theirs by gender (fighting, killing monsters, exercising political power), but here the contrast with their divine counterparts is less marked.

In making this point, I do not mean to say that a heroine's role – any more than that of a goddess – is only to give a somewhat distorted reflection of what is possible for women, significant though such a function may be. It is also often the case that the femaleness of heroines allows the expression of other ideas, such as human proximity to the divine, or the workings of a particular cult. In fact, a heroine's significance can rarely be summed up in one statement. There are some examples, however, which show particularly clearly how the same figure may display two or more specific, closely defined meanings, often depending on context. The heroine we have just been considering, Hyrnetho, has a political importance as patron of the non-Dorians at Argos. But her story also speaks especially to women: while she is a good daughter, acquiescing in her father's choice of husband, she chooses her husband again over her brothers. Though she suffers for it, she provides a model for a woman's proper choice between natal and conjugal family (unlike the 'bad woman' Althaia, who prefers her brothers to her son).[39] Iphigeneia is a more complex figure. She is the prototype of all the girls who perform the rite of passage at Brauron, and hence who move from childhood to adulthood, from maiden (*parthenos*) to woman (*gyne*). But she is also the first priestess of Artemis at the site, the cult's human institutor and mediator with the divine. Again, she has a special relationship with women who die in childbirth. Finally, moving into an area inhabited by men as well as women, she is the sacrificial victim in a story which has connections with the schema of patriotic self-sacrifice, but which can also be presented as a shocking abhorrence.

Aglauros is another heroine significant in both female and male worlds, though here her two spheres are more mutually exclusive. She has at least a mythical presence with her sister Pandrosos in the transitional rite of the Arrhephoria. Her more significant cult connection is with the uncanny, dangerous rites of Athena known as Plynteria and Kallynteria (washing and beautifying), and she may have been thought of as the institutor of these.[40] But she has also a connection in both cult and myth with Ares, not a very feminine deity, and the exclusively male ephebes took their oath in her sanctuary; at least in later times, she was said to have sacrificed herself to save Athens, a patriotic story suitable for those undergoing military training.[41] Here, then, a form of the sex inversion sometimes found in connection with transitional states (like that of the ephebes) has a more specific appropriateness, giving a heroine an unusual link with males on their own.

As a final example, we could take those heroines who appear as part of a couple acting together, as priests, givers of hospitality, or in other typically heroic modes. At Eleusis, for instance, Metaneira was worshipped alongside her husband Keleos; they had entertained Demeter on her wanderings, though it was perhaps their daughters who were really the prototype of the Eleusinian priestess of Demeter. At the Theban Kabeirion, Pelarge and her husband Isthmiades were the institutor figures for the cult. Heroines might act alongside their husbands as *trophoi*, nurses or foster-parents, like Klymene alongside Diktys, the saviours of the child Perseus.[42] Such heroines are significant for their particular role as part of a cult complex, but also conform to the pattern of the heroic couple, where the female is clearly the lesser partner.

Heroes and heroines reflect society, but like gods they also define another plane of existence, something which is more than merely human. A strong element of the unusual and paradoxical often characterises the heroic. But the gender divide goes deep in Greek thought, and it is rare to find a heroine – who was, after all, a woman in her lifetime – behaving in ways felt to be radically inappropriate to her sex. What is perhaps surprising, given that finding, is the range of functions and significances still open to the heroine. As priestess, hostess, institutor or *trophos* she performs essentially the same role as a male hero, and is worshipped in similar ways. Worshipped in connection with rites of passage, she is analogous to the heroes of similar rites for boys. Only political or military activity is scarce in the myths of heroines, and even here a few heroines make their appearance in a cult context. By contrast, heroines predominate over heroes as consorts of the gods and as saving victims, roles where passivity does not diminish importance. Other aspects and types of heroines have not been touched on – the heroine as old woman, like Hekale in Attica, expressing the tribulations of married life, like Hippodameia at Olympia, or afflicted with madness, like Antiope, Ino, or the daughters of Proitos.

Heroines also vary in their precise location between woman and goddess – it is seldom neatly in the middle – and additionally in the degree to which they display a divide between a human-style past and a contrasting goddess-like after-life, relatively free of gender restrictions. Such questions can make useful tools for analysis, but scarcely permit easy generalising answers. Even in the case of individual heroines, our evidence is in many cases pitifully thin and simply will not permit us to see how a particular heroine works.

What we do have is probably accurate in suggesting that heroines were fewer in number than male heroes (an instructive contrast with gods), but it is quite possible that were we suddenly able to view the Greek world as contemporaries, with access to a far wider range of documentation and with the ability to undertake fieldwork, we should find still more variety. Women's lives in Greece might in general have been comparatively restricted, but imagination — of both sexes, no doubt — was far less constrained.

NOTES

1 fr. 16 Diels-Kranz.
2 *ibid*. fr. 15.
3 Hom. *Il*. 6.492.
4 For a clear and concise statement of this point of view, see Pomeroy 1975: 4–9. The idea is developed in much more detail in Friedrich 1978. Essentially, it is a development, influenced in part by feminist theory, of the application of Jungian archetypes to Greek mythology, as pioneered by Kerényi and Jung himself.
5 See the critique of Loraux 1992.
6 See Nock 1944: 165 and n.81.
7 See Dowden 1989: esp. 43–6.
8 This is only partly explicable by the fact that a male sheep, in particular, would fetch more than a female, taken in conjunction with the (not invariable, B27, 44) norm prescribing victims of the same sex as the recipient. (See Van Straten 1987: 167–70.) This would account for the discrepancy between the offerings made to the *heros Pheraios* and his heroine at B15–16, but not for the 'extras' given to the male partner at B9, 19–21, 23–4, 25–6.
9 See Thönges-Stringaris 1965.
10 *SEG* 33 (1983) no. 147.
11 Xen. *Lac. Pol.* 1.3–4 (unmarried girls); less food needed, Arist. *Hist. An.* 608b15. The fourth-century Attic inscription Sokolowski 20 prescribes equal portions of sacrificial meat for the *orgeones* and their wives, but we cannot be sure that this is typical. However, it has been well demonstrated by Osborne (1993) that the classic article of Detienne (1989 [1979]), contending that women had virtually no access to flesh foods, goes much too far in extending structural patterns into everyday practice.
12 Vidal-Naquet 1986: 117–22.
13 To cite some prominent book-length examples: Brelich 1969, Calame 1977, Brulé 1987, Sourvinou-Inwood 1988, Dowden 1989.
14 Dowden 1989: 46.
15 Boys were also involved in both myth and ritual, but the girls are always mentioned first and seem to have been more important. There are further details in the Homeric Hymn to Apollo 146–64, Herodotus 4.33, and Pausanias 1.43.4. The evidence is of considerable complexity, and has been explored in Sale 1961; Calame 1977: 194–204; Robertson 1983a: 144–53. See also Larson 1995: 118–21.
16 Athena gave the sisters a chest or basket containing the child Erichthonios, and told them not to open it; they, or two of them, disobeyed and were driven by madness to hurl themselves off the Acropolis to their deaths. The *arrhephoroi* were also required to carry a container without knowing what was inside it.
17 IG II^2 3472, 3515 (second century BCE).
18 Compare Larson 1995: 116–21.
19 On Kallisto, see Henrichs 1987: 254–77.

II OBJECTS OF WORSHIP

20 For examples, see Brelich 1969: esp. 355–87.
21 Iliad 16.179–92.
22 Odyssey 11.225–332.
23 For instance, Triteia with Ares in the Achaian city called Triteia, Pausanias 7.22.8–9.
24 Generally when the son is divine or quasi-divine, as Semele with Dionysus and Alkmene with Heracles. Larson 1995: 60 sees this as a more general pattern.
25 See also Burkert 1979: 6–7.
26 He knew that any son Danae might have would kill him; however, the presence of the motif in the story speaks volumes.
27 Nymphs are a third category who bear children out of wedlock, but though they are sometimes represented as free of human family ties and conventions (like Maia, the mother of Hermes in the *Homeric Hymn*), they too are sometimes constrained to expose their children. The chorus of Sophocles' *Oedipus Tyrannus*, discovering that Oedipus was exposed after birth on Mount Kithairon, surmise that his mother was a nymph and his father a god (1098–1109). At times the line between nymphs and heroines appears rather blurred; however, see the caveats of Larson 1995: 22–4.
28 Accepting Pierson's emendation λείμακας for κλίμακας.
29 This is particularly noticeable in the case of Iphigeneia, who (called here Iphimede, but with the same story) is identified in the Hesiodic corpus (fr 23.17–26) with Artemis Enodia. Further, Iphigeneia was an epithet of Artemis at Hermione, Paus. 2.35.1: cf. 7.26.5.
30 On this group of eponyms and on the whole phenomenon, see Calame 1987.
31 Strabo 505 (11.5.4); cf. 573, 623, 633 (12.8.6, 13.3.6, 14.1.4).
32 Wife: Sparte, Messene (4.1.2), Arene, Oichalia, Helike. Mother: Triteia and probably Amphissa.
33 Paus. 8.8.4, 8.9.5.
34 Messene and Polykaon, 4.1.1–2, though the city is Andania, not Messene, which as Pausanias says was a fourth-century foundation. At an earlier period Messene, if she existed, would have been the eponym of the country Messenia/Messene and the people Messenians.
35 Paus. 9.1.1, 9.2.5. Plataia was also the name given to the supposed bride of Zeus, actually a log, in a bizarre complex of myth and ritual connected with the city and other parts of Boiotia. Her name, meaning 'broad', is exactly equivalent to Sanskrit *pṛthvī/pṛthivī*, 'earth', accounting for her exalted status: originally she was not a heroine at all, but Earth, consort of Sky. See Burkert 1979: 133–4. However, to the people of Plataia in classical times, their city took its name from a heroine, the daughter of Asopos.
36 Plutarch, *Moralia* 255D-E. Plutarch's source is probably Charon of Lampsakos, whose date is uncertain, but who is traditionally thought to be a predecessor of Herodotus.
37 Kearns 1989: 57–63; 1990: 31–2.
38 Notably the Amazons, who were worshipped as heroines both individually and as a group in Athens, and whose *raison d'être* was the inversion of norms; see most recently Blok 1994, also duBois 1982 and Tyrrell 1984; on their different role in the Asian cities, Larson 1995: 114–16. Huntresses, too, are well-known in myth (Prokris, Atalante) but are unlikely to have been so in real life.
39 See Sourvinou-Inwood 1990: 18–21. Although I have reservations about applying the pattern to the unmarried Antigone, the general idea is surely valid.
40 Photius s.v. Πλυντήρια, Hesychius s.v. Καλλυντήρια καὶ Πλυντήρια; Aglauros a priestess of Athena, Philochorus *FGrH* 328 F 106.
41 See Philochorus (above) F 105–6; Merkelbach (1972); Dontas (1983).
42 Paus. 2.18.1, probably at Athens, but possibly (with an emendation of the text) on Seriphos.

Part III

RITUAL AND GENDER

7

DEATH BECOMES HER
Gender and Athenian death ritual

Karen Stears

> A mourning woman is not simply a producer of pity, but dangerous.
> (Foley 1993: 143)

The lot of women in archaic and classical Athens has been characterised as an unhappy one. Denied access to avenues of social, political and economic power, their status has been identified as low, and their personal freedom of movement conceived of as being severely restricted. The funeral, so central to Athenian social and political life, has been singled out as a reification of the male and female power relationship, and the role of women within funerary practices has been adduced as evidence in the construction of this picture; the intensity of the display of their grief serves as an outlet for their own repressed frustrations. Such analyses tend to focus on gender at the expense of other issues. It is doubtful whether gender functioned as the sole means of group identity in ancient Athens. In many circumstances other aspects of social identity and relationship may have been uppermost, most notably familial relationships. By utilising jointly the tools of gender and kin in assessing women's duties in funerary rituals, this chapter hopes to present an alternative, more sanguine view of female status and power.

There is no single account of a contemporary Athenian funeral in the late archaic or classical periods. Instead, a composite picture has to be extrapolated from literary sources as disparate as the fifth-century tragedians, fourth-century orators and the Byzantine lexicographers, together with archaeological evidence from painted pottery and burials. Of all these sources, perhaps the pottery speaks most immediately with its scenes depicting funerary ritual. Athenian potters chose in the main to portray three scenes, the *prothesis* – the laying-out of the corpse, the *ekphora* – the procession to the grave, and the visit to the tomb. *Prothesis* and *ekphora* are attested in geometric pottery of the eighth century BCE (Ahlberg 1971) as well as in later styles, the *prothesis* being more common (Zschietzschmann 1928; Boardman 1955; Andronikos 1968; Kurtz 1984; Shapiro 1991).[1] Scenes of funerary ritual are most common in the sixth century in the black-figure style (Figure 7.1) and are less well attested in the red-figure period, ending altogether at

III RITUAL AND GENDER

Figure 7.1 Attic black-figure pinax depicting, on the upper level, a *prothesis*, and on the lower level, chariots. c.510 BCE.

the close of the fifth century. *Prothesis* itself still existed, as is witnessed in the arguments amongst inheritors in the fourth-century law-courts; perhaps it had lost something of its earlier significance.[2] However, in the fifth and fourth centuries it may well be that the tomb itself (a permanent arena for display as opposed to ephemeral funerary rituals), and expenditure on it became the centre for familial display within the *polis*; this would account for its popularity in the iconography of white-ground lekythoi (oil-jars specifically intended for the grave), and for its becoming the primary objective of funerary legislation (Snodgrass 1980; Shapiro 1991; Stears 1993).

From what we know of the *prothesis* it seems to have been a standardised set of rites: regardless of its sex, the corpse appears to have been prepared for disposal in the same manner. Upon death the eyes and mouth of the corpse were closed.[3] The body was, wherever possible, returned to its *oikos* where it was further treated by the women of the household. It was washed and then wrapped in a number of layers of fabric, including a shroud and a top-cover. On the bier it was laid out with the feet toward the door and a pillow under the head. It was then decked with herbs and sometimes with garlands and occasionally jewellery; an unmarried adolescent might be adorned as if for a wedding. A jar of oil was placed by the bier and a pot of water by the street door of the house, measures effecting the containment and purification of ritual pollution (*miasma*).

Thus decorated, the body was ready to be visited. It is uncertain where in the house *prothesis* took place. Funerary legislation attributed to Solon restricted the *prothesis* to the interior of the house, but the iconographic evidence is inconclusive (Boardman 1955; Garland 1985, 1989). It may well be that the location depended on the size and form of the house, the weather and the number of guests expected; the courtyard or the *andrôn* (the public room of the household reserved for men's dining) might have been particularly suitable given the semi-public nature of the proceedings (Jameson 1990; Nevett 1995). What the legislation did prohibit was the conduct of the *prothesis* in an overtly public space outside the domestic sphere, as appears to have been the practice in the Geometric period (Ahlberg 1971).

The *prothesis* lasted for one day, probably the day after death. Both men and women participated in mourning rituals, but the gestures of each sex are clearly differentiated in representations of *prothesis* scenes from the earliest examples onwards. In Geometric iconography, women adopt a pose with both arms raised to the head. With a single exception, men stand with only one arm to the head (Ahlberg 1971). Above the handles of some early pots, clay mourning women are attached, again with both arms lifted to the head, but with the addition of dashes of brown paint on their white-slip cheeks to indicate laceration.

In black- and red-figure scenes there is a similar gender division of position and gesture. Typically, the men enter the scene in a procession from left to right, with their arms raised in salutation, palms facing outwards, perhaps performing a prepared and orderly dirge (Shapiro 1991). They proceed no further than the feet of the corpse and are met by the male members of the household, who return their gesture. The women in the scene appear unresponsive to the procession but continue in their lamentation, standing closely around the corpse, which is their chief focus of interest. Children often appear near the corpse or under the bier. Occasionally, a male figure may stand nearby and these individuals are often distinguished as old by their white hair or beards and are perhaps to be recognised as fathers and grandfathers, their pose of lamentation marking them as distinct from the main body of male mourners (Shapiro 1991). Also in sharp contrast to the orderly procession of men, the women are depicted as being distraught. They tear at their hair as they sing their lament, moving around the bier as they grieve. The most important position in relation to the deceased appears to have been near the head, as this is where the chief female mourner (?the mother) stands, facing or behind the head, holding either it or the shoulders, or sometimes plumping the supporting pillow. Occasionally this position is occupied by an older woman with short hair who might be identified as the old wet-nurse of the deceased. Short hair, however, was a mark of grief as well as slavery and so may not be a simple indicator of servile status.

III RITUAL AND GENDER

A black-figure plaque in the Louvre MNB 1905 attributed to the Sappho painter is of particular interest in helping to determine whether there were special places or roles for familial members at the *prothesis*, since identifying labels are placed next to some of the figures. An *adelphos* (brother) of the deceased is a member of the procession of men which is greeted by the *pater* (father). Around the head of the male corpse stand the grandmother (*thethe*) and three aunts, each marked as *thesis*, and one of these is further identified as being paternal (*prospatros*). The *meter* (mother) holds the head of her dead son and next to her stands her daughter, his sister (*adelphe*). That the women are grieving is shown by the words *oimoi oimoi* placed next to the heads of the aunts.

On the third day after death, in the ceremony known as the *ekphora*, the corpse was taken out to the cemetery for burial. It was transported either on a bier or a cart in a procession which in vase-paintings usually leads from left to right. Both men and women attended the *ekphora*, males usually leading the procession and the women following, lamenting openly. They may have been accompanied in their lamentations by musicians since flautists also appear in depictions of the scene; perhaps this was meant to show that some of the women were hired professional mourners.

The burial or cremation of the corpse was presumably a male-led affair, since they would have to manhandle the body, sacrifice animals and perhaps dig or oversee the grave-digging and/or tomb construction. At the end of the burial rites the mourners returned to the home of the deceased to partake in the *perideipnon*, the funeral meal, and to bathe, purifying themselves from the ritual pollution to which they had been exposed. Further rituals were performed on behalf of the dead, the third and ninth day rites, *ta trita* and *ta enata*, in which food, libations and other offerings were placed on the new tomb. Death was followed by a mourning period of thirty days which was ritually closed by the performance of further rites on the thirtieth day (*triakostia*). At this point, the house of the deceased would be swept and the sweepings, *kallysmata*, were probably placed on the tomb; the *oikos* and the wider kin-groups were now free from the pollution of death.

It was these rites from *prothesis* to *triakostia* which were the kernel of Athenian funerary practice. Their correct performance might help to underpin a claim on the estate of the deceased by those who funded and dominated them. For this reason they could be rituals of great financial, legal and even political importance and hence liable to be used as arenas for conspicuous consumption and associated rivalry, perhaps even revenge. Funerary laws attributed both to Solon and, by Cicero, to a period some time after him are concerned with the size and extravagance of funerals. These laws, whatever their date, appear to be witness to the social and political tensions manifested at, and presumably by, funerals. These stresses on the system and the concomitant legislation have been associated with the rise of the Athenian *polis* and the changing relations between it and Athenian familial groupings, and with the growth of ideologies concerning political and legal equality – for instance, the establishment of the public burial of the war dead and the *epitaphios logos* (the annual state funeral speech) – as well as with the social control of women (Alexiou 1974; Humphreys 1980; Garland 1985; Loraux 1986 [1981]; Holst-Warhaft 1992; Foley 1993; Seaford 1994a).

The Solonian laws,[4] whilst advocating a general diminution of funerary rites, such as forbidding the sacrifice of an ox at the grave-side, specifically stipulate the expected roles and behaviour of women mourners. Only females within the kin-group of the *anchisteia* (a bilateral kinship grouping centred on an *ego* and extending to the children of cousins) were allowed to attend either the *prothesis* or the *ekphora*; the latter had to take place before dawn, and in it the women walked separately from the men. The only exceptions to this general prohibition were women over the age of sixty years. Those participating were forbidden to lacerate their faces or sing set dirges (*threnoi pepoiêmenoi*). Enforcement of this legislation may not have been entirely successful as some time afterwards a further law was enacted which attempted to limit large gatherings of men and women at funerals in order to control the amount of lamentation.[5]

This body of legislation should not be taken as being specifically aimed at women even though they were the central producers of noisy lamentation at the funerals.[6] The laws which prohibited the singing of *threnoi* and the laceration of the flesh, as well as the numbers of women, were probably aimed at curbing professional mourners as much as familial members; in which case, the legislation may have been specifically targeted against those families who were wealthy enough to indulge in such display. Thus the legislation was directed at excessively disruptive and even socially dangerous display by kin-groups and not at women *per se*. The inference of these laws is that women mourned in a more extrovert fashion than did men.

From this brief outline of funerary practice it appears that the tasks and roles undertaken by participants were for the most part allotted along the lines of a sexual division. Women tended the corpse before and during *prothesis*, and appear to have mourned in a more overt fashion than men, displaying greater levels of emotional grief. Furthermore, in general, men appear to have paid more attention to their guests than to the corpse at the *prothesis*, but then seem to have taken charge of proceedings during the *ekphora*. Lastly, the Solonian funerary legislation restricted the number of women who could attend a private, and indeed public funeral, whilst the attendance of men was unrestricted. We now need to ask why this division existed, and what it signified.

During the period from death to *triakostia* and the final release of the soul from this world, those near the dead, both physically and by blood or marital ties, were thought to be ritually polluted (Parker 1983). This ritual pollution (*miasma*) has been considered a factor in accounting for the prominent role of women in death ritual (Havelock 1982; Shapiro 1991). Like death, birth was regarded as a source of *miasma*, and women, because of their child-bearing capacity, were therefore seen as latently both polluted and polluting. For this reason, the argument goes, they were allotted the role of dealing with the pollution of death.

This argument requires closer examination. Here the parallel of childbirth is indeed instructive, though for rather different reasons from those outlined above. Like death, childbirth incurred a period of pollution for the household concerned, and was followed by a series of purificatory rites on the fifth, tenth and fortieth days. Anyone coming into contact with a woman who had just given birth was thought to be polluted for three days, and those who attended the birth were polluted until the fifth-day rites. The new mother was by this time no longer polluting, although she was apparently still regarded as polluted herself. It would seem then that it was the act of childbirth that was impure rather than the woman herself, although the *miasma* may have been centred on her.[7] One might maintain that 'since women could not escape the pollution of giving birth, as men could, they were presumably better suited to deal with the pollution of death' (Shapiro 1991: 635); but there were other sources of pollution from which men could not escape, namely the *miasma* surrounding sexual intercourse which appears to have been centred on semen (Parker 1983). Thus the argument that the 'natural' pollution of women made them particularly suitable as carers of the dead is inherently untenable. Indeed, women were not apparently considered to be any more affected than men by the pollution of death. Although measures were undertaken during *prothesis* to contain the *miasma* of the corpse, there is no evidence that it was considered less polluting at burial than at *prothesis*; thus, the men who carried the pall or buried the corpse were just as polluted as the women who prepared the body. Moreover, there is no evidence that women at Athens were obliged to undergo a longer period of mourning than were men. Rather, men and women associated with the household affected by death were considered equally ritually polluted until the *triakostia*. It was the degree of kin-relationship to the deceased, rather than the sex of the mourner, that determined the level of *miasma* encountered, and thus the level of correct ritual action necessary.

The ultimate implication of the line of argument linking women with the *miasma* of death is that men, as the power-holding section of society, would wherever possible have employed women to mediate pollution, which was seen as something to be feared and avoided. Females, in other words, were 'given' death because they were of a lower social status and held less power than men.[8] This reasoning is based on a number of assumptions: that the mediation of pollution is indicative of lower social status, and of marginality; and, even more importantly, that 'power' is a unified concept. These are, I think, fundamental errors and ones which I shall attempt to rectify in the remainder of this chapter. Participation in funerals, it will be argued, served in fact as a means for the construction and display of women's power in both the domestic and political arenas.

In seeking explanations for women's prominence in death ritual which go beyond that of inferior status, it is instructive to compare funerary practice with other rites of passage, such as those associated with marriage and, once again, childbirth. In these too, gender division was a significant feature. Marriage, which like death was a crucial transitional stage for members of both sexes, was marked by elaborate rituals. Wedding scenes are common in Athenian vase-painting and, as with funerary scenes, the artists developed a limited repertoire concentrating on a small group of images, the most popular scenes being the adornment of the bride and the procession to the house of the groom (Oakley and Sinos 1993). These scenes betray a startling similarity to the funerary scenes. The bride is dressed within the interior of the *oikos*, surrounded by women. She is washed, anointed, bejewelled and decked in fine cloths, a passive object just like the corpse. Then she makes the journey to her new home, often on a cart or chariot, accompanied by men and women and the sound of flutes. While the funerary *ekphora* was restricted to the dark hours before daylight, the bridal journey seems to have taken place in the darkness of the evening; it was certainly lit by special torches held by the bride's mother. Females played a major part in these aspects of marriage ritual although their presence was not required for the betrothal (*engye*) of the bride and groom. Indeed, the bride herself did not have to be at this ceremony, which took the form of a legally binding agreement between her present legal guardian, her father if alive, and her future husband, who would become her new legal guardian. This rite constituted a pledge which might be brought to public scrutiny if challenged or broken in any way. It was made between the head of an *oikos* and the potential head of another *oikos*; women did not need to be present, as this was essentially a public not a private concern. But the *gamos*, the marriage, was a different affair. The removal of a bride from her natal home and the consequent change in status from virgin (*parthenos*) to bride (*nymphe*), and ultimately through childbirth to that of woman (*gyne*), were personal rites which had to be undertaken carefully and properly in case of mistake. For, as with any rite of passage, the liminal state of those at its centre was a potential cause for concern; the bride might be considered as an individual capable of ritual pollution, as was the corpse (Van Gennep 1909).

The rituals surrounding childbirth are less well documented than those at marriage and death. As death witnessed the loss of a member of a household, an event marked by rituals of separation between the deceased and the living and the incorporation of the former into the company of the dead, so birth was marked by rites incorporating a new member into the family. The new mother did not take a very active role in these rites, most notably because she was thought to be still polluted by the birth, perhaps until the cessation of post-partum bleeding (see above, p.118). But the baby would undergo a series of gradually more public appearances, overseen by his or her father. For it was the acceptance of legitimate paternity by the father which sanctioned full incorporation both into the *oikos* and the wider social, religious and political body. The rituals concerning the mother, perhaps because of their private and therefore mainly female aspect, are largely unclear (Parker 1983; Garland 1990).

In both wedding and birth ritual we find men taking the lead when the public domain impinged on the rite. But rites of passage affected not only the public but the private sphere, and here women as members and, indeed, the recreators of the familial group were essential and sometimes dominant performers. Thus it may be useful when considering the different roles undertaken by the sexes at funerals to consider this public/private dimension.

The *prothesis* was an event staged within the house. As an area devoted chiefly to private life, this may be thought to have been ideologically the space which was properly female (Gould 1980); we might not be surprised to find women at the heart of this ritual. A comparison with wedding ritual is particularly illuminating in addressing the argument that women prepared the corpse because of some link between themselves and pollution inherent in ideologies concerning their biology. Instead, let us view the *prothesis* as an adornment of the corpse, comparable to that of the bride. It was a time when females might employ their most expensive unguents, bring out their most finely woven and embroidered textiles, produce their specially bought pottery, and sing songs most expressive of their emotion, albeit sorrow rather than joy. Women were the centre of the affair; it was their actions which held the attention of the pot-painter and which were thought worthy of depiction. Their proper enactment of these rituals ensured not only the peaceful departure of the soul of the deceased to Hades, but also the containment of the *miasma* of death and the ritual health of the household. It is easy for modern observers living in a society largely devoid of meaningful ritual to underplay the importance of correct praxis, but we should not under-estimate the latent power that those in charge of ritual performance might wield. It may not have been the financial, legal or political power which we ourselves value, but ritual knowledge was nevertheless a potent force. Hence, actions performed by women in the domestic domain may be thought of as enhancing their status rather than reinforcing their inferiority.

Men, usually associated with the 'male' political world as opposed to the 'female' domestic sphere (a distinction perhaps over-emphasised in modern studies), also inhabited this domestic space. Therefore, we find them present at the *prothesis* and sometimes, as close and in particular as elderly relatives of the deceased, they display their grief and mourn. But even within the house they were still linked to the public sphere; so it was they who greeted the visiting male mourners. At the *ekphora*, the funeral left the semi-public world of the *oikos* and entered fully the public world of the *polis*. Here the men, having played a secondary role at the *prothesis*, were required to take centre stage, leading the procession and perhaps carrying the corpse. Women were still present, but in the late archaic and classical city their attention-grabbing lamentations had been curtailed to some extent by legislation and they were obliged to walk separately from the men behind the pall or cart.

The sex-based divisions visible in Athenian funerary ritual may therefore be seen to be influenced by, as well as constructing, the concept of space as gendered. The distinction between private/female and public/male space should not be over-stated, for males and females operated in both spheres; however, it is a useful tool in attempting to explain patterns of thought and associated behaviour.

A distinction can also be discerned in the manner in which males and females expressed their grief. At the *prothesis* men are shown processing in orderly fashion, in contrast to the dishevelled women who stand around the corpse. This restrained behaviour may be as indicative of a form of social control as is the excessive emotionality of the women. Grief is a recognised psychological phenomenon comprising 'a stereotyped set of psychological and physiological reactions of biological origin' (Averill 1968: 721) whereas mourning consists of a set of conventional behavioural responses to death, both sanctioned and required by society (Lindemann 1944; Bowlby 1961). As has long been noted, individuals who experience grief may be socially compelled to either restrict or elaborate its display, whilst those who feel no emotion at all may be forced to undertake extreme forms of emotional behaviour in mourning (Mauss 1921; Rosenblatt, Walsh and Jackson 1971; Stears 1993). The contrast in male and female modes of mourning as portrayed in Athenian art may be witness to such strictures. The control of emotional display by Athenian men was a tenet central to the ideology of their gender construction and, moreover, their ethnic identity. Excessive emotionalism, of which mourning was a manifestation, was considered a typical female trait associated with lack of self-control. It was regarded not only as unmanly but also un-Greek and something undertaken by those who were opposite to both constructs, namely women and barbarians. Thus, the only male chorus that laments in Athenian tragedy is that of old men in *The Persians* (Dover 1974; Fortenbaugh 1975; Hall 1989). That is not to maintain that men did not grieve or mourn; indeed, it was thought odd that Demosthenes did not mourn properly when his daughter died, even though he was attempting to make a political gesture (Plutarch *Demosthenes* 22). The presence in the vase-paintings of grieving older men who are distinct from the processing men who greet the corpse more calmly points to the conclusion that emotional distress may have been culturally permissible for aged fathers but not for younger men; this has implications for Athenian concepts of masculinity. It also suggests that the relationship between ceremonial display and gender construction may provide an additional explanation for the prominence of women in funerary rituals.

Just as men may have been obliged by social constraint to conceal emotion on occasions (whether consciously or subconsciously), so women may well have been encouraged to express a level of grief in lamentation which they themselves did not feel. The task of lamenting the dead noisily may not have come naturally to more distant members of the *anchisteia* who might not have been personally well acquainted with the deceased. However, such women may not have felt 'compelled' to attend the funeral. On the contrary, they may have regarded attendance as a privilege. The fact that those who were allowed to attend were restricted by law may well have served to enhance their (self-perceived?) status, and this may have served as an encouragement to the level of emotion displayed, whether genuine grief or not. Moreover, the female members of a powerful kin-group may well have realised that public recognition, by non-familial males attending the funeral, of both the extent and the care with which they carried out proper ritual, including lamentation, was a means of acquiring reputation and honour, *philotimia*, for the kin-group as a whole. Modest and 'correct' female behaviour was after all a reflection of an ordered and properly run household. Such behaviour may also have secured the rights of a woman's legal guardian (*kyrios*) to inherit; thus women may have been extremely willing to participate. We might remember that self-awareness of gender and the associated solidarity that it implies may often take second place to kin or other affiliations.

I am not suggesting that all the female members of the *anchisteia* would have participated in every burial. The variable structure of the *oikos* and *anchisteia*, and the presumably varied reality of these terms for individuals in Athenian society, imply that there was no single model for participation by relatives at an Athenian funeral. There is however an ideological and legal norm displayed within the forensic literature of the fourth century, which often draws upon the Solonian legislation, with its references to the *anchisteia*. These speeches frequently imply that there is a direct correlation between possession of a corpse (occasionally involving its theft), being seen to bury it properly, and presenting a claim to an estate; and one aspect of a fitting burial is the requirement that the rites be overseen by the correct members of the deceased's household. Indeed, at [Demosthenes] 43.63, the absence of the opponent's wife and mother at the *prothesis* and *ekphora* is used as ammunition by the plaintiff against the rival claim to the estate. In fact, the plaintiff very cleverly turns around the Solonian legislation which stipulates that women outside the *anchisteia* may not attend by arguing that the law actually obliges (*keleuei*) women within that kinship limit to participate in the rites. Might we not then hypothesise that some women within kin-groups may well have recognised and even exploited the centrality of their role in funerary ritual in legitimising their *kyrios'* claim to an estate? This may have especially been the case if the *kyrios'* claim was dependent on a cognatic relationship, that is, a relationship through the female line.

As Van Gennep showed at the turn of the century, death rituals are a means of 'healing' a social group which has lost a member. That women were integral to the correct functioning of rites of passage, such as weddings, funerals and births – and therefore responsible for the actual and ritual health of the *oikos* and, by wider association, the *polis* – has been under-emphasised.

It may well be further proof that women were not simply passively confined within the *oikos*, but that they were its very life-blood and that without them it could not exist properly, either physically, economically or ritually. The establishment of an annual public funeral for the war-dead may have directly impinged on women's ritual authority within the *oikos*. With no corpse to care for (the dead were cremated on the battle-field) and with their lamentations effectively suppressed by the institution in the early fifth century of a state funeral speech, the *epitaphios logos*, they were handicapped to the level of silence (Loraux 1986; Holst-Warhaft 1992). As with the funerary legislation enacted by Solon and others, when the *polis* wished to curtail the powers of kin-groups in death ritual it struck out at its most vociferous members – its women.

Funerary legislation in particular shows that women's ritual activity within the *oikos* could be of significance for the *polis* as a whole. This link between private and public spheres is discernible in other aspects of women's involvement with rites of passage. These rites served to mark time within the history of a family and it may be that as keepers of ritual knowledge, and as essential witnesses of past kin-based events, women could become powerful figures within the household, and may have been the kernels of the *oikos'* self-knowledge and memory. Athenian marriage patterns may have served to increase this likelihood. Middle-aged men tended to marry girls who had just passed menarche (Garland 1990). If a woman was lucky enough to survive childbirth and reach middle or even old age, she was also likely to have been widowed; thus she may have lived on to become the oldest member of a household. When old women were associated with the telling of old-fashioned traditions, might these not include family histories? Plato writes of 'the sort of things old women sing' (*Lysis* 205b-e; Thomas 1989). Might this not include old familial traditions and stories as well as myths in our sense of the word? These 'songs' might be sung to children to educate them about their ancestors, but it seems as likely that the 'songs' were essentially laments.[9]

It is thus possible that female lamentations served as one of the media for the construction of a female and private history of the kin-group. This memory may have told of the fate of individuals over generations, both men and women. Women's important role as overseers of familial rites of passage may have been integral in their ability to construct a history of the family. Indeed, women may be regarded in a sense as the guardians and perhaps inventors of aspects of familial tradition, a tradition which could well have been more detailed and personal than the familial record constructed by the more archaeologically visible funerary inscriptions and tomb groupings (Stears 1995). Remembering the dead was of course only one aspect of lamentation; other elements might include the bewailing of one's loss and frustrations, expression of one's grief, and perhaps incitement to revenge (Alexiou 1974; Holst-Warhaft 1992; Foley 1993).

The funeral itself was not the only occasion at which laments might be sung: ethnographic comparisons suggest they may have been performed in non-funerary contexts, such as when toiling in the fields or wool-working (Caraveli 1986). But perhaps a more certain retelling of these familial histories within lamentation came at the monthly and annual visits to the tomb-site. The tombs themselves may have served as mnemonic devices for the inspiration of lament singing, and groups of burials, *periboloi*, may well have occasioned extended singing of laments for a number of recent ancestors. Tombs were situated on roadsides and outside city gates and walls, both in cemeteries and on private land. Lament singing here would have been one of the means by which the familial group could construct and project a public face, to draw attention to and to elaborate upon its funerary monuments, which grew in size and expenditure through the fifth and fourth centuries.

The foregoing discussion suggests that women's lamentations may have fulfilled a number of social functions. By providing demonstrations of their observance of 'correct' female behaviour in relation to ritual, they enhanced both the women's status and that of their kin-group. In addition, they may have helped to legitimate claims on an estate, have underpinned a family's ritual health, and have acted as a vehicle for the construction and promotion of family history. Functions such as these indicate that the impact of women's lamentations was by no means confined to the private sphere. In the course of funerary observances women were, moreover, able to cross the boundary between public and private in a more direct and physical way. It is something of a commonplace to write of women's confinement within the *oikos* in archaic and classical Athens and whilst one would not wish to refute the ideology and ideal of the gendered division of Athenian space, it may be worth restating a point made by John Gould:

> The world outside, the public world, is the world of men ... with one striking exception. In the sacred and ritual activities of the community the active presence of women in the public world is not merely tolerated but required.
>
> (Gould 1980: 50)

Funerary ritual not only required that women should participate noisily at the *prothesis* and *ekphora* but also that they should continue to visit the tomb, certainly on the anniversaries of an individual's death, and perhaps if they wished at other times. These visits, and the preparations for them, are a common motif on white-ground *lekythoi* (Shapiro 1991). We may need to reassess our picture of female usage of public space; it may be that women could utilise a visit to a tomb (and also a shrine or temple) to access the public world. A woman outside her house with no business to be so was an object of male concern, but a woman accompanied by other women, slaves or otherwise, and carrying objects for ritual use may have not only escaped censure, but may have even earned praise. The singing of laments at gravesides would have provided a meeting-place for related women otherwise isolated in their respective *oikoi*, and would have enabled them not only to become the focus of attention by lamenting, but also to catch up on family news and to glean other information by observing comings and goings from the vantage-point of the tomb, which was so helpfully placed in most conspicuous locations. We might characterise these actions as gossip and nosiness, but are they not also indirect ways of obtaining knowledge and hence a kind of power? Participation in birth- and wedding-rituals may have served much the same purpose. Clearly, the public/private distinction, though providing a useful basis for analysis, cannot be rigidly applied as an explanation for gender division in relation to funerary practices.

Death rituals are complex social and emotional phenomena and my analysis touches on only some aspects. Whilst arguing that women's participation in funerary rites needs to be re-evaluated in a more positive light than has previously been the case, it must not be forgotten that at the centre of women's lot in lamentation was a display of emotionality which both underpinned and reconstructed ideologies of the illogicality of a woman's nature and her essential lack of self-authority and control. For Aristotle, this was evidence enough that women needed to be controlled by men (Fortenbaugh 1975; Dover 1974). The display of emotion by women therefore confirmed and reinforced the belief that, if left uncontrolled, women would revert to a wild and untamed condition (Gould 1980). In this way women's behaviour at funerals helped to strengthen the dominant ideology concerning female gender, and thus the construction of femininity was maintained. When women who did not conform to expected behavioural patterns (*viz* adulteresses) were barred from participating in events, those who did take part may have valued their status of conformity all the more. This reinforced an imposed ideology which was already underpinning the women's behaviour and treatment, and indeed their very status and social value.[10] On this basis [Demosthenes] can claim that decent women would be outraged by the thought that Neiaira, a former prostitute and of non-citizen status, participated in public ritual ([Dem.] 59. 110ff).

It is always easy in this sort of study to overlook the fact that individuals in history did not merely function in terms of ideologies and structures, but were sentient beings. Athenian men and women mourned because many of them felt acute grief and loss. But the fact remains that as a sex, women were also a medium through which a kin-group was able to display 'correct' grief and emotion, even if not actually felt, both for the kin-group itself and for the social whole. This grief was 'required' as one of the means by which the social crisis initiated by a death was resolved. Female lamentation therefore constituted a mediating social strategy. As Rosenblatt, Walsh and Jackson (1971) have shown, the fact that females cross-culturally display emotion more than males may be indicative of the cross-cultural subordination and socialisation of women by men. However, whilst as a gender group women might have to conform to ideologically sanctioned norms of emotional behaviour at funerals and were expected to handle the polluting corpse more than were men, this was nevertheless a situation which could be exploited by women. The overseeing and performance of rituals within the private domain, which often overlapped into the public, could serve to express and enhance the status of an individual or a group of women as powerful members of the *oikos*, and indeed of their *oikos* within the *polis*. Women may be regarded as controllers of ritual pollution within society, as ritual timekeepers of the kin-group, as guardians of familial traditions and histories, and as media for the display of kin-group prestige. This is not to argue that females were empowered members of Athenian society, for in many important areas this was patently not the case. But these areas tend to be those most esteemed in our own societies: the economic, the legal and the political spheres. In religion and ritual, arenas which our own societies value little or indeed may even denigrate, we may find an alternative picture.

Although the funeral may have been one of those arenas of ritual practice which served to construct dominant ideologies about female gender, and hence reinforce notions of the inferiority of women as a sex, in the actual performance of the rites, women may have been able to wield some power and attempt to assert and enhance their status as active individuals within the kin-group. Ritual activity may also have functioned as an alternative access to other kinds of power, based on meetings with other women and on outings into the public world, a spatial domain that has for too long been viewed as simply male. Participation in funerary ritual would in this way have been one of the means of enhancing female status, rather than a way of emphasising the social inferiority of women as a gender. Hence, ideologies dominant in social discourse may have been subverted in social action.

ACKNOWLEDGEMENT

I would like to express my thanks to the editors for their patience *in extremis* and to Sally Humphreys, Lin Foxhall and Mark Trewin for their comments on various versions of this chapter.

NOTES

1 Other funerary scenes: Kurtz and Boardman 1971 plates 36–37; Mommsen 1984.
2 There may have been a shift in artistic taste or fashion with regard either to the extravagance of the practice, the scene itself or the ritual pots it adorned. The popularity of sculpted funerary monuments from the end of the fifth century onwards may also have been a contributing factor.

3 But see Shapiro 1991 for gender differences in associated iconography.
4 [Dem.] 43.62; Plut. *Solon* 21; Cic. *de leg.* 2.64.
5 Cic. *de leg.* 2.65.
6 Plato *Laws* 800e; Hdt. 2.61.
7 Menstruation was not considered polluting (Parker 1983: 101f). Contrast the lot of women as mourners among the Merina of Madagascar where the pollution associated with menstruation is of relevance for their role in funerary ritual; Bloch 1971; 1982.
8 On the danger of confusing gender roles with gender symbolism see Dubisch 1986.
9 For examples of laments constructed around the histories of past familial members see Holst-Warhaft 1992.
10 Slur on virginity at Panathenaia, Thuc. 6.56ff; [Arist.] *Ath. Pol.* 18. Cf. Ar. *Thesm.* 294; Isaeus 6.50; Luc. *Dial. Meretr.* 2.1.

8

IN THE MIRROR OF DIONYSOS

Richard Seaford

In one of the most striking scenes of Greek drama, King Pentheus of Thebes, after his violent opposition to the arrival of the new Dionysiac cult, is persuaded by Dionysos to appear on stage disguised as a maenad (i.e. a female follower of the god). What I propose is a new interpretation of this scene that tentatively suggests a possible relationship between initiation, identity and psychoanalysis. My concern is not with women (there are no women in the scene, and my other material is also male-centred) but with gender, in particular with the inversion of gender.

After some brief preliminary remarks about the liminal reversal of gender in Dionysiac cult (Section I), I argue that this liminality might involve the use of a mirror by the mystic initiand (Section II). Mystic initiation, like the rite of passage generally, involves a loss of previous identity. This loss may be expressed by the split implicit in the mirror-image of the initiand, but also by a series of inversions characteristic of the rite of passage (not only male–female, but also human–animal and alive–dead), with the result that the mirror-image of the initiand may be antithetical to himself, e.g. a female image of a male (Section III). Another mystic combination of opposites – the adult initiand assimilated to a child – suggests the possibility of a Lacanian interpretation (in terms of a regression to the formation of identity in the 'mirror stage') of the roles of reflection, dismemberment and inversion in Dionysiac myth and mystic ritual (Section IV). Finally, some of the themes thrown up by this interpretation – narcissistic delight, psychic fragmentation, alienation of the subject – are actually made more explicit in the use made of the metaphor of the mystic mirror by certain Pauline and Neoplatonic texts (Section V).

I

Maenadism is the performance, by a female *thiasos* (group), of a certain kind of cult, usually involving frenzy, in honour of Dionysos. We have descriptions of mythical maenads (notably in Euripides' *The Bacchae*) as well as evidence, such as inscriptions, for the actual practice of maenadism.[1] A central act of maenadism, in both myth and actual practice, was the *oreibasia* (going-on-the-mountain), in which females performed cult for Dionysos on the mountainside. I have shown elsewhere (1988: 124–7) that this sojourn in the wild resembles in various respects the sojourn in the wild undertaken by girls before their marriage, with the differences that the former belongs to Dionysos, the latter to Artemis, and that the former may include women who are already married. The effect of this latter difference is that the centrifugal female resistance to marriage that was supposedly overcome in the marital transition may, in maenadism, be thereafter regularly renewed. And so maenadism, besides involving the liminality of mystic initiation into the *thiasos*, also renews the liminality of the transition to marriage. Certainly it is marked by the inversions characteristic of liminality. In particular, the maenads of *The Bacchae* are like animals (165, 699–70, 731, 735–40, 748, 957, 977, 1056, 1090, 1125–36), and like males – acting as hunters and warriors (733, 752–64, 848, 977, 1144, 1181–91, etc.). In vase-paintings they are sometimes armed with swords.[2]

The maenadic *thiasos* is generally all-female. When maenads are imagined as accompanied by males, it is (in myth and vase-painting) generally by those mythical male companions of the god called satyrs. But, at least by the fifth century BCE, it is clear that males might be initiated into a Dionysiac *thiasos* (without necessarily dressing as satyrs). Xouthos in Euripides' *Ion*, for example, is said to have become (temporarily) part of a *thiasos* of 'maenads'.[3] Now there is evidence for male transvestism in the cult of Dionysos.[4] Transvestism is an inversion typical of the rite of passage.[5] But for the male the Dionysiac inversion of identity has no relation (as it does for the female) to the marital transition: rather, to the extent that it expresses a rite of passage, the rite is wholly that of mystic initiation. And in fact in *The Bacchae* the adoption of maenadic dress by Pentheus, which is not required by the plot, is one of a whole series of his experiences that reflect mystic initiation.[6]

II

The first thing that Pentheus says after adopting maenadic dress is that he sees two suns, two cities of Thebes, and Dionysos, in the form of a bull, leading him (918–22). Pentheus is newly docile, and clearly neither drunk nor hysterical. His simultaneous seeing of the same thing twice is best explained by the hypothesis that in some way *reflection* is involved, as in a mirror.[7] The evidence comes from various quite different directions:

1 The use of mirrors in Orphic and Dionysiac mysteries, apparently to stimulate and perhaps to confuse the initiand;

III RITUAL AND GENDER

2 The reflection of this ritual use in the Orphic myth of the infant Dionysos being enticed by a mirror to his death and dismemberment, a myth which exhibits a series of detailed correspondences with mystic initiation;
3 A mirror of the late sixth century BCE with a Dionysiac inscription, found in a tomb (at Olbia);
4 Aristophanes' parody of Aeschylus' *Lykourgeia* (with which *The Bacchae* displays various detailed similarities), which makes it very likely that Dionysos actually carried a mirror in the *Lykourgeia* (see below, p.131);
5 The suitability of a mirror to the detailed attention given in this scene to Pentheus' female appearance;
6 The power of the ancient mirror to give (sometimes obscure) access to hidden knowledge (as of Dionysos as a bull here).

I propose now to confirm this argument by evidence from yet another direction. This is a painting (Figure 8.1), on an Apulian bell-krater in Zurich, of the early fourth century BCE (i.e. not long after *The Bacchae*).[8] In it a maenad holds in one hand half a fawn and with the other raises a sword, with which she seems about to attack a near-naked young man who is holding up opposite his face a round object, almost certainly a *tympanon* (drum). In the *tympanon* there appears a female face in profile with headband and necklace. At one side is a *thyrsos* and at the other a satyr next to some ivy. Though the

Figure 8.1 Dionysiac scene. Apulian bell-krater, early fourth century BCE.

young man in this Dionysiac scene may be Pentheus, it hardly matters to my argument whether he is or not.

The overwhelming impression is that the face in the *tympanon* is a reflection. Moreover, the holding up of the *tympanon* to face level is absolutely characteristic of the holding up of a round mirror in numerous other vase-paintings of the period. For example, in a Lucanian vase-painting of the same period, the same position as our young man's is adopted by a maenad holding up a mirror in which her face is reflected.[9] And there have survived at least two other representations of reflections in a *tympanon* in a Dionysiac context. In one[10] a *silen* is staring at a *tympanon* held towards him by a female. In another[11] an Eros is reflected in a *tympanon* held up to it by a centaur, in a scene that also contains Dionysiac objects (including the mystic basket).[12] This phenomenon may explain the curious phrase 'image of a *tympanon*' (τυπάνου δ' εἰκών), in the context of Dionysiac mysteries, in a fragment of Aeschylus' *Lykourgeia*.[13]

Lilian Balensiefen, however, in her book on the mirror in ancient art, gives two reasons for believing that our Apulian bell-krater shows not a reflection but a painting on the *tympanon*. One is that the *tympanon* would reflect only if it was metal, and we do not hear of metal *tympana*. But this is an understandable lacuna in our exiguous written accounts of the *tympanon*. Moreover, it is in the spirit of the *thiasos* to use an instrument of Dionysiac activity for a purpose other than the one for which it was designed: for example, the young satyr in the frieze in the Villa of the Mysteries at Pompeii is looking into a metal bowl (almost certainly at a reflection) in a scene of Dionysiac mystic initiation.[14] Balensiefen's second objection is that the face in the *tympanon*, being female and with a headband and necklace, matches the face neither of the young man nor of the maenad. This is true. But we shall see how it is that the face may nevertheless be a (mysterious) reflection – not of the maenad, but of the young man – for it is the convention of this type that the reflected face faces its reflection.

Perhaps then, Pentheus in *The Bacchae* when adopting maenadic costume and *thyrsos* also acquired a *tympanon*, an instrument carried especially by maenads, and looks at its reflecting surface. Or perhaps he had a mirror, or a mirror was held towards him by Dionysos. Or perhaps no stage property was involved, and the 'double vision' merely derived from, or alluded to, the (secret) use of reflection in the mysteries. In any event, the case for reflection being involved in some way is overwhelming.

III

I move now onto the question of what the role of reflection may have been in the mysteries. We have seen in Section I that in Dionysiac cult females may be like males and males like females. This dual inversion may be expressed within the person of Dionysos. In *The Bacchae*, for example, he is both effeminate and leader of the hunt (353, 1189–91). And in Aeschylus' *Lykourgeia*, it appears from Aristophanes' parody,[15] he is mocked for simultaneously carrying a mirror (associated with the female) and a sword. In our Apulian painting the male carries a mirror and the female a sword. Sword and mirror appear together also in a Lucanian vase-painting[16] of about the same period but here it is the male, Orestes, who holds the sword while being harassed by two females, Furies, of whom one holds two snakes and the other a snake and a mirror.[17] In the mirror, which faces Orestes, is the face of a woman who does not appear elsewhere in the picture and is generally taken to be the (murdered) Klytaimestra. This face of Klytaimestra exemplifies the power of the mirror to display something other than by reflection of what can be seen. Similarly, it is in a reflecting surface, I would argue, that Pentheus in *The Bacchae* sees Dionysos as a bull (920–2; cf. 923–4). The revelatory power of the reflection is exemplified in Aristophanes' *Acharnians*, when Lamachos sees reflected in his shield an old man about to be indicted for cowardice (1124–30).[18]

In *The Bacchae* the reflection seen by Pentheus derives, I have claimed, from the use of reflection in Dionysiac mystic initiation. But what was the function of reflection in the mystic ritual? Mystic ritual involved revelation, to which the revelatory power of the mirror may have contributed. The mirror may reveal in two distinct ways. It may reveal you to yourself. Or it may reveal something that is not otherwise there (like the face of Klytaimestra or the bull-nature of Dionysos). For the young man in our Apulian painting, seeing himself as a maenad, these two ways are combined. So too, if the reflecting surface continues to be held up to Pentheus as (just after his 'double vision') he proudly invites attention to his new female appearance (925–42), then he too see himself reflected as a maenad, as the female he is not. According to Artemidorus, 'a mirror means a woman to a man, and a man to a woman'.[19] Seeing something that is not there was easier in ancient mirrors, which lacked the clarity of modern ones.

In each of the mirror images that we have discussed so far a boundary is confused, whether (a) between human (or god) and animal (Dionysos in *The Bacchae*), or (b) between living and dead (Klytaimestra), or (c) between male and female (our Apulian krater, Pentheus). It is significant that these are boundaries apt to be confused in the liminal inversions of identity required for mystic initiation. There is more to be said about each of them.

(a) To be initiated into the Dionysiac *thiasos* might be to become an (animal-like) satyr.[20] On various of the famous inscribed funerary gold leaves, which almost certainly contain formulae of Dionysiac initiation, the initiand is addressed as a kid, a bull, a ram, a god.[21] Pentheus is himself in *The Bacchae* mistaken for a bull, and elsewhere actually becomes a bull.[22] His cousin Aktaion, whose similar dismemberment as hunted prey is frequently alluded to in *The Bacchae*, sees a reflection of himself as a stag (see below).

(b) To become a satyr was to belong to a *thiasos* for eternity. A nice example is a verse epitaph in which the dead youth is imagined as a satyr surrounded by welcoming maenads in a field of flowers.[23] Mystic ritual may be imagined as taking place in Hades.[24] An example of the combination of life and death in mystic ritual is in the formula on the gold leaf 'now you died and now you were born, thrice blessed, on this day'. A fifth-century BCE bone plate from Olbia contains the words 'Dionysos' and 'Orphic' as well as the phrase 'life death life'.[25] Pentheus, as mystic initiand, is dressed in funerary costume (*The Bacchae* 857), as are the maenads in a fragment of Latin tragedy (Naevius *Lycurgus* fr.39 Warmington) that is no doubt influenced by a Greek model. Perhaps the mirror was used in the ritual to embody the dead double of the initiand. The word *eidolon* may mean image in a mirror or ghost. In Euripides' *Medea* the bride Glauke, preening herself, like Pentheus, in her new adornment, laughs at the 'lifeless' image of herself in the mirror[26] – just before her death. In the temple of Despoina at Lykosoura, Pausanias tells us, there was a mirror in which, whereas the reflections of the deities were clear, an onlooker saw himself either dimly or not at all.[27] This dimness of the image has been taken to imply death.[28] In the cult of Demeter at Patrai, a mirror was used to show a sick person as either alive or dead.[29] In numerous cultures, mirrors are associated with death in various ways, which include their presence in graves.[30] So too mirrors have frequently been found in Greeks tombs (e.g. the late sixth-century BCE mirror with a Dionysiac inscription found at Olbia) of males as well as females, which suggests that they were put there not as everyday objects but for a special connection with death. The mirror immediately precedes death for Dionysos, Pentheus, and Glauke. Narkissos dies gazing at his own reflection. Aktaion, seeing Artemis bathing, also sees reflected in the water his own head with horns, and will shortly be torn to pieces as a stag.[32]

(c) As we have already noted, transvestism is characteristic of the rite of passage, and occurs in the cult of Dionysos. The mystic transvestism of Pentheus marks his transition from aggression to docility, and from hostile ignorance to a degree of sympathetic enlightenment (*The Bacchae* 924, 944, 947–8). The same sequence – feminisation, docile enlightenment, death – is found also in Sophocles' Ajax (in a mystic pattern) and Herakles.[33] The power of the mirror to combine opposites (human–animal, living–dead, male–female) through reflection is especially striking in the case of a male initiand, because the ancient mirror, which appears very frequently in vase-painting, is associated almost exclusively with the female.[34] Exceptions tend to be effeminate: Pentheus, Dionysos, Hermaphrodite[35] and Narkissos. The *tympanon* too is largely associated with females (maenads) or effeminate males.[36]

IV

Another boundary sometimes confused in mystic initiation was, it seems, between adult and infant.[37] For this practice I will confine myself to some early evidence. One of the funerary gold leaves, probably from the first half of the fourth century BCE, contains the words 'I passed beneath the *kolpos* of the queen of the underworld'. This is almost certainly a formula uttered in Dionysiac mystic initiation.[38] The word *kolpos* may mean womb, female genitals or, more broadly, the hollow in which a woman may hold an infant. In the (sixth century BCE) *Homeric Hymn to Demeter*, Demeter receives in her *kolpos* the infant Demophon (231). Her attempt to immortalise him 'in much fire' (248) has (like much else in the Hymn) been related to the Eleusinian Mysteries, in particular to the announcement of the birth of a child (sometimes identified with Dionysos) 'with the accompaniment of much fire'.[39] This fire has been associated with the thunderbolt that was experienced in mystic initiation as accompanying the birth of Dionysos.[40] Sophocles' *Oedipus at Kolonos* 150–1, where the Eleusinian goddesses are said to 'nurse the awesome initiation rites for mortals (Πότνιαι σεμνὰ τιθηνοῦνται τέλη θνατοῖσιν)', implies that 'the initiate stands in the same relationship to the Eleusinian goddesses as Demophon to Demeter'.[41] Dionysos is in the *Iliad* received by Thetis in her *kolpos* (6.136), and in an *Orphic Hymn* (52.11) is called *hypokolpios* ('in the lap', or perhaps 'in the womb'). In an Athenian vase-painting of the fifth century BCE, a seated Dionysos holds on his knees a miniature version of his youthful self.[42] In a story that has a clear series of detailed connections with mystic initiation,[43] the Titans lure the *infant* Dionysos to his dismemberment with several objects, prominent among which is a mirror, into which Dionysos was looking as he was killed.[44] Returning to the scene of *The Bacchae* in which Pentheus sees a reflection, we find Dionysos predicting that Pentheus will return from Mount Kithairon 'carried ... in your mother's arms'. Pentheus, it seems, imagines that this means an embrace. But those who know what Dionysos really means (Agaue carrying Pentheus' head) must think of an infant carried in its mother's arms. She will, having led the dismemberment of her son, carry his head 'in her arms',[45] and recompose his body, just as the infant Dionysos' dismembered body was recomposed by his mother (though in his case for the rebirth that reflects the rebirth of the initiand). A central object of the Dionysiac mysteries was the *liknon*, a winnowing basket or cradle, in which, in a vase-painting contemporary with *The Bacchae*, an Attic *thiasos* of maenads attends the adult mask of Dionysos (as if he were a baby).[46] To the many experiences of Pentheus in *The Bacchae* that reflect the experiences of the mystic initiand,[47] we should add assimilation to an infant.[48]

The assimilation of Pentheus to an infant, with a relation to his mother that is both intimate and violent, occurs as part of a mystic pattern. Exactly the same can be said of the tragic Orestes. In Aeschylus' *Libation-Bearers*, the vengeance is clothed with mystic imagery,[49] and Orestes is first imagined as a baby by his nurse and then shown by his mother, whom he is about to kill, the breast from which, she reminds him, he once drew milk. Having killed her, he is violently attacked by the Furies she had invoked and, in the next play, the *Eumenides*, her image[50] appears on stage to incite the Furies to physical violence against him. We have seen that in a Lucanian vase-painting her image appears in a mirror held by a Fury. On first feeling the onslaught of the Furies, Orestes compares his mind to out-of-control horses pulling a chariot off the race-course.[51] In Sophocles' version, the fictive death of Orestes results from a chariot-race crash. His unrecognisable body is burnt and the ashes put in an urn (so the fiction goes), which is then held and lamented by Elektra as she remembers how she mothered him (1142–7). Then, on recognising him alive, she uses a series of mystic images to express the reversal into joy, including that of 'births, births of bodies dearest to me'.[52]

The same combination of violence and intimacy between mother and son occurs in the *Oedipus Tyrannos*. The physical intimacy of Oedipus with Jokasta turns out to be with mother as well as wife, and Oedipus' self-blinding with the brooches he tears from his mother's corpse[53] is represented in terms of a sexual act.[54] Oedipus goes on to express the desire to go out to Mount Kithairon (like Pentheus), where his mother and father had exposed him as an infant, 'so that my death may be caused by them, who tried to destroy me' (1451–4).

The destructive onslaught on Pentheus, Orestes and Oedipus is in each case associated with physical intimacy (as if an infant) with his mother.[55] In the case of Pentheus, the combination of physical intimacy and violence between mother and infant is exquisitely embodied in the line that follows Dionysos' remark that Pentheus will be carried in his mother's arms: 'You will compel me to be pampered (*truphan*) even', says Pentheus, to which Dionysos replies 'Pampering in my fashion' (a rough translation of *truphas ge toiasde*). Kepple (1976) observes on this passage that *truphan* and *truphas* are derived from *thrupto*, which means basically 'break into small pieces'. The parallel word *thrupsis* can mean 'breaking into small pieces' as well as, like *truphe*, 'softness', 'weakness', 'debauchery'. And so, Kepple suggests, there is a play on words.[56] Pentheus refers to his enjoyment of being pampered like an infant (such softness being expressed by the Greeks as being broken into pieces), to which Dionysos replies in a way that suggests the *physical* fragmentation that we know he will suffer. To the *psychological* fragmentation expressed by *truphan* that we have already seen in this scene in the soft, infantile, erratic behaviour of Pentheus, corresponds his physical fragmentation at the hands of his mother.

This implied association between psychological and physical fragmentation prompts me to make the tentative suggestion that the material under discussion might be illuminated from the perspective of Lacanian psychoanalysis. This suggestion implies no commitment on my part to this perspective, but may be of interest to those who are more qualified than I am to evaluate it.

Lacan writes of 'the signs of triumphant jubilation and playful discovery that characterise, from the sixth month, the child's encounter with its own image in the mirror'.[57] This institutes the 'mirror stage', which lasts until about the eighteenth month. The infant's jubilation is associated with the realisation that the image is his or her own (when he or she moves the image moves, etc.), a realisation that distinguishes the human subject from the chimpanzee (it seems). And yet the infant is in its sixth month backward in relation to a chimpanzee of the same age with respect to instrumental intelligence. The human infant depends on others for longer than any animal. This 'specific prematurity of birth' leaves the child in the first months of life relatively uncoordinated and uneasy. And so the 'mirror stage' anticipates for the infant the *imaginary* mastery of his or her body that *biologically* has not yet been achieved. And yet this imaginary mastery is, being associated with the mirror-image, *outside* the infant, and so involves a fundamental alienation. For Lacan it is this combination of fascination and alienation that initiates the formation of the ego.

As the infant develops, the anxiety associated with the early sense of being uncoordinated, of bodily fragmentation, strengthens the desire for a secure bodily identity, but also threatens this projection towards the ego with a 'retrospective pull towards fragmentation'.[58] Lacan writes:

> The mirror stage is a drama whose internal thrust is precipitated from insufficiency to anticipation – and which manufactures for the subject, caught up in the lure of spatial identification, the succession of fantasies that extends from a fragmented body-image to a form of its totality that I shall call orthopaedic – and, lastly, to the assumption of an alienating identity, which will mark with its rigid structure the subject's entire mental development.
>
> (Lacan 1977: 4)

And so the mirror phase represents

> a genetic moment: the setting up of the first roughcast of the ego . . . [and is moreover] responsible, retroactively, for the emergence of the phantasy of the body-in-pieces. This type of dialectical relation may be observed in the course of psychoanalytic treatment, where anxiety about fragmentation can at times be seen to arise as a consequence of loss of narcissistic identification and vice-versa.
>
> (Laplanche and Pontalis 1980 [1967]: 251–2)

Further, in Bowie's summary (26):

the very rigidity of the ego's armour can act as a violence upon the individual and scatter again his *disiecta membra*. Lacan insists that what is involved here is a Janus-faced phantasy structure rather than a simple set of memories associated with bodily parts. Whether the subject looks forward to the ego or backwards to the *corps morcelé* (fragmented body), he is contemplating a construction – the same one in alternative states.

(Bowie 1991: 26)

As an expression of the fragmented body, Lacan (1977: 4–5, 21) refers to the paintings of Hieronymous Bosch and, in connection with 'a peculiar satisfaction deriving from the integration of an original organic disarray', to Heracleitus' notion of discord being prior to harmony. Bowie (1991: 28–9) suggests that Lacan might have done better to refer to Empedocles' notion of disjointed limbs seeking union (*frr.* 57–8).

Entry into the mirror stage does not require the actual presence of a reflecting surface.[59] Rather, the function of the mirror stage is 'a particular case of the function of the *imago*'. It is an *identification*, 'the transformation that takes place in the subject when he assumes an image – whose predestination to this phase-effect is sufficiently indicated by the use, in analytic theory, of the ancient term *imago*' (Lacan 1977: 2). The infant identifies with his or her own reflection, but also (especially) with the mother (or primary nurturer),[60] and then with other human images. Identification with the mirror image is both recognition of self and alienation. The self is recognised by being identified with the other. And so subsequent interpersonal relations will be characterised by the confusion of self and other inherent in transitivism (the child who sees another fall, cries) and in narcissism. The *imago* of the infant's own body both alienates him/her from him/herself and is invested with the intraorganic disturbance of the first six months, making him/her into an aggressive rival both of him/herself and then of others, creating an 'internal conflictual tension which determines the awakening of his desire for the object of the other's desire' (Lacan 1977: 19). In this way, narcissism and aggressivity go together.

Let us now return, with this psychoanalytic theory in mind, to the ancient material and first to the myth in which the infant Dionysos is dismembered and eaten by the Titans, and then reconstituted and restored to life. In this myth the infant Dionysos delights in looking into the mirror. He is enticed by it, and led to the place of dismemberment 'by the desire of his puerile mind'.[61] It is apparently in connection with this myth that Plotinus speaks of the power of the mirror to seize (or capture, ἁρπάσαι) a form.[62] According to Olympiodorus, Dionysos 'followed' his mirror image and in this way (οὕτως) was divided into pieces.[63] In a late visual representation, it seems that the infant Dionysos is throwing up his arms in jubilation as he looks into a mirror while armed males dance on either side.[64] In Nonnus he is looking into a mirror as he is attacked (and dismembered) by the Titans (6.172–3, 206–7). The same poignant combination of dismemberment and fascination with the mirror-image is implicit, a thousand years earlier, in the combination of mirror and sword in our Zurich vase and in the fragment of Aeschylus' *Lykourgeia* (both discussed in Section II), as well as in *The Bacchae*.

We have seen that in *The Bacchae* the imagining of Pentheus as an infant also alludes to psychological and physical fragmentation and in the same scene, we have argued, his psychic transformation is marked by his looking into a reflecting surface. The reflecting surface is not explicitly mentioned, and may not have appeared on stage, perhaps out of the need to avoid profaning the mystic objects. But certainly the attention given to Pentheus' appearance, both by Dionysos and by Pentheus himself (925–44), goes well beyond what is required for a disguise. A striking feature of the sudden reversal of Pentheus' character is this self-consciousness about his appearance, of the kind manifested by the adorned female using a mirror (as we see in vase-painting, and at Euripides *Medea* 1161). Pentheus' attitude in this scene combines triumphant over-confidence in his own strength (945–50) with (feminine) delighted compliance. Significant, from the psychoanalytic perspective just sketched, is that he identifies his standing position[65] with that of his mother (926). He has become an object of vision, for himself and others. And although in this scene he imagines the maenads (his mother included) making love,[66] when he arrives on the mountainside it is he who 'was seen, rather than seeing the maenads' (1075).

One strand of psychoanalytic interpretation of *The Bacchae* has deployed Pentheus' desire to see his mother making love as part of a case for an Oedipal Pentheus.[67] Another has concentrated on his authoritarian and repressive personality. Focusing on the ambivalent attitude of Pentheus towards Dionysos, and on the numerous ways in which they resemble each other, Michael Parsons (1988) deploys the notions of *splitting* and *projection*: the infant needs to keep separate the loving from the aggressive aspects of its mother ('splitting the object'), and correspondingly to split the loving feelings within itself from the dangerous destructive ones ('splitting the ego'). Pentheus is like an adult who has failed to integrate such opposites and so cannot accept ambivalence. He insists on boundaries (between himself and others, male and female, etc.), and vehemently rejects what he takes to be alien to himself. Or rather, he *projects* onto Dionysos what he denies within himself: hence his simultaneous fascination with and hostility to Dionysos, especially to his sexuality. The resulting isolation is *narcissistic*: if Dionysos represents a split-off aspect of Pentheus, then Pentheus' fascination with Dionysos is fascination with himself.

What interests us about this argument of Parsons is that as part of it he attempts to do what almost no other critic does, namely to understand Pentheus' double vision.

> It is the split in Pentheus' world becoming visible ... Pentheus has been trying to keep two aspects of reality, and of his own self, so far apart that he does not have to know about both of them. Now this attempt is breaking down and the apparent unity of his world disintegrates. Both aspects are coming into view at the same time and the fragmentation of Pentheus' psyche declares itself.
>
> (Parsons 1988: 8)

The double vision is here interestingly associated with the doubleness within Pentheus that is expressed in his relationship with Dionysos. In accordance with this notion, but from a Lacanian perspective, and taking the double vision not as a mere abstraction but as produced by a reflecting surface, it would be possible to suggest that the split inherent in the reflected image expresses both the fundamental alienation (or doubleness) involved in the formation of the ego and the concomitant dialectic of narcissistic identification and aggressive rivalry (self as other, other as self) such as that of Pentheus with Dionysos.[69]

Characteristic of the liminal stage in the rite of passage is the breaking-down of the previous identity of the initiand through the confusion of boundaries, the destruction of form, as the precondition for the acquisition of a new identity.[70] An obvious way of achieving this breakdown is through regression to infancy. Accordingly, many rites of passage, including it seems (we have seen) Greek mystic initiation, do involve this regression.[71] In both *Oedipus Tyrannos* and *The Bacchae*, a tyrant with an armoured ego moves from basic ignorance about himself[72] to an enlightenment[73] which brings him destruction. Whereas in the *Oedipus Tyrannos* he is destroyed by the revelation of acts that (according to Freud) correspond to universal infantile desires, in *The Bacchae* (from a Lacanian perspective) he is destroyed by the 'backward pull towards fragmentation', by regression back through enactment of the 'succession of phantasies' created by the infantile mirror stage: the 'Janus-faced phantasy structure' includes, in quick succession, narcissistic ambivalence towards the double (Dionysos), fundamental psychic transformation marked by seeing reflected images, identification with the mother, assimilation to an infant in its mother's arms, and finally physical fragmentation (associated with psychological fragmentation).[74]

Apart from regression to infancy, another obvious way to break down identity is by inversion of gender, and so this too is found generally in rites of passage. In the case of Pentheus we have a remarkable combination of inversion with regression. The breakdown of his earlier, rigidly aggressive identity occurs along with his dressing as a female (inversion). Along with this breakdown through inversion comes a new identity, marked by the doubleness of reflection, by a new sense of his appearance, by enlightenment, and by self-confidence: that is to say, the identity is acquired as by an infant in the mirror stage (*regression*). But characteristic of the identity acquired in the

III RITUAL AND GENDER

mirror stage is its *otherness* (alienation). In the case of Pentheus, because this regression occurs along with inversion (and the mirror is in antiquity associated with the female), the otherness of the new identity takes the specific form of gender: it is female.[75] Further, because this inversion occurs along with regression, the new (female) identity is that of his mother. Pentheus first identifies his new appearance with that of his mother, and then imagines himself as physically as close to her as possible – as a baby in her arms (and she will indeed hold the head of his fragmented body). The liminal confusion of boundaries between male and female has become the confusion of boundaries between the male infant and his mother. The triumphant acquisition of identity (characteristic of the mirror stage and of the rite of passage) is (as it may be in life) undermined, put into tragic reverse by the backward pull towards fragmentation and towards identification and merging with the mother.

V

We have argued so far that the reflected image was used in Dionysiac mystic initiation to embody the double identity of the initiand, and that the myths in which this use was expressed might be illuminated from a Lacanian perspective. We now conclude by looking at some Pauline and Neoplatonic texts, in which mystic imagery and mystic Dionysiac myth is raised to a higher level of abstraction in order to indicate a relation with the divine that, although influenced by mystic revelation, goes beyond that found in the mysteries as actually practised. The relevance of these texts to what precedes consists in the fact that in this process of abstraction they actually draw out the themes of narcissistic delight, psychic fragmentation, and alienation of the subject that we have suggested may be useful in analysing the mystic ritual and its myths. We start with a famous passage from the First Epistle to the Corinthians (13.9–12).

> For now we know in part [ἐκ μέρους: 'fragmentarisch' Conzelmann]. But when the totality [τὸ τέλειον] comes [i.e. at the Eschaton], that which is partial/fragmentary shall be done away with. When I was an infant, I used to speak as an infant, I used to reckon as an infant; but now I have become a man, I have done away with the things of the infant. For now we look through a mirror in a riddle [δι' ἐσόπτρου ἐν αἰνίγματι], but then [we shall see] face to face. Now I have known in part/fragmentarily; then I shall know even as also I have been known.

The curious conjunction of images 'through a mirror in a riddle' derives in part from the use of both mirror and riddle in the mysteries. Riddling language indicates indirectly and obscurely what is eventually fully revealed. Ancient mirrors, which were never as clear as ours, could have the same function in ritual: they might reveal indirectly and obscurely something that would later in the ritual be revealed 'face to face', i.e. deity.[76] Paul is deploying a mystic pattern to express the higher truth that God cannot in fact be revealed face-to-face in this world. We are all still in the relative ignorance of the liminal stage of mystic initiation, as it were. Further, it is in accord with what we suggested earlier as a function of the mystic mirror that there is in this passage too the implication that what is indirectly and obscurely revealed to us who look in the mirror is an image of ourselves. For just as looking in a mirror is aligned in the text with knowing in part, so looking 'face to face' is aligned with knowing 'even as also I have been known'. This implies that even in a mirror (and even in mystic initiation), I cannot know myself in the direct and clear way that 'I have been known' by another,[77] i.e. that seeing myself in a mirror is (being indirect and obscure) inferior to the face-to-face sight others have of me, and to seeing myself face-to-face – which in this world I can never do.[78] And so mystery cult is inadequate: to be more specific, it cannot go beyond the ignorance of its liminal stage. We should also note, in view of our earlier discussion, that looking in the mirror is also aligned with being an infant (νήπιος).[79]

There is a similar association between seeing ourselves and seeing deity at 2 *Corinthians* 3.18: 'But we all with unveiled face beholding as in a mirror the glory of the Lord are transformed into the same image . . .'. The influences on this passage are numerous, and so are the possibilities of interpreting it.[80] We note only that (a) the 'unveiled face' corresponds to the unveiling of the mystic initiand (to allow him to see);[81] (b) looking as into the mirror is accompanied by the transformation of the beholder (as in mystic initiation); (c) the transformation is into the 'same image' as the image in the mirror (i.e. of the Lord) – we become one with what we see in the mirror.[82]

A reflected image may do various things. It may (1) reveal (a) oneself to oneself, and (b) other things that are out of view (and so it may be imagined to reveal what is otherwise invisible). It may (2) delight, especially by (1a). On the other hand it represents indirectly, and so may (3) obscure what it represents (ancient mirrors did not achieve the clarity of modern ones), or (4) deceive, by presenting as a reality what is in fact an insubstantial image.

Some of these functions are antithetical to others: especially (1) is to (3) and (4). When the mirror is used in ritual or as a metaphor, it may be that more than one function is involved, and sometimes it is hard to tell which.[83] Its use in the mysteries may have involved all functions except (4). The Pauline passages that we have seen alluding to the mystic mirror involve (1a), (1b), and (3).

A striking combination of (1), (2), and (4) is to be found in Neoplatonism. Here the myth of Dionysos seeing his image in a mirror is used as a metaphor or allegory of fundamental significance, and in a way which combines

III RITUAL AND GENDER

our themes of narcissistic delight and the consequences of this delight – physical and psychic fragmentation, radical alienation and desire for a return to unity. According to Plotinus (*Enneads* IV 3.12), 'the souls of humans, having seen their images as in the mirror of Dionysos, became there [ἐκεῖ ἐγένοντο, i.e where the images are], having leapt from above; but not even these souls are cut off from their principle and from intellect.' The fall is a consequence of the narcissistic delight of souls in their own mirror-image. Souls descend into the sensible world because they are ensnared by their own beautiful but insubstantial reflections, like Narkissos.[84]

According to Proclus, Dionysos sees his own image in the mirror and goes out into the whole divided creation.[85] Proclus assimilates the dismemberment of Dionysos to the fragmentation of the soul in its insertion into the sensible world,[86] and maintains that within us the intellect (νοῦς) is Dionysiac, and that to offend against it by tearing apart its undivided nature is to offend, like the Titans, against Dionysos.[87] Olympiodorus claims that just as Dionysos followed his own mirror-image and was divided into the all, so the soul enters into sympathy with its own corporeal image and is consequently torn apart.[88]

The separation of the soul from its true (unified, incorporeal) self occurs at two points of the myth, which are in a sense one: the narcissistic delight at its (corporeal) image in the mirror, and its consequent fragmentation (in the corporeal). At the level of ritual, the anxious liminality of looking into the mirror might be followed by direct revelation, just as imagined (or threatened) bodily fragmentation might be followed by restoration to wholeness and life.[89] In myth this restoration is reflected by the recomposition and rebirth of Dionysos from his still-living heart. For Proclus this heart represents the (undivided) intellect. Olympiodorus maintains that the recomposition signifies the transition from the Titanic (torn apart by passions) to the unitary life[90] and, again with reference to the myth of Dionysos, that the soul may reobtain unity by gathering itself from its dispersal,[91] loosing the bond of sympathy with its corporeal image, and returning to its original autonomous life without the image.[92] Similarly, Plotinus writes (I 6.5) of the sight of your own internal beauty resulting in your 'longing to be with yourselves, gathering yourselves away from your body' with an excitement that he calls a 'bacchic revel' (ἀναβακχεύεσθε).

For Plotinus the goal of the philosophical and spiritual life is to find the One. This is achieved by a turning inward, in which one sees god and oneself as god (VI 9.9). The one who sees will see himself as above reason, or rather 'he will be in union with himself as like this', as he has become single. What sees and what is seen become one. The one who sees 'does not imagine two, but it is as if he had become someone else'. The vision is not of another but of 'one with himself'. It is 'hard to put into words. For how could he announce that as another when he did not see ... another, but one with himself? This is the intention in the command given in the mysteries here below not to disclose to the uninitiated.' Here again, as is implied by the other texts discussed in this section, mystic overcoming of our separation from the divine is associated with eliminating the otherness that separates our image from ourselves.[93]

ACKNOWLEDGEMENT

My thanks go to Darian Leader, Pauline Meredith-Yates, John Wilkins, and the editors of this volume for their comments on this chapter; also to the Archäologische Sammlung der Universität Zurich for permission to reproduce the photograph (taken by Silvia Hertig) on p. 130.

NOTES

1. See most recently Seaford 1996: 36–7.
2. Usually when attacking Pentheus: cf. below on Figure 8.1. See now also Hatzopoulos: index s. Dionysos Pseudanor.
3. *Ion* 552; cf. also Hdt. 4.79–80; Hclt. B15 D-K; Sokolowski 1962: no.120; Bérard *et al.* 1989: figs 179, 191, 199; Seaford 1994a: 272; Versnel 1990: 119 n.94, 133 n.154, 151–2.
4. Seaford 1994a: 273; Henrichs 1982: 158–9; Turcan 1959.
5. See e.g. Brelich 1969: 31, 72; Leitao 1995.
6. Seaford 1996: 42.
7. The evidence for these statements is in Seaford 1987a. The question why he sees double is, oddly, hardly ever asked. The question why specifically sun and Thebes has never been asked. Part of the answer to this latter question may be that both sun and Thebes are unmistakably single, whereas (e.g.) 'I see two mountains and two trees' would not unequivocally imply doubling.
8. Trendall 1978: 50 n.34.
9. Trendall 1973: 168 n.533a, pl. 32,3; Balensiefen 1990: pl. 6,2.
10. On a *kylix* from Falerii at the Villa Giulia (26013); Jucker 1956: 105. Balensiefen (1990: 216) maintains that a reflection may not be involved.
11. On a silver *skyphos* of the Tiberian-Claudian era from Berthouville: Paris, Cab.Méd.Cat. Nr.60; reproduced by Balensiefen (1990: pl. 24).
12. A third possible example is a fragment in Boston (*MFA* 03.857; Neumann 1986: 107 Abb.2). Balensiefen (1990: 217) does not accept E.Robinson's view (*Museum of Fine Arts. Annual Report* 1903, 72, 64d) that the face in the *tympanon* is a reflection.
13. *Fr.*57.10. The phrase is thus generally restored. For εἰκών meaning an image in a mirror see e.g. Eur. *Med.* 1162 cited on p. 133.
14. On bowls used as mirrors, see Pliny *NH* 33.129, Theopompos Comicus *Nemea fr.*33 K-A.
15. *Thesm.*140 = Aesch. *fr.*61; τίς δαὶ κατόπτρου καὶ ξίφους κοινωνία;, 'what association (is this) then of mirror and sword?'; Cf. also Alexander *fr.*1 *PCG*.
16. Balensiefen 1990 pl. 43; *LIMC* s. Erinys 834 n.68; Trendall 1967: 113, 588. It must be kept in mind that this vase has suffered some repainting: Balensiefen 1990: 35.
17. Furies were sometimes envisaged as maenads (Aesch. *Eum.* 500), who also carry snakes.
18. For the ancient practice of catoptromancy (divination by mirror), see Delatte 1932.
19. *Oneir.* 2.7. This property of the mirror is mentioned as explaining why seeing a mirror-image similar to yourself is good for those about to marry. (Cf. Chester Beatty Papyrus III

143

7,11: 'If a man sees his face in a mirror in a dream, it is bad: it means another wife'.) The explanation he gives of the property ('since it shows their faces as these (show) each other their children') seems laboured, as does his explanation of why a mirror is fatal for the ill ('for a mirror is of the earth, whatever material it is made of').
20 A striking expression of this is the Villa of the Mysteries frieze at Pompeii. See also Pl. *Laws* 815c; *et al.* (Seaford 1994a: 266).
21 Zuntz 1971; Tsantsanoglou and Parassoglou 1987.
22 Seaford 1994a: 289 n.33.
23 *CIL* III 686 (Philippi).
24 Pl. *Phaedo* 108a; Ps.Pl. *Axiochus* 371de; Ar. *Frogs* 154–8, 313–459; Burkert 1987: 22–3, 100–1, 105.
25 West 1983: 17–19; cf. Hclt. *fr.* 62.
26 *Med.* 1162; cf. 1165 with *Ba.* 938.
27 8.37.7. Next to the temple were celebrated the goddess' mysteries, in which (to judge from terracotta figures found there) the participants wore the heads of animals.
28 By Vernant 1991: 142. He calls the word for dim, ἀμυδρός, 'a doublet of ἀμαυρός' – a word used of the dead.
29 Paus. 7.21.12; see also an anonymous poem in I.U.Powell *Collectanea Alexandrina*, p. 199, 25–8.
30 See e.g. Von Negerlein 1902; Hartlaub 1951: 26–7; Thimme 1965: 85–6.
31 See e.g. Hartlaub 1951: 81; Kerenyi 1964; Thimme 1965: 85–6.
32 Ov. *Met.* 3.200–3; Sen. *Oed.* 751–63; Ap. *Met.* 2.4.1–6; Balensiefen 1990: pls 40, 41.1.
33 Soph. *Ajax* 651 (see Seaford 1994b) and *Trach.* 1071, 1174.
34 For a male to possess a mirror might be used in an accusation of magic against him: Apul. *Apol.* 13.
35 In a Pompeian wall-painting: Balensiefen, 1990: pl. 12.
36 West 1992: 124.
37 This phenomenon may be related to the practice of initiating children (or even babies): for this in the Dionysiac mysteries see West 1983: 168–9 and Nilsson 1957: 106–15, and generally the bibliography in Burkert 1987: 151 n.115.
38 Seaford 1996: 41.
39 Richardson 1974: 26–7, 233.
40 Seaford 1996: 195–7.
41 Richardson 1974: 236.
42 Ferrara, *Nat. Arch. Mus.* T381 (Altamura Painter) = ARV^2 589.3.
43 West 1983: 140–75. The story may well be early: Seaford 1994: 284 n.17.
44 Kern 1922: frags. 209, 214 (also 34–6, 210–21). See further below.
45 1277: the phrase implies a child carried in its mother's arms (Seaford 1996: 248).
46 Cf. Plutarch *Mor.* 365a; Seaford (1996) on *Ba.* 969.
47 Seaford 1996: 42.
48 Cf., as a curiosity from a much earlier period, the suggestion by Thimme (1965: 85) that the prehistoric 'Kykladenpfannen' were filled with water for use as a mirror, and that to look into the water was to look into the lap of the goddess (they were decorated with the vulva).
49 Thomson 1966: 178–82.
50 I write 'image' because the Greeks had no word that only meant 'ghost'; *eidolon* (the word written into the Medicean manuscript) could mean (reflected) image as well as ghost.
51 The turmoil of the chariot-race seems to have been an image for the initial sufferings of the mystic initiands: Seaford 1994b: 279–80.
52 For these and other mystic allusions in Orestes' revenge in the play, see Seaford 1994b.
53 They are associated with her nipples by Devereux 1973: 48–9.
54 Seaford 1987b: 120.

IN THE MIRROR OF DIONYSOS

55 The self-blinding of Oedipus is associated by Devereux (1973) with castration. With the mask of Pentheus cradled by Agaue I (1996: 248) have compared the mask of Dionysos in the liknon cradle, which also regularly contained the phallos. From a Lacanian psychoanalytic perspective (cf. below) it could no doubt be suggested that the implied equivalence of mask and phallos in the cradle implies Pentheus' desire (at 966–70) to become the phallos for his mother (cf. Lemaire 1977 [1970]: 82) as well as her castration of him. For castration as an image of bodily fragmentation, see e.g. Lacan 1977: 11.
56 He compares *Ba.* 292ff., 367–8, 507–8, and esp. *Ion* 1375–7.
57 Lacan 1977: 18 (also 1–2).
58 The phrase is Bowie's (1991: 26).
59 Benvenuto and Kennedy 1986: 54; Ragland-Sullivan 1986: 29.
60 Benvenuto and Kennedy 1986: 58; Lemaire 1977 [1970]: 78; Ragland-Sullivan 1986: 24–7, 269, 278; Grosz 1990: 32, 42–3, 46–7.
61 ... *inlexit* ... *puerilis animi desiderio*: Firm. Mat. *Err.* 6 p.15, 2 Ziegler (= Kern *fr.* 214). In a Hellenistic text the bacchic cry *euoi* was first exclaimed by the Titans in praise of the invention of the mirror: Ps. Arignote ap. Harpocrat. s. εὐοῖ: West 157.
62 *Enneads* IV 3. 11. 7–8 (cf. IV 3. 12. 1–4 = *fr.* 209 Kern).
63 *In Phaedonem* p. 111, 14 Norvin (= *fr.* 209 Kern). See further Section V, this chapter.
64 Pyxis in Bologna: *LIMC* s. Dionysos/Bacchus 559 n.267.
65 Cf. the emphasis placed on the totality of bodily form (Gestalt), like a 'statue', perceived in the mirror by the infant: Lacan 1953: 15 and 1977: 2; Benvenuto and Kennedy 1986: 54–5; Grosz 1990: 42.
66 957-8 (cf. Aktaion seeing the naked Artemis). Devereux (1974: 38) argues that this exemplifies the phenomenon of the professed interest in a group disguising actual interest in an individual within it.
67 e.g. Zeitlin 1990: 135–6; Devereux 1974.
68 e.g. Dodds in his commentary (Dodds 1960) on the play.
69 Along with all the *similarities* that have been pointed out between Dionysos and Pentheus, it is interesting that in this scene Dionysos claims to be Pentheus' 'first of φίλοι (friends or kin)' (939).
70 Turner 1969: ch.3.
71 See the bibliography listed by West 1983: 169 n.97.
72 Cf. *OT* 413–5 with *Ba.* 506.
73 Note esp. *Ba.* 924, 947–8.
74 It is tempting to add, as the first stage of this reverse process, the earlier imprisonment of Dionysos within Pentheus' house. In the 'succession of phantasies' manufactured (according to Lacan) by the mirror stage, the fragmented body may manifest itself in dreams (under certain circumstances) as disjointed limbs, whereas 'correlatively, the formation of the *I* is symbolised in dreams by a fortress, or a stadium' (Lacan 1977: 4–5). Psychoanalytic criticism of *The Bacchae* has associated the interior of Pentheus' house with his defended unconscious, penetrated by the mysterious light that breaks forth along with the earthquake (Sale 1972: 68–9; Segal 1986: 305). Attention has also been drawn to the way in which the play implies an equivalence between Pentheus and the house (with the god in both): Wohlberg 1968. From our perspective, it is interesting that the shaking of the house is imagined in terms of the frenzy of a Dionysiac worshipper, that the house is fragmented by the earthquake, and that the concomitant thunderbolt belongs to a pattern of mystic initiation and evokes the birth of a child (Dionysos): 587–8, 592, 606, 633; Seaford 1996: 196–7.
75 This inversion is of course antithetical to the sameness of the mirror-image. Given that the function of inversion in the rite of passage may be to prepare the way for a new place in the *symbolic order* (with a new status, name, etc.), we may, from a Lacanian perspective, see transvestism in the rite of passage as dramatising the 'unrealistic', the substitution, the

III RITUAL AND GENDER

displacement, the inversion, etc. that characterise the symbolic order. And so inasmuch as the mirror relation must be mediated by and become subsumed in the symbolic, and inasmuch as the rite of passage involves regression to the imaginary so as to create a movement from the imaginary to the symbolic, then the failure of Pentheus to complete the rite of passage is a failure to move beyond the (unmediated) imaginary: transvestism, that generally prepares for a new place in the symbolic order, means in his case a lethal narcissistic identification with his *mother*. I owe much in this suggestion to Darian Leader.

76 For this whole argument see Seaford 1984. For seeing deity in mystic ritual see Riedweg 1987: 24–5, 142–9; Ap. *Met.* 11.23 (cf. 9 deity in mirror); etc.
77 This other is generally taken to be God, but this does not affect my point.
78 Cf. Eur. *Hipp.* 1078–9, 'Would that it were possible to stand opposite and look at myself, at my tears at what I am suffering'.
79 The usual translation 'child' is misleading. That would be παῖς. Νήπιος means an infant or a very young child: cf. e.g. Paul's *Letter to the Hebrews* 5.11 'For everybody who partakes of milk has no experience of the word of justice, for he is νήπιος'.
80 See esp. Lambrecht 1994 and Thrall 1994.
81 On the veiled initiand see *h. hom. Dem.* 192 (with Richardson 1974: 26–7, 233); Aesch. *Cho.* 811 (with Thomson 1966: 178–82); Burkert 1985 [1977]: 286; Nilsson 1957: figs 11 and 14.
82 Cf. *Odes of Solomon* 13 (late first or early second century CE): 'Behold the Lord is our mirror. Open (your) eyes and see them in him. And learn the manner of your face' (J.H. Charlesworth, *The Old Testament Pseudepigrapha* vol.2: 747).
83 From the fifth century BCE note Aesch. *Ag.* 839 – (1b), (4), with a hint of (1a) (Fraenkel misunderstands the passage); Aesch. *fr.* 393 – (1a) and (1b); Eur. *Hipp.* 429 – (1a) and (1b) oddly combined; Pi. *Nem.* 7.14 – (1b) or (2).
84 *Enneads* I 6.8, V 8.2. Although for Plotinus the notion of reflection is involved in the creation of the sensible world (III 6.7 and 14), this is distinct from the notion, to be found in a hermetic text, that the sensible world was created by the narcissistic love of the archetypal man for his own reflection in nature, with the result that man alone of creatures is 'double': *Poimandres* 14 (*Corpus Hermeticum*, ed. Nock and Festugière, Paris 1945, I p.11): Hadot 1976: 100–1.
85 *In Tim.* 33b II, 8, 19 Diehl (*fr.* 209 Kern).
86 Kern *frr.* 198, 210, 215, 216.
87 *In Crat.* 400d, 133, ed. Pasquali pp.77–8.
88 *In Phaedonem* p.111 Norvin, 4–19.
89 The myth corresponds (as we have seen) to the mystic ritual. And so presumably the mystic initiand may have imagined his experiences in terms of the dismemberment and rebirth of Dionysos: cf. *RE* IX A,2 s. Zagreus, p. 2278.
90 *In Phaedonem* p.43,14 Norvin (= *fr.* 211 Kern).
91 This notion is found as early as Pl. *Phaedo* 67c, where purification consists (in part) of the soul 'collecting and gathering itself (συναγείρεσθαί τε καὶ ἀθροίζεσθαι) from all parts of the body.' The *Phaedo* was clearly influenced by mystic doctrine (e.g. 69c).
92 *In Phaedonem* p.111, 4–19 Norvin.
93 Cf. also the Gnostic *Acts of Thomas* 112: 'Suddenly when I saw the robe made like (me) as though in a mirror, I also saw my whole self in it. And through it I knew and saw myself, that we have been divided into parts, though being from the same. And again we are one through one form'.

Part IV

SOURCES AND INTERPRETERS

9

THESMOPHORIA AND HALOA
Myth, Physics and mysteries

N. J. Lowe

The Thesmophoria was the most widespread and conspicuous of Greek women's festivals, celebrated at the end of summer all over the Greek world, its mysteries forbidden to men. In Athens especially, as Aristophanes opportunistically appreciated in setting two of his comedies of gender in and around the festival,[1] it constructed an exclusively-female collective religious space in the very heart of the male city; and in many ways it seems tailor-made to meet certain prevailing modern expectations about the feminine strand in ancient religion. First, its roots seem very ancient, to judge from its early distribution over a wide geographical range; and what we are told of its strange ritual has certainly savoured to many of the primitive, even the primeval. Second, its central rites were 'mysteries', secret ceremonies from which the uninitiated – in this case, all males – were excluded, and of which they were forbidden all knowledge. Third, it honoured Demeter, whose complex divine portfolio included not only the earth and its gifts, but the mysteries themselves, and the ancient world's archetypal narrative of mothers, daughters and the feminine condition – to all of which the Thesmophoria myth and ritual made reference. But perhaps above all, it is the one ancient rite to be explicitly discussed by our sources in terms of 'fertility', the manipulation of its symbols and its promotion by supernatural means: a nexus of ideas so powerfully in harmony with the influential nineteenth-century paradigm enshrined in Frazer's *Golden Bough* as to ensure its largely unquestioned dominance in modern interpretation of the festival,[2] long after the fertility paradigm itself has been disowned by anthropologists.[3] This chapter sets out to question that heritage of interpretation, by taking a closer look at how it has used its central document and, in so doing, to raise some uneasy wider questions about the nature of religious 'sources' and their reading, both ancient and modern.

IV SOURCES AND INTERPRETERS

I

The four passages A–D at the end of this chapter together make up the single most extraordinary and challenging document in our entire corpus of literary evidence for the interpretation of Greek religion. I stress this at the outset because it is surprising how unsurprised scholars have managed to be by this group of texts, and how uninterested in the document which the four fragments comprise, in the century and a quarter since A and C were first published. There is nothing remotely like them in our other ancient evidence for Greek ritual and its interpretation; many important features of the fragments' interrelation, both internally and in the history of the text, have been overlooked, including the remarkable *analytic* model that is surely their most striking feature of all. In addition, the use that has been made of them has tended at best to ignore, and at worst to contradict, their actual content. I want to suggest that a consideration of the document *as a whole* invites a re-evaluation not merely of the two Attic women's festivals discussed, but of the shibboleth of 'fertility' in the interpretation of women's cult, and perhaps even of some fundamental orthodoxies about the nature of Greek mysteries in general.

The two long texts A and C are scholia on Lucian's *Dialogues of Hetaerae*: marginal notes by a medieval scribe glossing the names of two Attic women's festivals, the Thesmophoria and Haloa, mentioned in Lucian's text. They lie a few pages apart in a single thirteenth-century manuscript of Lucian, and were first published and discussed by Erwin Rohde in 1870. Passage B is from Clement of Alexandria's famous tirade against Greek mystery cults in the second chapter of his *Protrepticus* or *Exhortation to the Greeks*, composed around AD 190. Passage D is a scholion on Lucian's *Council of the Gods*, preserved in six separate manuscripts dating between the early tenth and the fifteenth centuries. This last passage says nothing about women's festivals at all, but it gives a bizarre variant of the celebrated myth of Icarius that is otherwise found only in the Haloa scholion, C – where it has been bowdlerised to the point of incomprehensibility, but still shows unmistakable parallels of wording. What we have, then, is two versions each of a pair of texts, whose fuller versions (A and C) each take the form of an account of a particular Attic women's festival.

Strangely, no writer on these texts in 125 years has made explicit the elementary observation from which any discussion ought to begin: that *all four* passages must go back to a single ancient source. Indeed, only Rohde (1870) and Robertson (1984) have even remarked that the key texts A and C, besides turning up in the same medieval manuscript, derive from a common *ancient* author. It has, since Rohde, been routinely recognised that passages A and B share a single original (though there has never been an attempt to reconstruct it from the parallels and divergences between the two texts[4]); while the similar relationship between C and D has never been remarked on at all beyond a laconic 'cf.' in Rabe's edition.[5] At the risk of labouring the obvious, I list the most indicative verbal parallels, and point out that, if A and B share a source, A and C share a source, and C and D share a source, then a common source must lie behind all *four* passages – a source, moreover, that predates, and was directly or indirectly used by, Clement of Alexandria for the section of the *Protrepticus* that deals with the mysteries. Since, however, this section is a virtuoso pot-pourri of the entire corpus of pagan religious scholarship, this may not in practice significantly narrow the field.[6] But the main contention of this chapter is that, once these passages are read as parts of a whole, some very unusual features emerge. In particular, their ancient author used a highly distinctive, sophisticated, and consistent methodology of interpretation for which there is no easy parallel in known ancient writers on religion, and which so strongly colours his presentation and analysis of the two festivals as to raise urgent questions not merely about his own sources, affinities, and authority, but about the construction of meaning in ancient religion generally.

An account of the traditional reading of these texts can usefully begin with A, the famous Thesmophoria scholion.[7] Here we seem to have our one surviving account of the central mysteries, knowledge of which was forbidden to men. Yet this unique text lifts the veil on that deepest of ritual secrets: an uncanny, primeval-sounding rite involving underground chambers, decaying pigs and phantom serpents, too strange to seem anything but authentic. Astonishingly, however, the account does not stop there. Not only does it tell us what the mystery was, but it even tells us what it *meant*: its origins in an obscure Eleusinian myth, and its true symbolic meaning, which is connected with fertility magic. In 1870, when a daring new paradigm was emerging to argue that *all* religion was really about fertility magic, this was the one ancient text to come out and offer such an interpretation explicitly.[8] And so, I should stress, it remains – a point of some significance for the question of the texts' larger use discussed below.

From the beginning, however, it has been recognised that the scholion is desperately garbled or obscure, and perhaps corrupt, on some of the most important points of detail. Commentators from Rohde onwards have been alarmed by the airy claim that 'the same things' (whatever that means) 'are also known as Skirophoria and Arretophoria' – since we know enough about both of these intriguing Attic festivals to know that they were not the same thing at all. They took place in different months; unlike the Thesmophoria, they were confined to Athens; neither had anything to do with Demeter and/or Persephone; and they seem to have involved completely different rituals, though Pausanias' famous and tantalising account of the rites of the Arrephoria (i.27.3) does show some intriguing general parallels with the Thesmophoria ritual described in the scholion, inasmuch as both are to do with going down to underground chambers and bringing some manner of mystic baggage back up.[9] It would be convenient to be able to believe that the claim that all three festivals are 'the same' is the result of textual corruption in the scholion's transmission; unfortunately, however, it recurs in the equivalent passage in Clement, even down to the pedantic etymological respelling of the festival name as 'Arre<to>phoria' (found in no other source).

There are also internal problems. The technical term *megara*, 'chambers', is introduced in line 9 but not actually explained until 23–4; the 'models' (*plasmata*) of 16 are mentioned as though they have already been explained, but the explanation is actually in 20–2 below; and in 18 'the same explanation' refers to an interpretation of the ritual not introduced in our text until seven lines later at 25ff. Finally, somewhere between lines 22 and 29 the subject of discussion has switched back from the Arretophoria to the Thesmophoria, leaving the worrying question of which festival is being discussed in the lines from 'And they take' down to 'is physical' (λαμβάνουσι δέ ... φυσικός). Even if all three festivals are to be understood as *exactly* 'the same', the text as it stands begins to start talking about the Arretophoria as a separate event in 17, yet by the final sentence has somehow drifted back to the Thesmophoria.

When we turn to the Haloa scholion (C), the textual problems if anything increase.[10] There are passages where the Greek stops making any kind of sense; and were it not for the survival of the parallel passage D, the nature of Dionysus' vengeance on the unfortunate farmers would have been quite unintelligible from phrases like 'having remained under the very aspect of shame' (C10–11). More seriously still, a key element of the ritual is left obscure by the vagueness over which of the various sets of genital models are under discussion at any particular point. Those in the myth are made of clay and are dedicated; those in line 33 are made of cake and are laid on the table; but those at 4 and 22 could be either (though not both). The cart-before-horse pattern seen in the Thesmophoria note recurs at, for example, 32–3, where the obscenely shaped cakes of the Haloa banquet have become separated from the description of the banquet itself at 22–7. It has not helped that our author's ubiquitous interest in pornographic confectionery was clearly not shared by some of the Christian hands that have reshaped his text in the course of transmission – at least one of whom (as we shall see, it is possible to make a fair guess at his identity) seems to have found a number of details in the Haloa ritual a little too strong to stand unedited.

Clearly, then, the two long texts have been through a drastic process of repeated abridgment, précis, rewording, reshaping, and reordering in the course of transmission, resulting in several different kinds of obscurity and *non sequitur* all too characteristic of scholiastic literature in general. To speak of textual 'corruption' here, as though this were the sort of thing we could simply emend to restore the original, is to misunderstand the nature of how such texts are composed and transmitted. If we look, for example, at a passage like A20–29, it is hard to resist the impression that from line 15 to the end some struggling scribe has gone back over his source more or less grasshopper-fashion, picking out piecemeal odd points passed over in his précis of the text as a whole, so that from 'On that occasion too . . .' to the end (ἀναφέρονται κτλ) we have a series of disconnected points whose stringing-together into a pretence of order is entirely the work of the rewriter. Even to talk of 'deliberate ambiguity' (Robertson 1983: 257) gives a misleading picture of the haphazard, anything-but-purposeful way in which such texts come into being.

II

The modern literature on these texts has not always shrugged off this difficult textual and transmissional history. But even the wariest discussions have tended to treat the accounts of the ritual as the problematic part and the interpretative comment, whatever its actual authority, as comparatively straightforward. Now, certainly it would be interesting to know, for example, the actual location of the Athenian Thesmophorion with its pig-chambers, or how long the pigs were left to decay, or the relationship (if any) between the Thesmophoria ritual and the Skirophoria and Arrephoria. But I want to suggest that the most challenging questions centre on the model of *interpretation* used – indeed, shared – by both scholia: the way they answer the basic question of what, if anything, ritual means. It is here, I want to argue, that the real uniqueness of this set of texts lies, and that their implications reverberate through the whole enterprise of 'understanding' Greek religion.

Again I begin with passage A and the Thesmophoria. The historical significance of this text's publication for the then-emerging discipline of comparative religion has never been as fully recognised as it deserves. As the first – and only – explicit ancient evidence for the concept of 'fertility magic' as a major component of the 'meaning' of ancient Greek ritual, it was a cornerstone text for the general application to antiquity of what has been variously called the 'Mannhardt–Frazer hypothesis' or 'fertility paradigm': the doctrine that religious ritual historically originates in, and preserves the more or less atrophied traces of, the attempt to compel the productivity of the natural world by supernatural means. Though the doctrine itself is by now long discredited, it still demands a considerable effort of intellectual disrobing to read the text innocent of its late-Victorian intellectual baggage of sympathetic magic and fertility cults. Yet if we do so, we find that what it actually says is far more complex, more interesting, and (perhaps above all) more recognisably Greek.

The scholion firmly distinguishes between *two* explanations (*logoi*) of the ritual, which it calls 'mythical' and 'physical' (or 'scientific', or 'natural'; more on the usage of *phusikos* below). The 'more mythical', *muthodesteros*, explanation is aetiological, using narratives about the past to explain institutions in the present. In this case, the ritual commemorates an episode from Eleusinian myth through a stylised re-enactment of the incident. A swineherd called Eubouleus witnessed the rape of Persephone/Kore, and his pigs tumbled down the hole into the underworld after her; and this Eubouleus (who in the Orphic poem on the rape apparently was able to help Demeter with her inquiries, and whom we know from inscriptions to have been already worshipped at Eleusis in the fifth century) is then honoured by the ritual sacrifice of other people's pigs in an appropriately similar way.

But this, the scholion tells us, is only part of the story: there is a second *logos* of the festival which is 'physical'. On this level of explanation, the reason for throwing pigs and pine branches down holes is because pigs are *polutokos* (they give birth to many offspring), and pines are *polugonos* (they 'produce a lot' – of seeds, or cones, or other pines). The detail that especially attracted the generation of Frazer, and has seemed central to readings of the scholion ever since, is the reported belief that anyone who sowed some of the decayed remains of this mixture with their seedcorn would find that their crops grew better. It needs to be said, however, that this is not what the text itself claims to be the physical *logos* of the Thesmophoria; on the contrary, that the earth is sown with fertile things in order to transfer their fertility magically to the soil is precisely what the scholion does *not* say. The reason, rather, for the offerings is not an act of sympathetic magic but a thank-offering (*charisterion*) to Demeter; and the reason they are selected for their fertility is not to transfer this effect to something else but because they are symbols of generation (*sunthemata tes geneseos*) and specifically of the generation of crops and of humans – crops, because that is what Demeter is being thanked for providing, and humans, because that is who benefited from it. And *how* did they benefit? Not, as we might expect and as might seem more symbolically appropriate, by enhancements to their own fertility – but by becoming *hemeros*, civilised.

Many points could be made about the details of this *logos*; I should like for now to single out just three. First, it offers no support at all for the Mannhardt–Frazer paradigm; on the contrary, it raises it only to discount it. This is, I stress again, the only ancient text to offer anything like the nineteenth-century concept of 'fertility' – in asserting a symbolic connection in a religious context between the reproductivity of crops, animals and humans, in generalising from this connection to an abstract notion of *genesis*, and in suggesting a magico-religious connection of cause and effect between the manipulation of 'fertility' symbols and the prospect of an abundant crop. Yet only the most naively linear reading of the text could refer *ton auton logon* ('the same explanation', A18–19) to the belief in its fertilising power (A11–13). On the contrary, the *logos* that is to do with 'vegetable fertility and human procreation' is the one stated at 25–7, where the motive is thanksgiving and commemoration for the gift of civilization.

Second, and in significant contrast to the fertility-magic reading, this *logos* itself is a characteristically Greek, and perhaps specifically Eleusinian, pattern of ideas. The idea that agriculture is one of the key tokens of civilization is one of the most ancient and pervasive in Greek thought; and it is a keynote of Eleusinian and Attic religious propaganda that Demeter is thus a panhellenic culture goddess, responsible not just for the gift of corn but for the rise to civilization that it entails.[11] What is more, the term *charisterion* ('thank-offering') is a widespread and well-formed technical term, one of a family of *-terion* words used from Aeschylus to Heliodorus[12] to describe an offering made to a god for a particular purpose.

The final, and most crucial, observation I want to make about this physical *logos* is that it is mirrored point-for-point in the Haloa scholion C, where once again we have two separate, but interlinked, explanations of the festival: one aetiological, and one symbolic. The aetiology in this case is a bizarre and unparalleled variant of the myth of Icarius, the Attic farmer who first received the gift of wine from Dionysus, got all the other farmers drunk on it, and was then murdered in misplaced revenge because they mistook the unfamiliar sensation of drunkenness for poisoning. Now, this story was a famous one in Hellenistic poetry: mainly for a sequel excluded here, according to which Icarius's daughter Erigone was led to the corpse by the faithful family dog. Erigone then hanged herself in grief, whereupon Dionysus sent a plague upon the land which the farmers eventually discharged by instituting, in honour of the hanged Erigone, the festival of the Aiora: the ritual involving little girls on swings that fell on the last day of Dionysus' spring festival of the Anthesteria. Callimachus alluded to this sequel in the *Aetia* (fr. 178.1–6 Pfeiffer), and it was told at length in Eratosthenes' epyllion *Erigone*.

That is not, however, the sequel we get here, which is altogether stranger and – some might be tempted to say – more archaic-looking. In this version, unintelligible in C's own bowdlerised summary, but spelled out in the Icarius scholion D, Dionysus arouses the farmers by taking the form of a sexually alluring youth, and then teasingly disappears leaving them with permanent erections, until an oracle (in a familiar aetiological pattern) prompts them to ritualise the problem away by instituting a commemorative rite in which the incident is symbolically re-enacted. This in itself raises important questions about the version of the myth we have here. Is it an early or late variant? Is it (as I strongly suspect) an early version that was later displaced by a cleaned-up Hellenistic variant? Or is it a late and clumsy *ad hoc* rewrite? Such questions need to be filed with larger questions of date and authorship, raised – but not resolved – below. For now, the important thing is to note how closely parallel this aetiology is to the one raised in the Thesmophoria scholion: an Attic peasant suffers a disastrous side-effect of the god's actions, and is repaid by the institution of a ritual commemorating the original incident in a stylised re-enactment.

Yet the most striking parallel of all is in the 'physical' *logoi* given for the two festivals. Here too, the ritual objects are a symbol of human reproduction;

but here too, what the scholion does *not* claim is that they somehow promote male potency and/or human fertility. On the contrary, once more they are a commemorative symbol, and what they commemorate is the primal gift of the god's miraculous crop and its effect on human behaviour. The link drawn between wine and phalli might seem tenuous; but it is explicitly bridged here by the ancient commonplace that wine is a sexual stimulant, which is apparently why the gift of wine has been such an important gift to humanity. We can see both the logic and the parallel with the Thesmophoria scholion at once if we mentally interpolate 'as a thank-offering to Dionysus' after 'of men's generation' in line 6 (γινομένων <οἷον χαριστήρια τῷ Διονυσῷ>, ὅτι κτλ). And the clinching connection is that, at lines 30f. below, the message of the festival to outsiders is that *hemeroi trophai*, 'civilised foods', originated in Attica and were disseminated from there to the rest of the world. In other words, the god's gift is once again a crop whose arrival and cultivation has been a mark of civilization, and specifically of the Attic origins of agriculture and thus Athenian primacy in the hierarchy of civilised peoples.

Now, it needs saying that by ancient standards this is an interpretative model of quite exceptional sophistication. Aetiology and allegory are of course the two standard modes of religious explanation in ancient scholarship, the two available ways to answer the question, 'What does this ritual mean?' To my knowledge, however, there is no other ancient text that treats aetiology and allegory as complementary modes of explanation, let alone tries to apply them to the same institution in a way that demonstrates the close relationship between them. Yet here we have a writer who not only attempts to do just that, but seeks to extend and generalise the complementary model into a form that can be applied to two separate festivals – festivals, moreover, whose more than usually outré and meaningless-looking ritual challenges the interpreter to make *any* kind of sense of these bizarre goings-on, let alone a kind of sense that will satisfy on all the different moral, political and intellectual levels that a convincing ritual explanation demands. Finally, he is also a writer who has penetrated the secrets of mysteries undocumented by any other ancient scholar, and whose extraordinary and riveting account of those mysteries seems to have bypassed the mainstream of antiquarian scholarship (as drawn on, for example, by the lexicographic tradition), escaping the attention of all but a handful of late, Christian writers and the author of a trio of scholia to Lucian. Whether his interpretation is that of a researcher who has succeeding in probing to the very heart of the mysteries, or simply the artefact of a brilliant intellectual synthesis, I can think of few questions in the scholarship on Greek religion as exciting as the hunt for who this writer can possibly be.

III

First, we need to dispose of a red herring that has distracted that hunt since its beginnings. Rohde thought that the two festival scholia were probably composed in the tenth century by Arethas of Caesarea, bishop, scholar and bibliophile, whose annotations to authors who passed through his collection draw on a wide range of material from earlier lexica and commentaries now lost.[13] A key figure in the history of the text of Lucian, Arethas augmented the older scholia with some learned, distinctive, often quirky notes of his own;[14] and scholars who have considered the matter at all have tended to follow Rohde's lead, despite the absence of any parallel to this extraordinary material in Arethas' own copious writings.

In fact, though, two overlooked points in the manuscript history tell against Arethas as the notes' composer, and suggest instead that Arethas found these notes in the older scholia and merely passed them on in an edited form. First, the Icarius scholion D is found in the first hand of a tenth-century manuscript[15] whose text, at least, certainly lay outside the Arethan tradition. This in itself, however, is less conclusive than may seem, since the scholia follow a more open tradition than the text; and there are internal signs that these notes have at least passed through Arethas' hands. Several passages as we have them, especially the first two-thirds of the Haloa scholion, show signs of interference by a Christian editor with a distinctive line in baroque Greek, who seems characterised by a tendency to strange prudish circumlocutions and indignation at the excesses of paganism.[16] By contrast, most of A and D, and the Haloa scholion from 22 to the end, seems free of this sort of phraseology. That the periphrast is Arethas is suggested by his fondness for 'Byzantine' perfects, something of an Arethan trademark, in those areas of the text where the rewriter's hand is apparent (C8 δέδωκε, 11 καταμεμενηκότες; D16 ὡρμήκεσαν, 17 μεμενήκεσαν).

Yet though Arethas may have had a hand in the reshaping of these scholia, the strongest argument against Arethas as their original author lies in an unremarked coincidence in the history of the text. Fortunately, Arethas' own copy of Lucian survives: Harley 5694, the manuscript nowadays known as E. Unfortunately, the part that originally contained the text and scholia of the *Dialogues of Hetaerae* is lost. But we do have another manuscript Arethas had copied in the same year, 914: Parisinus Graecus 451 (P), which by a twist of chance includes the archetype of Clement's *Protrepticus*, annotated with scholia in the hands of Arethas himself and of his secretary Baanes. Surprisingly, no treatment of passage A has noted that on the Clement passage B, and specifically the very rare technical term *megarizontes*,[17] Baanes has written the brief note (p. 192.1f. Marcovich) '*megarising*: they call the trenches "megara"; thus "megarising" instead of "sacrificing"' (μεγαρίζοντες. μέγαρα καλοῦσι τοὺς βόθρους. μεγαρίζοντες οὖν ἀντὶ τοῦ θύοντες). Baanes knows that the word means a kind of sacrifice and that there were pits involved, two details that cannot possibly be inferred from Clement's word alone and in fact are explained in precisely one other surviving Greek text, the scholion on the Lucian passage whose closing etymology is unmistakably echoed in a further note by Baanes (p. 193. 29ff. Marcovich) on the very next page of the manuscript. Yet when it comes to glossing the Skirophoria, unhelpfully and ambiguously treated by the scholion in the elliptical form in which it has survived, Baanes and Arethas fall back on a rival tradition in their scholia on Clement and on Pausanias.[18] Clearly, then, when Baanes made that note in 914, he (and his employer Arethas) already knew the Thesmophoria scholion – but apparently not in a form significantly more helpful than the state in which it survives,[19] and Arethas merely bowdlerised some of the more interesting passages, especially of C, in his own distinctive style.

The spectre of Arethan authorship exorcised, the search must turn to the identity and nature of the ancient source. To my knowledge, only five candidates have ever been proposed, with dates ranging from the second century BCE to the second century AD. Rohde originally suggested Didymus on the somewhat vague, and debatable, grounds that he was a 'pragmatising mythologist' (1870: 554n.); but the kind of theoretical elaboration we get here is far outside Didymus' range both practically and intellectually. Rohde himself perhaps felt this, since in the reprint of his article he added a parenthesis suggesting Aelius Dionysius (1901: 361); but we now have considerably more of Aelius than was available to Rohde, and his surviving notes on religious terms are all rather brief and summary. Jacoby recognised that the key must be the source's unusual theoretical approach, which severely restricts the field of eligible authors known to us: 'we have the choice between Poseidonios and Apollodoros Περὶ Θεῶν, the only ancient authors who wrote real history of religion; the fact that it was Clement and the Scholiast on Lucian who used the authority tells in favour of Apollodoros.' (Jacoby 1954: ii.204) Jacoby's splendidly characteristic *ex cathedra* assertion has bowled most later and lesser scholars into a kind of dazed assent. Posidonius was a bad guess; his own *On the Gods* (*Peri theon*) was a work of philosophical theology, and nothing in the fragments suggests any interest in the fine details of cultic *realia*. But Apollodorus has several attractions: he was resident in Athens; his massive and widely influential survey of cult shared a lot of the interests that seem to have animated our writer; and he was drawn on by Clement for *Protrepticus* ii.

Yet the really distinctive features of our source cannot easily be reconciled with either the contents or the arrangement of Apollodorus' great work. The positive parallels between the festival scholia and the remains of the *On the Gods* are of a very general and unsurprising kind, while the Apollodoran fragments offer no support for the genuinely unique features of our source: the double-*logos* model, *muthikos/phusikos* distinction, extensive ritual detail, privileged information on secret women's rites, philosophical language like *sunthemata* and *genesis* and the allegorical techniques they express.[20] Nor is it at all clear that the contents and arrangement of the *On the Gods*, generous though they seem to have been, could easily have accommodated a discussion of this unusual form. Much remains uncertain, but it seems that the twenty-four books were arranged by deity, and the material within each as a series of mythico-etymological glosses on the different epithets of the god in question; it is not easy to see how our texts, in whatever original shape, could have fitted in a work of this design. Finally, if the two texts were adjacent in the source, it must have been the Demetrian book 16; but the Haloa scholion makes far more of the Dionysiac elements in the cult and myth, and the closely analogous model of interpretation suggests a connection more theoretical than phenomenological.

So Robertson (1984: 4–5, n15) and Riedweg (1987: 118–23), independently and for very different reasons, proposed a fifth possibility. The form and content of our texts, as well as the context for which they have been drawn on by Clement and the scholiast, most naturally suggests one of the numerous pre-Apollodoran treatises *On Festivals* produced by Attic antiquarians in the Hellenistic period.[21] The prodigiously widely-read Clement, whose intellectual interest in the mysteries has sometimes been thought to go back to a pagan youth in Athens, was unusually well placed and motivated to draw on such writers, though a compendium source is perhaps more characteristic. But there were a great many such writers about whom we know very little today: writers such as Apollonius of Acharnae, whose fragments show the same glossary form as the scholia and a similar depth of detail on festival matters. And there were many similar books, some emanating from the shadowy class of ritual experts known as 'exegetes', of whose content we now know nothing at all, such as the works of Theophrastus *On Festivals*, Habron the Exegete, Aristodicus and Sotades *On Mysteries*. Neanthes of Cyzicus' *On Initiations* is another possible source, though the few extant fragments do not actually discuss Attic mysteries. Riedweg, who would like the whole of Clement's section on the mysteries to go back to a single pagan treatise, suggests an unidentified exegetic work *On Mysteries*; while Robertson cautiously nominates Theophrastus, which would be attractive inasmuch as we would know we were dealing with a work of genius.

We know so little of this lost exegetic literature that such a hypothesis cannot be excluded, and it has the advantage of proposing a convincing form for the original document. Nevertheless, there remain serious difficulties with the exegetic hypothesis. In particular, the pairing of 'mythical' and 'physical' looks anything but third century. Rather, it strongly recalls what is arguably the most famous of all ancient models for religious interpretation, the so-called 'tripartite theology' of Varro's *Religious Antiquities*, which analyses the meaning of the gods in three different ways: in Greek mythical, physical and political, in Latin fabulous, natural and civil, and associated respectively with poets, philosophers and states.[22] The first of these three hermeneutic models seeks 'meaning' by telling stories about the gods (including what we would call *aitia*); type two is the kind of nature allegory pioneered by the early Homeric critics, elaborated by the Sophists, and taken up at length by the Stoics; and the third concerns the practical administrative details of ritual regulations and proprieties. Varro is usually thought to have taken his model from an unidentified author of the middle Stoa: perhaps Posidonius, writer of *On the Gods*, but other suggestions have included Panaetius or Dionysius of Heraclea.

The problem is that the Thesmophoria scholion uses the terms 'mythical' and 'physical' in a way quite different from any of the extant discussions of the tripartite model. It is not primarily that our texts, at least as we have them, say nothing about the political level; a case might conceivably be made that the ritual details themselves constitute the political *logos*. Far more important is the fact that the scholion treats the mythical and physical modes of explanation as complementary and mutually reinforcing, whereas in the tripartite model they are alternative and mutually exclusive, and certainly not applicable simultaneously to the analysis of a single figure or institution. Finally, the word *phusikos* is used in a quite different way from all other applications of the term to the analysis of myth and religion. Classical Stoic physicising *rejects* myth, by reducing it to an underlying allegory of natural processes; but our writer rejects allegory by subordinating it to the ends of myth. Far from displacing the theology of myth, the two scholia's elaborate symbolic analyses of fertility imagery in the ritual actually *reinforce* the culture myth of the deity's primal agricultural gift, through the use of symbols, *sunthemata*, that embody the blessings brought by that gift.

These considerations make it difficult to reconcile the use of these terms here with the model in which they are otherwise encountered. Either we are faced with a very idiosyncratic and deviant version of the tripartite terminology, or two of its keywords have been hijacked (the exegetic hypothesis would have to say 'anticipated') in the service of a different kind of model altogether. One possible explanation might be that a comparatively late writer[23] has seized for convenience on what were once precise technical terms, as imperial and Byzantine commentators tend to do, for example, with ancient literary-theoretical terminology. But there are no easy parallels, and it remains extremely difficult to locate even such a putative maverick within *any* recognisable ancient intellectual tradition. We cannot strictly rule out the possibility that the Stoic terminology has been overlaid by a later writer, paraphrasing an earlier account which did not use these labels; but this would then posit two interventions of unparalleled sophistication in the history of a single document.[24]

IV

It is at this point that the texts themselves present us with an unsettling further possibility. I consider it here with some reluctance, as it threatens some of our most basic assumptions about the nature of Greek religion in general. Until now, I have stressed the intellectual sophistication of the ancient source, with the tacit implication that this undermines the usefulness to us of the interpretations, and perhaps even the ritual reportage, in the text. At the very least, such a model-driven interpretative account, offering such idiosyncratic yet closely parallel interpretations of apparently unrelated Demetrian rites, raises the question of the extent to which the interpretation is the reporter's own, rather than that of his informants. To invoke a common anthropological distinction, how much of the interpretation belongs to the *actors* (the participants in the activity or belief and how much to the *observers* the outsiders who are trying to make sense of it)?

And it is precisely here that an unremarked feature of texts A and C raises the stakes still higher. At least as the texts stand, they seem to make a number of strong attributive statements ascribing elements of the interpretative content to sources other than, and anterior to, the voice of the author. At five points in the two scholia, interpretations are presented in indirect-speech constructions governed by a third-person verb in the plural: *nomizousi*, 'they think that' at A12 and A17; *legousi*, 'they say' at A13; *diegountai*, 'they explain' at C5; and the participle *epideiknumenoi*, 'demonstrating', at C29.[25] Tacit judgments about the syntax and sense of these attributions have been crucial to scholars' interpretations of the festivals. But just who *are* the subjects of these verbs?

In A, the subjects of *nomizousi* (both occurrences) and *legousi* ought, like that of *lambanousi* ('they take') at 22, to be the women who participate in the festival: specifically, if we can press the syntax, the *antletriai* or 'dredger-women' who were the subject of the last main verb before the first *nomizousi*. Significantly, however, the beliefs attributed by these verbs are not the actual *logos* of the ritual, but incidental, unverifiable superstitions from which the author seems to want to distance himself: the imaginary snakes guarding the chambers, the belief in the fertilising power of the remains. For the actual statements of what the rite as a whole means, the text drops quietly into defocalising passives. *Diegountai*, similarly, could credit the participants or other sources for the author's information; but it could equally well be the kind of vague attribution to earlier authorities we see so often in imperial antiquarians and miscellanists (especially Aelian), in whom 'They say that . . .' means no more than that 'It is said that . . .' or 'Some scholars think that . . .'. As Clement's (presumably coincidental) usage in B1 illustrates, the verb is also used by Christian writers in a contemptuously ironic and dismissive stance towards the material reported. As for *epideiknumenoi*, its subject should, if we press the text as it stands, be the archons; Brumfield (1981:

113) takes this at face value, and imagines the archons hovering at the gates of the sanctuary to deliver lectures on the Attic origins of civilization to parties of visiting tourists. But even if the syntax is trustworthy there are likelier ways of reading the verb: it could just mean that the archons' role in the banquet arrangements is itself interpretable as a demonstration or endorsement of the nationalistic principle that civilised foods originated in Attica.

Thus the rhetoric of ascription is extremely complex and ambiguous. It can be a discourse of validation, claiming actorly authority for observerly interpretations; but it may also be a strategy of embarrassment, evasion, obfuscation or open disavowal. Taken literally, *legousi* seems to claim that the explanation of the 'clatter' (*krotos*) is derived from oral reports by the 'dredgers'; while *nomizousi* seems to report an actual belief of the participants. But their reservation for unobservable, credulity-stretching 'beliefs' may be a focalising device, distinguishing the authoritative voice of the interpreting observer from a more provisional viewpoint conveniently attributed to the actors – especially if the wording is that of a Christian paraphraser for whom the actors are deluded pagans and the observer a beneficiary of revealed truth. And such attributions become peculiarly difficult and insistent in the case of a (presumably) male author writing about cults from which men were specifically excluded. How secret were these rituals, and were there legal sanctions for profanation? Who could his informants, even if unambiguously credited, have been? His wife or other family? Hetaerae or other acquaintances? Religious or civic officials? Archons? Exegetes?

For it is here that the quest for the source of the myth-and-physics model of women's mysteries has to reckon with the near-heretical possibility that it goes beyond the author to an actorly source. When we introduce Greek religion to beginners, we usually begin with a series of negatives: that, in tandem with the absence of sacred texts and central institutions, there was no dogma, no official version, no received wisdom as to what a particular ritual activity meant. But was this, in fact, true? Even outside the so-called 'mysteries', was Greek religion entirely a religion of doing rather than 'believing'?[26] Was there no doctrinal, interpretative element? Take aetiology, for instance: who, if anyone, is actually responsible for the attachment of a myth to a ritual? Is it a spontaneous, authorless process of collective tradition, or do the appointed priests of a cult or sanctuary endorse and propagate both the general method and a particular official version?

A thought-experiment: suppose one were actually able to ask the Hierophant, the chief priest of the Eleusinian mysteries, as one initiate to another what the secret ritual of revelation really meant. It is hard to imagine he would simply answer, 'Oh, it doesn't mean anything really; it's just something you *do*'. But one could easily envisage an answer of the kind we meet in these scholia: that the ritual makes an elaborate, edifying symbolic statement about the nature of the god and the reasons why she or he is being honoured.

Unfortunately, this is also precisely the kind of answer that an intellectual commentator might seek or invent; and even if he obtained it from a priestly source, in the very act of recording it he would transcribe it into the kind of language (such as the appropriated terminology of myth and physics) that would validate it for an intellectual readership. Nevertheless, one could imagine certain diagnostic signs that might argue for a priestly rather than a scholarly ultimate source: if, for example, the interpretation lay outside the theological mainstream; if it preserved aetiologically customised variants of myths at odds with their more familiar versions in the literary tradition; if it was integrated with uniquely detailed inside knowledge of ritual procedure; and if it was couched in terms that, though intellectual in manner, would in content seem less philosophical and more cultically orthodox than we would expect from Hellenistic antiquarians and philosophers of religion. And perhaps one of the lost and, even in antiquity little-read, treatises by Hellenistic exegetes, who wrote at an intriguing interface between the scholarly and the priestly, might be the least unlikely channel by which such material could enter the margins of the literary tradition.

To go even this far, however, would be a bolder solution to the challenge of these texts than I would feel comfortable in proposing. I merely want to open this unique document up to the kind of debate its content, sophistication and implications demand, and to indicate how much is at stake in the search for its source – even if its importance should turn out to lie less in what it may or may not tell us about women's mysteries and their secret meaning than in the processes by which an account of those secrets has come down to us, in the uses we make of that account and in the questions they force us to face about both. What happens when a male writer looks for the meaning of a women's festival? What agenda does he bring to the process, what sources does he use and how does his sense of the answers he wants shape his use of the answers he gets? How many times is that process repeated in the transmission, reception and interpretation of 'sources'? How far can rival discourses for making sense of ritual – myth, allegory, regulation – coexist, and who owns and propagates those discourses? Athenian housewives with bags of fertiliser? Women called dredgers? The priestess with her whispered exhortations to sin? The exegete, the philosopher, the scholiast? The Christian polemicist, the Byzantine bishop, the Cambridge ritualist, the Paris structuralist, the London seminar? On what grounds do we so privilege our own interpretations over our sources' that we feel entitled to dismantle their readings and reassemble them to suit our own (considerably more ideologically gendered) sense of what women's religion ought to mean? When our one ancient statement of a fertility interpretation turns out to be nothing of the kind, is there any reason to cling to a model discarded half a century ago by anthropologists? Was Greek religion itself as dogma-free, as empty of indigenous 'meaning', as we like to claim in our scramble to colonise its signifying space with meanings of our own devising? These are uncomfortable questions, but they are the dues we owe for the rights to mine this material. In particular, it should no longer be possible to treat this document as an inert and innocent 'source', without dirtying our hands with the attempt to excavate the complex layers of textual and intellectual history that created it. Clearly, in these four texts, we are faced with a middenful of the decayed remains of something that was once alive and vigorous, and which if recovered might actually bring new life to our field. But first we have to descend where no man has gone: to climb down into the darkness and dredge.

A. Scholion to Lucian, *Dialogi Meretricii* ii.1

Θεσμοφόρια· Θεσμοφόρια ἑορτὴ Ἑλλήνων μυστήρια περιέχουσα, τὰ δὲ αὐτὰ καὶ Σκιροφόρια καλεῖται. ἤγετο δὲ κατὰ τὸν μυθωδέστερον λόγον, ὅτι, [ὅτε] ἀνθολογοῦσα ἥρπάζετο ἡ Κόρη ὑπὸ τοῦ Πλούτωνος, τότε κατ' ἐκεῖνον τὸν τόπον Εὐβουλεύς τις συβώτης ἔνεμεν ὗς καὶ συγκατεπόθησαν τῷ χάσματι τῆς Κόρης· εἰς οὖν τιμὴν τοῦ Εὐβουλέως ῥιπτεῖσθαι τοὺς χοίρους εἰς τὰ χάσματα τῆς Δήμητρος καὶ τῆς Κόρης. τὰ δὲ σαπέντα τῶν ἐμβληθέντων εἰς τὰ μέγαρα κάτω ἀναφέρουσιν ἀντλήτριαι καλούμεναι γυναῖκες καθαρεύσασαι τριῶν ἡμερῶν καὶ καταβαίνουσιν εἰς τὰ ἄδυτα καὶ ἀνενέγκασαι ἐπιτιθέασιν ἐπὶ τῶν βωμῶν· ὧν νομίζουσι τὸν λαμβάνοντα καὶ τῷ σπόρῳ συγκαταβάλλοντα εὐφορίαν ἕξειν. λέγουσι δὲ καὶ δράκοντας κάτω εἶναι περὶ τὰ χάσματα, οὓς τὰ πολλὰ τῶν βληθέντων κατεσθίειν· διὸ καὶ κρότον γίνεσθαι, ὁπόταν ἀντλῶσιν αἱ γυναῖκες καὶ ὅταν ἀποτιθῶνται πάλιν τὰ πλάσματα ἐκεῖνα, ἵνα ἀναχωρήσωσιν οἱ δράκοντες, οὓς νομίζουσι φρουροὺς τῶν ἀδύτων. τὰ δὲ αὐτὰ καὶ Ἀρρητοφόρια καλεῖται καὶ ἄγεται τὸν αὐτὸν λόγον ἔχοντα περὶ τῆς τῶν καρπῶν γενέσεως καὶ τῆς τῶν ἀνθρώπων σπορᾶς. ἀναφέρονται δὲ κἀνταῦθα ἄρρητα ἱερὰ ἐκ στέατος τοῦ σίτου κατεσκευασμένα, μιμήματα δρακόντων καὶ ἀνδρείων σχημάτων. λαμβάνουσι δὲ κώνου θαλλοὺς διὰ

Thesmophoria: a festival of the Greeks encompassing mysteries, also known as Skirophoria. It was [or 'they were'] held, according to the more mythological explanation, because [when] Kore, picking flowers, was being carried off by Pluto, one Eubouleus, a swineherd, was at the time grazing his pigs on that spot, and they were swallowed up together in Kore's pit; wherefore, in honour of Eubouleus, piglets are thrown into the pits of Demeter and Kore. The rotten remains of what was thrown into the megara below are recovered by women called 'dredgers', who have spent three days in ritual purity and descend into the shrines and when they have recovered the remains deposit them on the altars. They believe that anyone who takes some and sows it with the seed will have a good crop. They say that there are also serpents below about the pits, which eat up the great part of the material thrown in; for which reason they also make a clatter whenever the women dredge and whenever they set those models down again, so that the serpents they believe to be guarding the shrines will withdraw. The same thing is also known as Arretophoria, and is held with the same explanation to do with vegetable fertility and human procreation. On that occasion too they bring unnameable holy things fashioned out of wheat-dough: images of snakes and of male members. And they take pine

τὸ πολύγονον τοῦ φυτοῦ. ἐμβάλλονται δὲ καὶ εἰς τὰ μέγαρα οὕτω καλούμενα ἄδυτα ἐκεῖνά τε καὶ χοῖροι, ὡς ἤδη ἔφαμεν, καὶ αὐτοὶ διὰ τὸ πολύτοκον εἰς σύνθημα τῆς γενέσεως τῶν καρπῶν καὶ τῶν ἀνθρώπων οἷον χαριστήρια τῇ Δήμητρι, ἐπειδὴ τοὺς Δημητρίους καρποὺς παρέχουσα ἐποίησεν ἥμερον τὸ τῶν ἀνθρώπων γένος. ὁ μὲν οὖν ἄνω τῆς ἑορτῆς λόγος ὁ μυθικός, ὁ δὲ προκείμενος φυσικός. Θεσμοφόρια δὲ καλεῖται, καθότι θεσμοφόρος ἡ Δημήτηρ κατονομάζεται τιθεῖσα νόμους ἤτοι θεσμούς, καθ' οὓς τὴν τροφὴν πορίζεσθαί τε καὶ κατεργάζεσθαι ἀνθρώπους δέον.

branches because of that plant's fertility. There are also thrown into the megara (so the shrines are called) those things, and piglets, as mentioned above – the latter because of their fecundity as a symbol of vegetable and human generation, for a thanksgiving offering to Demeter; because in providing the fruits of Demeter she civilized the race of humans. Thus the former reason for the festival is the mythological one, but the present one is physical. It is called Thesmophoria because Demeter is given the epithet 'Lawgiver' for having set down customs, which is to say laws, under which men have to acquire and work for their food.

(Rabe 1906: 275.23ff.)

B. Clement of Alexandria, *Protrepticus* xvii.1

βούλει καὶ τὰ Φερεφάττης ἀνθολόγια διηγήσομαί σοι καὶ τὸν κάλαθον καὶ τὴν ἁρπαγὴν ὑπὸ Ἀιδονέως καὶ τὸ σχίσμα τῆς γῆς καὶ τὰς ὗς τὰς Εὐβουλέως τὰς συγκαταποθείσας τοῖν θεοῖν, δι' ἣν αἰτίαν ἐν τοῖς Θεσμοφορίοις μεγαρίζοντες χοίρους ἐμβάλλουσιν; ταύτην τὴν μυθολογίαν αἱ γυναῖκες ποικίλως κατὰ πόλιν ἑορτάζουσι, Θεσμοφόρια, Σκιρόφορια, [Ἀρρητοφόρια] πολυτρόπως τὴν Φερεφάττης ἐκτραγῳδοῦσαι ἁρπαγήν.

Would you like me to explain to you also Pherephatta's flower-picking, and her rape by Aidoneus, and the cleft in the earth, and the pigs of Eubouleus that were swallowed up with the Two Goddesses [*sic*], according to which aetiology the 'megarising' women at the Thesmophoria throw in pigs? This myth the women celebrate variously in festival around the city, Thesmophoria, Skirophoria, Arretophoria, acting out the rape of Pherephatta in many ways.

(Marcovich 1995: 26.1ff.)

C. Scholion to Lucian, *Dialogi Meretricii* vii.4

Ἀλῷα· ἑορτὴ Ἀθήνησι μυστήρια περιέχουσα Δήμητρος καὶ Κόρης καὶ Διονύσου ἐπὶ τῇ τομῇ τῆς ἀμπέλου καὶ τῇ γεύσει τοῦ ἀποκειμένου ἤδη οἴνου γινόμενα παρὰ Ἀθηναίοις, ἐν οἷς προτίθεται αἰσχύναις ἀνδρείοις ἐοικότα, 5 περὶ ὧν διηγοῦνται ὡς πρὸς σύνθημα τῆς τῶν ἀνθρώπων σπορᾶς γινομένων, ὅτι ὁ Διόνυσος δοὺς τὸν οἶνον παροξυντικὸν φάρμακον τοῦτο πρὸς τὴν μῖξιν παρέσχεν. δέδωκε δὲ αὐτὸ Ἰκαρίῳ, ὃν καὶ ἀποκτείναντες ποιμένες τῷ ἀγνοῆσαι, ὅπως διαιτίθησι ποθεὶς οἶνος, εἶτα μανέντες διὰ 10 τὸ καὶ πρὸς τὸν Διόνυσον ὑβριστικῶς κινηθῆναι καὶ ἐπ' αὐτοῦ τοῦ τῆς αἰσχύνης σχήματος καταμεμενηκότες χρησμὸς παύσασθαι τῆς μανίας αὐτοὺς διηγόρευσε πήλινα ποιήσαντας αἰδοῖα καὶ ἀναθέντας· οὗ δὴ γενομένου αὐτοὶ μὲν ἐστησαν τοῦ κακοῦ, ὑπόμνημα δὲ τοῦ πάθους ἡ τοιαύτη 15 ἑορτή. ἐν ταύτῃ καὶ τελετή τις εἰσάγεται γυναικῶν ἐν Ἐλευσῖνι καὶ παιδιαὶ λέγονται πολλαὶ καὶ σκώμματα. μόναι δὲ γυναῖκες εἰσπορευόμεναι ἐπ' ἀδείας ἔχουσιν ἃ βούλονται λέγειν· καὶ δὴ τὰ αἴσχιστα ἀλλήλαις λέγουσι τότε, αἱ δὲ ἱέρειαι λάθρᾳ προσιοῦσαι ταῖς γυναιξὶ κλεψιγαμίας πρὸς τὸ 20 οὖς ὡς ἀπόρρητόν τι συμβουλεύουσιν. ἀναφωνοῦσι δὲ πρὸς ἀλλήλας πᾶσαι αἱ γυναῖκες αἰσχρά τε καὶ ἄσεμνα βαστάζουσαι εἴδη σωμάτων ἀπρεπῆ πρόκειται καὶ τράπεζαι ἀνδρῶν τε καὶ γυναικεῖα. ἐνταῦθα οἶνός τε πολὺς πρόκειται καὶ τράπεζαι πάντων τῶν τῆς γῆς καὶ θαλάσσης γέμουσαι βρωμάτων πλὴν τῶν

Haloa: A festival at Athens of Demeter and Kore and of Dionysus, encompassing mysteries, held among the Athenians at the cutting of the vine and the tasting of the wine previously laid in storage. In these, [*subject missing*] in the form of male privates are set out, which they explain as symbolic of the seed of men's generation, because Dionysus in making the gift of wine provided that stimulating drug as an incitement to sex. He gave it to Icarius, whom the shepherds having also [?] slain through their ignorance of the effects of wine-drinking, and subsequently being driven mad on account first of their blasphemous impulse towards Dionysus, and secondly having remained under the very aspect of shame [?] – an oracle commanded them to desist from their madness by fashioning clay genitals and dedicating them. This done, they were released from the curse, and the present festival commemorates the events. In it, there is also presented a women's *telete* at Eleusis, and many jokes and frivolities are uttered. The women go in alone, and may say what they wish; and indeed they do then say the most disgusting things to one another, and the priestesses approach the women secretly and into their ear urge them to commit adultery, as though it were some holy secret. All the women shout disgusting, blasphemous things at one another, handling the while indecent images of the body, male and female alike. Here there is a great deal of wine laid ready, and tables laden with all the victuals of earth and sea save those forbidden in the mysteries: I mean

ἀπειρημένον ἐν τῷ μυστικῷ, ῥοιᾶς φημι καὶ μήλου καὶ ὀρνίθων κατοικιδίων καὶ ᾠῶν καὶ θαλαττίων τρίγλης, ἐρυθίνου, μελανούρου, καράβου, γαλεοῦ. παρατιθέασι δὲ τὰς τραπέζας οἱ ἄρχοντες καὶ ἔνδον καταλιπόντες ταῖς γυναιξὶν αὐτοὶ χωρίζονται ἔξω διαμένοντες ἐπιδεικνύμενοι τοῖς ἐπιδημοῦσι πᾶσι τὰς ἡμέρους τροφὰς παρὰ αὐτοῖς εὑρεθῆναι καὶ πᾶσι κοινωνηθῆναι τοῖς ἀνθρώποις παρ᾿ αὐτῶν. πρόσκειται δὲ ταῖς τραπέξαις καὶ ἐκ πλακοῦντος κατεσκευασμένα ἀμφοτέρων γενῶν αἰδοῖα. Ἁλῷα δὲ ἐκλήθη διὰ τὸν καρπὸν τοῦ Διονύσου· ἅλῳαί γὰρ αἱ τῶν ἀμπέλων φυτεῖαι. 25, 30

pomegranate, apple, domestic fowl, eggs, and among fish the red mullet, erythinus, black-tail, crayfish and dogfish. The Archons prepare the tables and leave them inside for the women, while they themselves depart and wait outside to show all visiting foreigners that civilized foods originated with them and were communicated to all mankind by them. Also laid on the table are private parts of both sexes fashioned of cake. It is called Haloa after the fruit of Dionysus, for *aloai* are where vines are grown.

(Rabe 1906: 279.24ff.)

D. Scholion to Lucian, *Deorum Concilium* 5

Ἰκάριον· ὁ Ἰκάριος οὗτος Ἀθηναῖος ἐγεγόνει γεωργός· τούτῳ φασὶ τὸν Διόνυσον δοῦναι τὸ κλῆμα πρῶτῳ, ἀφ᾿ οὗ Ἰκαρία ἡ πρώτη ἄμπελος ὠνομάσθη καὶ ἡ χώρα ἡ ἐνέγκασα τὸ φυτόν. οὗτος ὁ Ἰκάριος ἔδωκε ποιμέσι τοῦ καρποῦ πιεῖν Ἀττικοῖς, οἳ πιόντας νομίσαντας τοὺς λοιπούς, ὅτι τεθνήκοιεν τῷ βαθεῖ τῷ ὕπνῳ διὰ τὴν οἰνοποσίαν κατασχεθέντες, ἀποκτεῖναι τὸν Ἰκάριον νομίσαντας θανάσιμον φάρμακον δεδωκέναι οὐ μόνον τοῖς καθεύδουσιν ἀλλὰ δὴ καὶ τοῖς ἐγρηγορόσι καὶ τῇ μέθῃ βακχεύουσι μανίας ἐμποιητικόν. οὕτω μὲν οὖν τὸν Ἰκάριον ἀποθανεῖν. ἐπεὶ δὲ κατέστησαν ἀπὸ τῆς μέθης, τὸν Διόνυσον χόλον αὐτοῖς ἐμβαλεῖν τοιόνδε· ἐλθὼν γὰρ πρὸς αὐτοὺς ἐν 5, 10

Icarius: This Icarius was an Athenian farmer. He was, they say, the first man to whom Dionysus gave the vine, and after him the first vineyard and the area that bore the fruit came to be called Icaria. This Icarius gave the Attic shepherds to drink of the crop. When they had drunk, the others believed that the ones who had been overcome by sleep thanks to their wine-drinking were dead, and they murdered Icarius thinking he had given a lethal drug not only to those who were asleep but also one that brought on madness to those who were awake and intoxicated by the drunkenness. So that is how Icarius died; but when they had recovered from the drunkenness, Dionysus wrought the following revenge on them. Coming among them in the form of a comely

σχήματι ὡραίου παιδὸς ἐξέμηνεν αὐτοὺς πρὸς ὁρμὴν μίξεος· καὶ δὴ ἐπιβουλεύειν αὐτὸν διαφθεῖραι. ἀλλ' ὁ μὲν ἀφανὴς εὐθὺς ἐγεγόνει, οἱ δὲ ἅτε δὴ ἐκείνου ὑποσχομένου 15 τὸ καθ' ὁρμὴν αὐτοῖς ἐᾶν ἐκτελέσαι ὡρμήκεσαν ἄχρι κινήσεως καὶ δὴ μεμενήκεσαν οὕτως ἀεὶ ἐκ τῆς ὀργῆς Διονύσου ἀκατάπαυστον τὴν ὁρμὴν ἔχοντες. ἐφ' οἷς ἐξιλασάμενοι τὸν θεὸν τοιαῦτα κατὰ χρησμὸν πεποιηκότες πήλινα σχήματα καὶ ἀνθ' ἑαυτῶν ἀναθέντες ἐπαύσαντο τῆς 20 μανίας.

youth, he maddened them with sexual desire; and accordingly they wanted to abuse him. But then he suddenly disappeared; and because he had promised to allow them consummation in accordance with their desire, they were sexually excited and indeed remained so, thanks to the wrath of Dionysus, their desire never remitting. Finally they placated the god by making clay images of this kind in response to an oracle, and dedicating them on their own behalf; and so were released from their madness.

(Rabe 1906: 211.14ff.)

Some significant verbal parallels

Clement	Thesmophoria scholion
B1 ἀνθολόγῳ	ἀνθολόγουσα A3
2, 8 ἁρπαγὴν	ἡρπάζετο 4
2 χάσμα	χάσματι 6, χάσματα 7, 14
3 συγκαταποθείσας	συγκατεπόθησαν 6
3, 5 ὗς ... χοίρους	ὗς ... χοίρους 5, 7
5 ἐμβάλλουσιν	ἐμβληθέντων 8, ἐμβάλλονται 23
5 μυθολογίαν	μυθωδέστερον λόγον 3, λόγος ... μυθικός 29
6 ἑορτάζουσι	ἑορτή 1, ἑορτῆς 29
7 Ἀρρητοφόρια	Ἀρρητοφόρια 18

Thesmophoria scholion

A1 Θεσμοφόρια ἑορτὴ Ἑλλήνων μυστήρια περιέχουσα
25f. εἰς σύνθημα τῆς γενέσεως τῶν καρπῶν καὶ τῶν ἀνθρώπων
15 τῆς τῶν ἀνθρώπων σπορᾶς
30 Θεσμοφόρια δὲ καλεῖται, καθότι. . . .

Haloa scholion

Ἁλῷα· ἑορτὴ Ἀθήνησι μυστήρια περιέχουσα C1 πρὸς σύνθημα τῆς τῶν ἀνθρώπων σπορᾶς 5f.

Ἁλῷα δὲ ἐκλήθη διὰ . . . 33f.

Haloa scholion

C8 δέδωκε δὲ αὐτὸ Ἰκαρίῳ 8 ποιμένες
8 ὃν καὶ ἀποκτείναντες 11 καταμεμενηκότες
12f. χρησμὸς παύσασθαι τῆς μανίας αὐτοὺς διηγόρευσε πήλινα ποιήσαντας αἰδοῖα καὶ ἀναθέντας

Icarius scholion

τούτῳ φασὶ τὸν Διόνυσον δοῦναι τὸ κλῆμα D2
ποιμέσι 4
ἀποκτεῖναι τὸν Ἰκάριον 7
μεμενήκεσαν 17
κατὰ χρησμὸν πεποιηκότες πήλινα σχήματα καὶ ἀνθ' ἑαυτῶν ἀναθέντες ἐπαύσαντο τῆς μανίας 19–21

ACKNOWLEDGEMENT

This material began life as a chapter of a 1983 Cambridge PhD thesis; I should like to thank Robert Parker, Geoffrey Lloyd, Richard Gordon and Matthew MacLeod for help and advice with the earlier version, and Robert Garland, Colin Austin and the editors for encouragement to revisit the problems. Above all I am indebted to my thesis supervisor, Geoffrey Kirk, to whom this chapter is dedicated with deep affection and gratitude.

NOTES

1 Enough survives of the lost second *Thesmophoriazusae* to make it clear that, in contrast to other duplicate titles in the Aristophanic canon, it was a quite different play on a quite different plot that so far has defied plausible reconstruction.
2 'The core of this Demeter festival is the concern for the promotion of human and cereal fertility' (Versnel 1994: 236, cf. 1992: 34); 'It was celebrated to convey fertility to the soil and to married women' (Simon 1983: 21); 'The Greeks typically associated together all natural birth, and Demeter though chiefly goddess of the corn-crop also presided over human fertility' (Parke 1977: 87): 'the clearest example in Greek religion of agrarian magic. The remains are, in Deubner's words, "bearers of fertility . . . sucked full with the forces of the earth . . . employed as fertility magic for the new sowing"' (Burkert 1985 [1977]: 244). For salutary scepticism, see now Nixon 1995: 92 and Foxhall 1995: 97.
3 'For contemporary social anthropologists, the category "fertility god" is as void of meaning as its coeval "totemism"' (Leach 1978).
4 Clement follows the broad contents of the first eight lines of the scholion, with close correspondences in language and sequence that imply neither version has diverged radically from this part of the common source. His first sentence might almost have been based on the verbatim narrative preserved in the scholion, though he salvages one extra detail, the *kalathos* or basket, and leaves others out. He then makes a remark about the relationship between the three festivals that substantially clarifies the scholion's ambiguous 'also known as Skirophoria. . . . The same thing is also known as Arretophoria' (A2, A17f.) and preserves two details not explicit in the scholion: all three festivals are celebrated by women, and (if 'variously around the city' is taken in its natural sense) at three different locations in Athens. Both these data are confirmed by other sources, and presumably derive from the common original. See also n.18 below.
5 Robertson (1983b: 257 n.51) suggests that the same source may lie behind a damaged passage in Stephanus s.v. *Miletos*; but *genesis* there must surely mean 'race'. In contrast, Epiphanius *De fide* p. 510.10 Holl clearly *does* derive from the scholiast's and Clement's source, but at too far a remove to be useful; it may not be independent of Clement.
6 I list, purely for demonstration, simply those authorities, other than poets, Clement mentions *by name* in *Protrepticus* ii-iii – all of whom can, I think, be safely eliminated as the original source of these scholia: Anticlides; Antiochus; Apollodorus; Aristotle; Diagoras of Melos; Demaratus; Dicaearchus; Didymus; Dorotheus; Dosidas/iades; Heraclides; Heraclitus; Hieronymus; Leandrius; Monimus; Myrsilus of Lesbos; Phanocles; Philochorus; Polemon; Ptolemy son of Agesarchus; Pythocles; Sosibius; Staphylus; Zeno of Myndos. Riedweg's hypothesis of a single handbook source, if accepted, merely shifts the search a step further back.
7 The key treatments are Rohde 1870; Robert 1885; Mommsen 1891; Mommsen 1898: 308–22; Nilsson 1955: 461–6 119f.; Farnell 1907: 89–93; Frazer 1912: ii.16–22; van

der Loeff 1916; Gjerstad 1929; Deubner 1932: 40–60; Eitrem 1944; Jacoby 1954: i.285–305 with nn.; Burkert 1966: 7–9; Brumfield 1981: 73–9; Simms 1980: 180–2; Robertson 1983b; Simon 1983: 18–24; Winkler 1990; Robertson 1992: 14–21; Metzger 1985: 45–8; Sfameni Gasparro 1986: 259–77; Brulé 1987: 82; Riedweg 1987: 116–23; Van Sichelen 1987. For more general treatments of the Thesmophoria see also Preller 1837: 335–65; Harrison 1903: 120–31; Nilsson 1906: 313–25; Nilsson 1955: 461–6; Farnell 1907: 75–112; Frazer 1911; Stengel 1920: 231f.; Arbesmann 1936; Johansen 1975; Dahl 1976; Parke 1977: 82–8; Burkert 1985 [1977]: 242–6; Brumfield 1981: 70–103; Simon 1983: 18–22; Detienne 1989 [1979]: 129–47; Zeitlin 1982: 138–53; Metzger 1985: 44–53; Sfameni Gasparro 1986: 223–83; Clinton 1988; Clinton 1992 (index s.v. 'Thesmophoria'); Versnel 1994: 235–60, 274–88 (cf. 1992); Foxhall 1995; Nixon 1995.

8 Mannhardt's *Die Korndämonen* had appeared in 1867; *Wald- und Feldkulte* followed in 1875–7, and its theories were canonised in the first edition of Frazer's *Golden Bough* in 1890.

9 Burkert 1966 (q.v. for earlier treatments), 1983: 150–4, 1985 [1977]: 228f.; Parke 1977: 141–3; Simms 1980: 121–40, 144–5; Robertson 1983b; Simon 1983: 39–46; Brulé 1987: 79–98; Van Sichelen 1987.

10 Discussions of the Haloa in Rohde 1870: 557–60 = 1901: 367–9; Mommsen 1878: 270–5; Mommsen 1889: 250–6; Mommsen 1898: 359–69; Nilsson 1900: 95–100; Nilsson 1941–57: i^3.466f.; Farnell 1907: 45f.; Stengel 1910; Stengel 1920: 231f.; Foucart 1914: 54–6; Frazer 1912 i.60–3; Deubner 1932: 60–7; Jacoby 1954: i.362f.; Skov 1975; Parke 1977: 98–100; Parker 1979; Brumfield 1981: 104–31; Simon 1983: 35–7; Robertson 1984: 2–5, esp. n.15.; Sfameni Gasparro 1986: 285–93; Winkler 1990: 194–6; Foxhall 1995.

11 Graf 1974: 38f., 158–81.

12 In the opening of *Libation Bearers*, Orestes lays two locks of hair on the grave: a *pentheterion* or 'grief-offering' in token of his mourning for his father, and a *threpterion* or 'growing-up-offering' to mark his successful growth to manhood. For Heliodoran wordplay with *charisterion* and cognates, see especially *Aethiopica* iv.16.8, but also iv.14.1, v.15.3, v.27.9, x.6.2.

13 An accessible sketch in Wilson 1983: 120–35.

14 Useful accounts in Rabe 1903; Bidez 1934, esp. 396–9.

15 Vaticanus 90 (Γ).

16 To this writer I would assign the phrases A21–2 μιμήματα δρακόντων καὶ ἀνδρείων σχημάτων ('images of snakes and of male members'); C4 αἰσχύναις ἀνδρείοις ἐοικότα ('in the form of male privates'); C7 παροξυντικὸν φάρμακον τοῦτο πρὸς τὴν μῖξιν παρέσχεν ('provided that stimulating drug as an incitement to sex'); the whole sentence C8–11 but especially ὅπως διατίθησι ποθεὶς οἶνος (literally, 'how wine disposes having been drunk'), ὑβριστικῶς κινηθῆναι ('their blasphemous impulse'), ἐπ αὐτοῦ ... καταμεμενηκότες ('having remained under the very aspect of shame'); 18 τὰ αἴσχιστα ('the most disgusting things'); 19–20 κλεψιγαμίας πρὸς τὸ οὖς ὡς ἀπόρρητόν τι συμβουλεύουσιν ('urge them into their ear to commit adultery as though it were some holy secret'); 21 αἰσχρὰ καὶ ἄσεμνα ('disgusting, blasphemous things'); 19–20 εἴδη σωμάτων ἀπρεπῆ ἀνδρεῖά τε καὶ γυναικεῖα ('indecent images of bodies, male and female'); and perhaps in the Icarius scholion the sentence D14–18 ('he suddenly disappeared ... remitting').

17 All citations seem to derive from two ancient occurrences; the second, mysteriously glossed by Hesychius and Suda as 'famished', came in an unknown comedy (perhaps a *Thesmophoriazusae*). The participle is the only form found.

18 302.18 Stählin; cf. Jacoby 1954: i.216–18.

19 Regrettably, the part of P is lost that included Eusebius' *Praeparatio*, in which the *Protrepticus* is cited *in extenso* (and would have attracted further glosses from Arethas and his notary).

20 With the exception discussed below, there seem no strikingly parallel uses or conjunctions

anywhere in classical Greek of what would seem the most diagnostic features of the scholia's terminology: *musteria periechein, sunthema geneseos, karpon genesis, anthropon spora*.
21 Tresp 1914, 1924: 1119–23; Jacoby 1949: 8–70 and Fragmente der griechischen Historiker: 352–6.
22 Lieberg 1973 (*q.v.* for earlier treatments); Pépin 1976: 13–32; Cardauns 1976; Jocelyn 1980, 1982–3.
23 If the identification of Thesmophoria and 'Arretophoria' is the result of imperfect information on the Arrephoria, Pausanias' guidebook would presumably be a *terminus ante*.
24 Note, however, that Clement's second sentence combines, in *muthologian . . . heortazousi* ('myth . . . celebrate in festival'), three terms associated at two different locations in the scholion: *heorte . . . muthodesteron logon* A1–3, and *heortes logos ho muthikos* A29 (both perhaps based on the same sentence in the source). This suggests the terminology of mythical and physical *logoi* was already in Clement's source; *muthologia* of course means something rather different from *muthikos logos*, but Clement is interested only in the grotesqueries of pagan aetiology, not in the theory of ritual exegesis, and may have retained the author's language while simplifying the sense.
25 Baanes' *kalousi* ('they call') in his gloss on B may qualify as a sixth, if A24's *houto kaloumena aduta* ('so the shrines are called') is a variant of the same original phrase.
26 On the difficulties in defining 'belief' cross-culturally, see Needham 1972.

BIBLIOGRAPHY

Aebli, D. (1971) *Klassischer Zeus*, Munich: Dissertationsdruck: Schön.
Ahlberg, G. (1971) *Prothesis and Ekphora in Greek Geometric Art = Studies in Mediterranean Archaeology* 32, Göteborg: Astrom.
Aleshire, S.B. (1989) *The Athenian Asklepieion: the People, their Dedications, and the Inventories*, Amsterdam: Giessen.
Alexiou, M. (1974) *The Ritual Lament in Greek Tradition*, Cambridge: Cambridge University Press.
Andronikos, M. (1968) 'Totenkult' in *Archaeologica Homerica 3*, Göttingen: Vandenhoeck and Ruprecht.
Arafat, K. (1990) *Classical Zeus*, Oxford: Clarendon Press.
Arbesmann, P. (1936) 'Thesmophoria', *Real-Encyclopädie der Klassischen Altertumswissenschaft* 6.1: 15–28.
Avagianou, A. (1991) *Sacred Marriage in the Rituals of Greek Religion*, Bern: Lang.
Averill, R. (1968) 'Grief: its nature and significance', *Psychological Bulletin* 70: 721–48.
Balensiefen, L. (1990) *Die Bedeutung des Spiegelbildes als Iconographisches Motiv in der Antiken Kunst*, Tübingen: Ernst Wasmuth.
Beaumont, L.A. (1995) 'Mythological childhood: a male preserve? An interpretation of classical Athenian iconography in its socio-historical context', *Annual of the British School at Athens* 90: 339–61.
Benvenuto, B. and Kennedy, R. (1986) *The Works of Jacques Lacan. An Introduction*, London: Free Association Books.
Bérard, C. (1974) *Anodoi: essai sur l'imagerie des passages chthoniens*, Rome: Institut Suisse de Rome.
Bérard, C. *et al.* (1989) *A City of Images*, Princeton: Princeton University Press.
Bidez, C. (1934) 'Arethas de Césarée', *Byzantion* 9: 391–408.
Bloch, M. (1971) *Placing the Dead: Tombs, Ancestral Villages and Kinship Organisations in Madagascar*, London: Seminar Press.
Bloch, M. (1982) 'Death, women and power' in M. Bloch and J. Parry (eds), *Death and the Regeneration of Life*, Cambridge: Cambridge University Press, pp.211–30.
Blok, J. (1994) *The Early Amazons: Modern and Ancient Perspectives on an Ancient Myth*, Leiden: Brill.
Blundell, S. (1995) *Women in Ancient Greece*, London: British Museum Press and Cambridge, Mass.: Harvard University Press.
Boardman, J. (1955) 'Painted funerary plaques and some remarks on prothesis', *Annual of the British School at Athens* 50: 55ff.

Boardman, J. (1977) 'The Parthenon frieze – another view' in U. Höckmann and A. Krug (eds), *Festschrift für Frank Brommer*, Mainz: von Zabern, pp.39–49.

Boardman, J. (1982) 'Heracles, Theseus and Amazons' in D.C. Kurtz and B. Sparkes (eds), *The Eye of Greece: Studies in the Art of Athens*, Cambridge: Cambridge University Press, pp.1–28.

Boardman, J. (1984) 'The Parthenon frieze' in E.Berger (ed.), *Parthenon-Kongress Basel, Referate und Berichte 4 bis 8 April 1982*, Mainz: von Zabern, vol. 1, pp.210–15.

Boardman, J. (1985) *The Parthenon and its Sculptures*, London: Thames and Hudson.

Bonnechere, P. (1994) *Le sacrifice humain en Grèce ancienne*, Kernos, Supplément 3, Athens and Liège: Centre International d' Étude de la Religion Grecque Antique.

Bowie, M. (1991) *Lacan*, London: Fontana.

Bowlby, J. (1961) 'Processes of mourning', *International Journal of Psycho-Analysis* 42: 317–40.

Brelich, A. (1969) *Paides e Parthenoi*, Rome: Edizioni dell' Ateneo.

Bremmer, J.N. (ed.) (1987) *Interpretations of Greek Mythology*, London and Sydney: Croom Helm.

Brijder, H.A.G. (ed.) (1984) *Ancient Greek and Related Pottery Symposium 5*, Amsterdam: Allard Pierson Series.

Brommer, F. (1979) *The Sculptures of the Parthenon*, London: Thames and Hudson.

Brommer, F. (1980) *Göttersagen in Vasenlisten*, Marburg: Elwert.

Broude, N. and Garrard, M.D. (eds) (1982) *Feminism and Art History*, New York, London and Cambridge: Harper & Row.

Brulé, P. (1987) *La Fille d'Athènes: la religion des filles à Athènes à l'époque classique*, Paris: Belles Lettres.

Brulotte, E.L. (1994) 'The placement of votive offerings and dedications in the Peloponnesian sanctuaries of Artemis', Diss., University of Minnesota.

Brumfield, A.C. (1981) *The Attic Festivals of Demeter and their Relation to the Agricultural Year*, New York: Arno.

Burkert, W. (1966) 'Kekropidensage und Arrhephoria', *Hermes* 94: 1–25.

Burkert, W. (1979) *Structure and History in Greek Mythology and Ritual*, Berkeley and Los Angeles: University of California Press.

Burkert, W. (1983 [1970]) *Homo Necans*, Berkeley and Los Angeles: University of California Press.

Burkert, W. (1985 [1977]) *Greek Religion*, Oxford: Blackwell.

Burkert, W. (1987) *Ancient Mystery Cults*, Cambridge, Mass.: Harvard University Press.

Calame, C. (1977) *Les Choeurs de jeunes filles en Grèce archaïque*, Rome: Edizioni dell' Ateneo e Bizzarri.

Calame, C. (1987) 'Spartan genealogies: the mythological representation of a spatial organisation' in J.N. Bremmer (ed.) (1987) pp.153–86.

Campbell, B. (1987) *The Iron Ladies. Why do Women Vote Tory?* London: Virago Press.

Cameron, A. and Kuhrt, A. (eds) (1983) *Images of Women in Antiquity*, London: Croom Helm.

Cantarella, E. (1987) *Pandora's Daughters: The Role and Status of Women in Greek and Roman Antiquity*, trans. M.B. Fant, Baltimore: Johns Hopkins University Press.

Caraveli, A. (1986) 'The bitter wounding: the lament as social protest in rural Greece' in J. Dubisch (ed.), *Gender and Power in Rural Greece*, Princeton: Princeton University Press, pp.169–94.

Cardauns, B. (1976) *M. Terentius Varro: Antiquitates Rerum Divinarum*, Wiesbaden: Steiner.

Castriota, D. (1992) *Myth, Ethos and Actuality. Official Art in Fifth-Century Athens*, Madison: University of Wisconsin Press.

Chantraine, P. (1946–7) 'Les noms du mari et de la femme, du père et de la mère', *Revue des Études Grecques* 59–60: 228–31.
Clairmont, C.W. (1993) *Classical Attic Tombstones*, Introductory volume, Kilchberg: Akanthus.
Clement, P. (1934) 'New evidence for the origin of the Iphigeneia legend', *L'Antiquité Classique* 3: 393–409.
Clinton, K. (1988) 'Sacrifice at the Eleusinian mysteries' in R. Hägg *et al.* (eds) (1988) pp.69–80.
Clinton, K. (1992) *Myth and Cult: The Iconography of the Eleusinian Mysteries*, Stockholm: Svenska Institutet i Athen.
Cohen, B. (1983) 'Paragone: sculpture versus painting. Kaineus and the Kleophrades painter' in W.G. Moon (ed.), *Ancient Art and Iconography*, Madison: University of Wisconsin Press, pp.171–92.
Cohen, D. (1989) 'Seclusion, separation, and the status of women in classical Athens', *Greece and Rome* 36: 3–15.
Cole, S.G. (1984) 'The social function of rituals of maturation', *Zeitschrift für Papyrologie und Epigraphik* 55: 233–44.
Connelly, J.B. (1996) 'Parthenon and *parthenoi*: a mythological interpretation of the Parthenon frieze', *American Journal of Archaeology* 100: 53–80.
Dahl, K. (1976) *Thesmophoria: en graesk kvindefest*, Opuscula Graecolatina 6, Copenhagen: Museum Tusculanum.
Dakoronia, F. and Gounaropoulou, L. (1992) 'Artemiskult auf einem neuen Weihrelief aus Achinos bei Lamia', *Mitteilungen des Deutschen Archäologischen Instituts (Athenische Abteilung)* 107: 219–27.
Daux, G. (1983) 'Le calendrier de Thorikos au Musée J. Paul Getty', *L'Antiquité Classique* 52: 150–74.
De Polignac, F. (1994) 'Mediation, competition, and sovereignty: the evolution of rural sanctuaries in geometric Greece' in S. Alcock and R. Osborne (eds), *Placing the Gods: Sanctuaries and Sacred Space in Ancient Greece*, Oxford: Clarendon Press, pp.3–18.
De Polignac, F. (1995 [1984]) *Cults, Territory, and the Origins of the Greek City-State*, Chicago: University of Chicago Press.
Deissmann-Merten, M. (1984) 'Zur Sozialgeschichte des Kindes im Antiken Griechenland' in J. Martin and A. Nitschke (eds), *Zur Sozialgeschichte der Kindheit*, Freiburg and Munich.
Delatte, A. (1932) *La Catoptromancie grecque et ses dérivés*. Bibliothèque de la Faculté de Philosophie et Lettres de l'Université de Liège 18, Paris: Droz.
Delcourt, M. (1938) *Stérilités mystérieuses et naissances maléfiques dans l'antiquité classique*. Bibliothèque de la Faculté de Philosophie et Lettres de l'Université de Liège 83, Paris: Droz.
Demand, N. (1994) *Birth, Death and Motherhood in Classical Greece*, Baltimore and London: Johns Hopkins University Press.
Detienne, M. (1989 [1979]) 'The violence of wellborn ladies: women at the Thesmophoria' in M. Detienne and J.-P. Vernant (eds), *The Cuisine of Sacrifice*, Chicago: University of Chicago Press, pp.129–47.
Deubner, L. (1925) 'Hochzeit und Opferkorb', *Jahrbuch des Deutschen Archäologischen Instituts* 40: 210–12.
Deubner, L. (1932) *Attische Feste*, Berlin: Keller.
Devereux, G. (1970) 'La naissance d'Aphrodite' in J. Pouillon and P. Maranda (eds), *Echanges et Communications: Mélanges Offerts à Claude Lévi-Strauss* ii, Paris: Mouton, pp.1229–52.
Devereux, G. (1973) 'The self-blinding of Oidipous in Sophokles: *Oidipous Tyrannos*, *Journal of Hellenic Studies* 93: 36–49.

Devereux, G. (1974) 'Trance and organism in Euripides' *Bacchae*' in A. Angoff and D. Barth (eds), *Parapsychology and Anthropology*, New York: Parapsychology Foundation, pp.36–58.
Dodds, E.R. (1960) *Euripides' Bacchae* (2nd edn), Oxford: Clarendon Press.
Dontas, G.S. (1983) 'The true Aglaurion', *Hesperia* 52: 48–63.
Dover, K.J. (1974) *Greek Popular Morality in the Time of Plato and Aristotle*, Oxford: Oxford University Press.
Dowden, K. (1989) *Death and the Maiden: Girls' Initiation Rites in Greek Mythology*. London: Routledge.
Dubisch, J. (1986) 'Culture enters through the kitchen: women, food and social boundaries in rural Greece' in J. Dubisch (ed.) *Gender and Power in Rural Greece*, Princeton: Princeton University Press, pp.195–214.
duBois, P. (1982) *Centaurs and Amazons: Women and the Prehistory of the Great Chain of Being*, Ann Arbor: University of Michigan Press.
Eitrem, S. (1944) 'Les Thesmophoria, les Skirophoria et les Arrhétophoria', *Symbolae Osloenses* 23: 32–45.
Ellinger, P. (1987) 'Hymapolis et le sanctuaire d'Artemis Elaphébolos dans l'histoire, la légende et l'espace de la Phocide', *Archäologischer Anzeiger* 102: 88–99.
Evelyn-White, H.G. (1954) *Hesiod, the Homeric Hymns and Homerica*, Loeb Classical Library; London: Heinemann; Cambridge, Mass.: Harvard University Press.
Fantham, E. (1975) 'Sex, status and survival in Hellenistic Athens: a study of women in new comedy', *Phoenix* 29: 44–74.
Fantham, E., Foley, H., Kampen, N., Pomeroy, S. and Shapiro, H.A. (1994) *Women in the Classical World: Image and Text*, New York and Oxford: Oxford University Press.
Farnell, L.R. (1907) *Cults of the Greek States III*, Oxford: Clarendon Press.
Fehl, P. (1961) 'The rocks on the Parthenon frieze', *Journal of the Warburg and Courtauld Institutes* 24: 1–44.
Foley, H.P. (1993) 'The politics of tragic lamentation' in A.H. Sommerstein *et al.* (eds) *Tragedy, Comedy and the Polis*, Bari: Levante, pp.101–43.
Fontenrose, J. (1959) *Python: A Study of Delphic Myth and its Origins*, California: University of California Press.
Fortenbaugh, W.W. (1975) *Aristotle on Emotion*, London: Duckworth.
Foucart, P. (1914) *Les Mystères d'Eleusis*, Paris: Picard.
Foxhall, L. (1995) 'Women's ritual and men's work in ancient Athens' in R. Hawley and B. Levick (eds) (1995), pp.97–110.
Frazer, J.G. and 'X' (1911) 'Thesmophoria', *Encyclopedia Britannica* (11th edition) 26: pp.838–40.
Frazer, J.G. (1912) *Spirits of the Corn and of the Wild*, 2 vols = vii–viii of *The Golden Bough* (3rd edition, 1911–15), London: Macmillan.
Friedrich, P. (1978) *The Meaning of Aphrodite*, Chicago: University of Chicago Press.
Frontisi-Ducroux, F. (1975) *Dédale: mythologie de l'artisan en Grèce ancienne*, Paris: Maspero.
Furley, W.D. (1981) *Studies in the Use of Fire in Ancient Religion*, Salem: Ayer Co.
Garland, R.S.J. (1985) *The Greek Way of Death*, London: Duckworth.
Garland, R.S.J. (1989) 'The well-ordered corpse: an investigation into the motives behind Greek funerary legislation', *Bulletin of the Institute of Classical Studies* 36: 3ff.
Garland, R.S.J. (1990) *The Greek Way of Life*, London: Duckworth.
Gjerstad, E. (1929) 'Das attische Fest der Skira', *Archiv für Religionswissenschaft* 27: 189–240.
Golden, M. (1985) '*Pais*, "child" and "slave"', *L'Antiquité Classique* 54: 91–104.

Golden, M. (1990) *Children and Childhood in Classical Athens*, Baltimore and London: Johns Hopkins University Press.

Gomme, A.W. (1925) 'The position of women in Athens in the fifth and fourth centuries', *Classical Philology* 20: 1–25.

Gould, J.P. (1980) 'Law, custom and myth: aspects of the social position of women in classical Athens', *Journal of Hellenic Studies* 100: 38–59.

Graf, F. (1974) *Eleusis und die orphische Dichtung Athens im vorhellenistischer Zeit*, Berlin and New York: De Gruyter.

Grosz, E. (1990) *Jacques Lacan: A Feminist Introduction*, London and New York: Routledge.

Günther, W. (1988) ' "Vieux et inutilisable" dans un inventaire inédit de Milet' in D. Knoepfler and N. Quellet (eds), *Comptes et inventaires dans la cité grecque*, Geneva and Paris: Droz, pp.215–37.

Hadot, P. (1976) 'Le mythe de Narcisse et son interpretation par Plotin', *Nouvelle Revue de Psychanalyse* 13: 81–108.

Hadzisteliou Price, T. (1978) *Kourotrophos: Cults and Representations of the Greek Nursing Deities*, Leiden: Brill.

Hägg, R., Marinatos, M., and Nordquist, G.C. (eds) (1988) *Early Greek Cult Practice*, Stockholm: Svenska Institutet: Athen.

Hall, E. (1989) *Inventing the Barbarian: Greek Self-Definition through Tragedy*, Oxford: Oxford University Press.

Harrison, E.B. (1967) 'Athena and Athens in the east pediment of the Parthenon', *American Journal of Archaeology* 71: 27–58.

Harrison, E.B. (1989) 'Hellenic identity and Athenian identity in the fifth century BC' in *Cultural Differentiation and Cultural Identity in the Visual Arts. Studies in the History of Art* 27, Washington: National Gallery, pp.41–61.

Harrison, E.B. (1994) 'The web of history: a conservative reading of the Parthenon frieze'. Paper presented at a symposium, 'Parthenon and Panathenaia', at Princeton University, 1991, as reported by S. Peirce and A. Steiner, *Bryn Mawr Classical Review* 5: 78–80.

Harrison, J.E. (1903) *Prolegomena to the Study of Greek Religion*, Cambridge: Cambridge University Press.

Hartlaub, G. F. (1951) *Zauber des Spiegels*, Munich: Piper.

Hatzopoulos, M.B. (1994) *Cultes et rites de passage en Macedoine*, Athens and Paris: Boccard.

Havelock, C.M. (1982) 'Mourners on Greek vases: remarks on the social history of women' in N. Broude and M.D. Garrard (eds) (1982), pp.45–61.

Hawley, R. and Levick, B. (eds) *Women in Antiquity: New Assessments*, London and New York: Routledge.

Henrichs, A. (1982) 'Changing Dionysiac identities', in B.F. Meyer and E.P. Sanders (eds), *Self-Definition in the Graeco-Roman World*, London: SCM Press, pp.137–60.

Henrichs, A. (1987) 'Three approaches to Greek mythography' in J.N. Bremmer (1987) (ed.) pp.242–77.

Herington, C.J. (1955) *Athena Parthenos and Athena Polias*, Manchester: Manchester University Press.

Himmelmann, N. (1971) *Archäologisches zum Problem der griechischen Sklaverei*, Mainz: Akademie der Wissenschaften und der Literatur.

Hirsch-Dyczek, O. (1983) *Les Représentations des enfants sur les stèles funéraires attiques*, Warsaw and Cracow: Nakl. Uniwersytetu Jagiello'nskicgo.

Holst-Warhaft, G. (1992) *Dangerous Voices: Women's Laments and Greek Literature*, London: Routledge.

Humphreys, S.C. (1974) 'The *nothoi* of Kynosarges', *Journal of Hellenic Studies* 94: 88–95.
Humphreys, S.C. (1980) 'Family tombs and tomb cult in ancient Athens – tradition or traditionalism?', *Journal of Hellenic Studies* 100: 96–126.
Hunter, V.J. (1989) 'Women's authority in classical Athens', *Échos du Monde Classique* 33: 39–48.
Hurwit, J.M. (1995) 'Beautiful evil: Pandora and the Athena parthenos', *American Journal of Archaeology* 99: 171–86.
Jacoby, F. (1949) *Atthis*, Oxford: Clarendon Press.
Jacoby, F. (1954) *A Commentary on the Ancient Historians of Athens*, 2 vols (*Die Fragmente der griechischen Historiker*, IIIb Supplement), Leiden: Brill.
Jameson, M.H. (1990) 'Domestic space in the Greek city-state' in S. Kent (ed.) (1990), pp.92–113.
Jenkins, I. (1994) *The Parthenon Frieze*, London: British Museum Press.
Jocelyn, H.D. (1980) 'On editing the remains of Varro's *Antiquitates Rerum Divinarum*', *Rivista di Filologia e di Istruzione Classica* 108: 100–22.
Jocelyn, H.D. (1982–3) 'Varro's *Antiquitates rerum divinarum* and religious affairs in the late Roman republic', *Bulletin of the John Rylands Library* 65:148–205.
Johansen, J.P. (1975) 'The Thesmophoria as a women's festival', *Temenos* 11: 78–87.
Johnston, S.I. (1995) 'Defining the dreadful: remarks on the Greek child-killing demon' in M. Meyer and P. Mirecki (eds), *Ancient Magic and Ritual Power*, Leiden: Brill, pp.361–87.
Jost, M. (1985) *Sanctuaires et cultes d'Arcadie*, Paris: J. Vrin.
Jucker, I. (1956) *Der Gestus des Aposkopein*, Zurich: Juris.
Just, R. (1989) *Women in Athenian Law and Life*, London: Routledge.
Kahil, L. (1965) 'Autour de l'Artémis attique', *Antike Kunst* 8: 20–33.
Kahil, L. (1977) 'Rites et mystère', *Antike Kunst* 20: 86–98.
Kahil, L. (1981) 'Le cratérisque d'Artémis et le Brauronion de l'Acropole', *Hesperia* 50: 252–63.
Kästner, U. (1981) 'Bezeichnungen für Sklaven' in E. C. Welskopf (ed.), *Soziale Typenbegriffe im alten Griechenland und ihr Fortleben in den Sprachen der Welt* iii, Berlin: Akademie Verlag, pp.282–318.
Kearns, E. (1989) 'The heroes of Attica' (*Bulletin of the Institute of Classical Studies*, Suppl 57), London: Institute of Classical Studies.
Kearns, E. (1990) 'Saving the city', in O. Murray and S. Price (eds), *The Greek City: From Homer to Alexander*, Oxford: Clarendon Press, pp.323–44.
Kent, S. (ed.) (1990) *Domestic Architecture and the Use of Space*, Cambridge: Cambridge University Press.
Kepple, L.R. (1976) 'The broken victim: Euripides' *Bacchae* 969–970', *Harvard Studies in Classical Philology* 80: 107–9.
Kerenyi, K. (1964) 'Der spiegelnde Spiegel' in E. Haberland *et al.* (eds), *Festschrift für A. E. Jensen*, Munich.
Kern, O. (1922) *Orphicorum Fragmenta*, Berlin: Weidmann.
King, H. (1983) 'Bound to bleed: Artemis and Greek women' in A. Cameron and A. Kuhrt (eds), (1983), pp.109–27.
Knoepfler, D. and Quellet, N. (eds) (1988) *Comptes et inventaires dans la cité grecqu*, Geneva: Droz.
Kondis, I.D. (1967) 'Artemis Brauronia', Ἀρχαιολογικὸν Δελτίον 22:156–206.
Kurtz, D.C. (1984) 'Vases for the dead, an Attic selection, 750 – 400' in H.A.G. Brijder (ed.) (1984), pp.314–28.

BIBLIOGRAPHY

Kurtz, D.C. and Boardman, J. (1971) *Greek Burial Customs*, London: Thames and Hudson.
Laager, J. (1957) *Geburt und Kindheit des Göttes in der griechischen Mythologie*, Winterthur: Keller.
Lacan, J. (1953) 'Some reflections on the ego', *International Journal of Psychoanalysis* 34: 11–17.
Lacan, J. (1977) *Écrits. A Selection*, trans. A. Sheridan, London: Routledge.
Lambrecht, J. (1994) 'Transformations in 2 Corinthians 3.18' in R. Bieringer and J. Lambrecht, *Studies on 2 Corinthians*, Leuven: Leuven University Press, pp.295–307. Reprinted (with an additional note) from *Biblica* 64 (1983): 243–54.
Laplanche, J. and Pontalis, J.-B. (1980 [1967]) *The Language of Psycho-analysis* (trans. D. Nicholson-Smith of *Vocabulaire de la psychanalyse*), London: Hogarth Press.
Larson, J. (1995) *Greek Heroine Cults*, Madison, Wisconsin: University of Wisconsin Press.
Leach, E.R. (1978) 'Lettuces', letter in *Times Literary Supplement*, 22 September: 1055.
Lebeck, A. (1971) *The Oresteia: a Study in Language and Structure*, Cambridge, Mass.: Center for Hellenic Studies/ Harvard University Press.
Leipen, N. (1971) *Athena Parthenos: a Reconstruction*, Toronto: Royal Ontario Museum.
Leitao, D. (1995) 'The perils of Leukippos', *Classical Antiquity* 14: 130–63.
Lemaire, A. (1977 [1970]) *Jacques Lacan*, trans. David Macey, London: Doubleday.
Lieberg, G. (1973) 'Die "theologia tripertita" in Forschung und Bezeugung', *Aufstieg und Niedergang der römischen Welt* 1.4: 63–115.
Lindemann, E. (1944) 'The symptomatology and management of acute grief', *American Journal of Psychiatry* 101: 141–8.
Linders, T. (1972) *Studies in the Treasure Records of Artemis Brauronia Found in Athens*, Stockholm: Svenska Institutet i Athen.
Lissarrague, F. (1992) 'Figures of women' in P. Schmitt Pantel (ed.) (1992), pp.139–229.
Loeb, E. H. (1979) *Die Geburt der Götter in der griechischen Kunst der klassischen Zeit*, Jerusalem: Shikmona.
Loraux, N. (1986 [1981]) *The Invention of Athens: The Funeral Oration in the Classical City*, Cambridge, Massachusetts: Harvard University Press.
Loraux, N. (1991) 'Qu'est-ce qu'une déesse?' in P. Schmitt Pantel (ed.), *Histoire des femmes en occident*, vol.1, Paris: Plon, pp.31–62. (French version of N. Loraux (1992).)
Loraux, N. (1992) 'What is a goddess?' in P. Schmitt Pantel (ed.) (1992), pp.11–44.
Lyons, D. (1996) *Gender and Immortality: Heroines in Ancient Greek Myth and Cult*, Princeton: Princeton University Press.
Mansfield, J.M. (1985) 'The robe of Athena and the panathenaic peplos' unpublished Ph.D. Diss., University of California at Berkeley.
Marcovich, M. (1995) *Clementis Alexandrini Protrepticus*, Leiden, New York and Cologne: Brill.
Mark, I. (1984) 'The gods on the east frieze of the Parthenon', *Hesperia* 53: 289–342.
Mauss, M. (1921) 'L'Expression obligatoire des sentiments (rituels oraux funéraires australiens)', *Journal de Psychologie* 18: 425 ff.
Merkelbach, R. (1972) 'Aglauros: die Religion der Epheben', *Zeitschrift für Papyrologie und Epigraphik* 9: 277–83.
Merkelbach, R. and West, M. L. (1967) *Fragmenta Hesiodea*, Oxford: Clarendon Press.
Metzger, I.R. (1985) *Das Thesmophorion von Eretria: Funde und Befunde eines Heiligtums* (Eretria: Ausgrabungen und Forschungen 7), Bern: Francke.
Mikalson, J. D. (1983) *Athenian Popular Religion*, Chapel Hill and London: University of North Carolina Press.
Mommsen, A. (1878) *Delphika*, Leipzig: Teubner.
Mommsen, A. (1889) 'Jahresbericht über die griechischen Sakralaltertümer', *Bursians Jahresbericht* 60.3: 222–59.

Mommsen, A. (1891) 'Die attische Skirabraüche', *Philologus* 50: 108–36.
Mommsen, A. (1898) *Feste der Stadt Athen im Altertum*, Leipzig: Teubner.
Mommsen, H. (1984) 'Der Grabpinax des Exekias mit den trauernden Frauen' in H.A.G. Brijder (ed.), pp.329–33.
Morris, S. (1992) *Daidalos and the Origins of Greek Art*, Princeton: Princeton University Press.
Needham, R. (1972) *Belief, Language and Experience*, Oxford: Blackwell.
Neils, J. (1992) *Goddess and Polis: The Panathenaic Festival in Ancient Athens*, Hanover: Hood Museum of Art and Princeton: Princeton University Press.
Neumann, G. (1986) 'Alkibiades', *Archäologischer Anzeiger*: 103–12.
Nevett, L. (1995) 'The organisation of space in classical and Hellenistic houses' in N. Spencer (ed.) (1995), pp.89–108.
Nilsson, M.P. (1900) *Studia de Dionysiis Atticis*, Lund: Möller.
Nilsson, M.P. (1906) *Griechische Feste*, Leipzig: Teubner.
Nilsson, M.P. (1940) *Greek Folk Religion*, New York: Columbia University Press.
Nilsson, M.P. (1948) *Greek Piety*, Oxford: Clarendon Press.
Nilsson, M.P. (1955) *Geschichte der griechischen Religion I* (2nd edn), Munich: Beck.
Nilsson, M.P. (1957) *The Dionysiac Mysteries of the Hellenistic and Roman Age*, Lund: C.W.K. Leerup.
Nixon, L. (1995) 'The cults of Demeter and Kore' in R. Hawley and B. Levick (eds) (1995), pp.75–96.
Nock, A.D. (1944) 'The cult of heroes', *Harvard Theological Review* 37: 141–74 (reprinted in Nock, A.D (1986)) *Essays on Religion and the Ancient World* (2nd edn), Oxford: Clarendon Press, vol. 2, pp.575–602.)
Norvin, W. (1913) *Olympiodori philosophi in Platonis Phaedonem Commentaria*, Leipzig: Teubner.
Oakley, J. and Sinos, R. (1993) *The Wedding in Ancient Athens*, Madison, Wisconsin: University of Wisconsin Press.
Osborne, R. (1985) 'Artemis Brauronia', in *Demos: The Discovery of Classical Attika*, Cambridge: Cambridge University Press, pp.154–72.
Osborne, R. (1987) 'The viewing and obscuring of the Parthenon frieze', *Journal of Hellenic Studies* 107: 98–106.
Osborne, R. (1993) 'Women and sacrifice in classical Greece', *Classical Quarterly* n.s. 43: 392–405.
Osborne, R. (1994) 'Looking on – Greek style. Does the sculpted girl speak to women too?' in I. Morris (ed.), *Classical Greece: Ancient Histories and Modern Archaeologies*, Cambridge: Cambridge University Press, pp.81–96.
Padel, R. (1983) 'Women: model for possession by Greek daemons' in A. Cameron and A. Kuhrt (eds) (1983), 3–19.
Padel, R. (1992) *In and Out of the Mind: Greek Images of the Tragic Self*, Princeton: Princeton University Press.
Padel, R. (1995) *Whom Gods Destroy: Elements of Greek and Tragic Madness*, Princeton: Princeton University Press.
Palagia, O. (1980) *Euphranor*, Leiden: Brill.
Parke, H.W. (1977) *Festivals of the Athenians*, London: Thames and Hudson.
Parker, R. (1979) 'Dionysus at the Haloa', *Hermes* 107: 256–7.
Parker, R. (1983) *Miasma: Pollution and Purification in Early Greek Religion*, Oxford: Oxford University Press.
Parsons, M. (1988) 'Self-knowledge refused and accepted: a psychoanalytic perspective on the *Bacchae* and the *Oedipus at Colonus*', *Bulletin of the Institute of Classical Studies* 35: 1–14.

BIBLIOGRAPHY

Pasquali, G. (1908) *Procli Diadochi in Platonis Cratylum Commentaria*, Leipzig: Teubner.
Patterson, C. (1981) *Pericles' Citizenship Law of 451–50*, Salem: The Ayer Company.
Patterson, C. (1987) '*Hai Attikai:* the other Athenians' in M. Skinner (ed.), *Rescuing Creusa: new methodological approaches to women in antiquity*. Special issue of *Helios*, n.s. 13.2, Lubbock, Texas: Texas Tech University Press, pp.49–67.
Pearson, A.C. (1917) *The Fragments of Sophocles*, Cambridge: Cambridge University Press.
Pembroke, S. (1967) 'Women in charge: the function of alternatives in early Greek tradition and the ancient idea of matriarchy', *Journal of the Warburg and Courtauld Institutes* 30: 1–35.
Pépin, J. (1976) *Mythe et Allégorie* (2nd edn), Paris: Études Augustiniennes.
Peppas-Delmousou, D. (1988) 'Autour des inventaires de Brauron' in D. Knoepfler and N. Quellet (eds) (1988), pp.323–46.
Peradotto, J. and Sullivan, J.P. (eds) (1984) *Women in the Ancient World*, Albany: State University of New York Press.
Perlman, P. (1989) 'Acting the she-bear for Artemis', *Arethusa* 22: 111–33.
Pingiatoglou, S. (1981) *Eileithyia*, Würzburg: Königshausen and Neuman.
Pipili, M. (1991) 'Hermes and the child Dionysos: what did Pausanias see on the Amyklai throne?' in M. Gnade (ed.), *Stips Votiva: Papers Presented to C. M. Stibbe*, Amsterdam: Allard Pierson Museum, pp.143–70.
Pomeroy, S.B. (1975) *Goddesses, Whores, Wives and Slaves: Women in Classical Antiquity*, New York: Schocken.
Pomeroy, S.B. (1977) '"Technikai kai mousikai": the education of women in the fourth century and the Hellenistic period', *American Journal of Ancient History* 2: 51–68.
Pötscher, W. (1987) *Hera: Eine Strukturanalyse im Vergleich mit Athena*, Darmstadt: Wissenschaftliche Buchgesellschaft.
Prandi, L. (1983) 'L'heraion de Platea e la festa de Δαιδαλα' in M. Stordi (ed.), *Santuari e Politica nel Mondo Antico*, Milan: Vita e Pensieri, pp.82–94.
Preller, L. (1837) *Demeter und Persephone: ein Cyclus mythologischer Untersuchungen*, Hamburg: Perthes-Besser & Mauke.
Price, T.H. (1978) *Kourotrophos: Cults and Representations of the Greek Nursing Deities*, Leiden: Brill.
Rabe, H. (1903) 'Die Lukienstudien des Arethas'. *Nachrichten von der Königlicher Gesellschaft des Wissenschaften zu Göttingen* 59: 643–56.
Rabe, H. (1906) *Scholia in Lucianum*, Leipzig: Teubner.
Ragland-Sullivan, E. (1986) *Jacques Lacan and the philosophy of psycho-analysis*, London: Croom Helm.
Redfield, J. (1982) 'Notes on the Greek wedding', *Arethusa* 15: 188–201.
Rhodes, R.F. (1995) *Architecture and Meaning on the Athenian Acropolis*, Cambridge: Cambridge University Press.
Rhodes, R.F. and Dobbins, J.J. (1979) 'The sanctuary of Artemis Brauronia on the Athenian Acropolis', *Hesperia* 48: 325–41.
Richardson, N.J. (1974) *The Homeric Hymn to Demeter*, Oxford: Oxford University Press.
Ridgway, B.S. (1992) 'Images of Athena on the Akropolis' in J. Neils (1992), pp.119–42.
Riedweg, C. (1987) *Mysterienterminologie bei Platon, Philon und Klemens von Alexandrien*, Berlin and New York: De Gruyter.
Rizzo, G.E. (1932–40) *Prassitele*, Milan: Treves.
Robert, C. (1885) 'Athena Skiras und die Skirophorien', *Hermes* 20: 349–79.
Robertson, N. (1983a) 'Greek ritual begging in aid of women's fertility and childbirth', *Transactions of the American Philological Association* 113, 143–68.

Robertson, N. (1983b) 'The riddle of the Arrephoria at Athens', *Harvard Studies in Classical Philology* 87: 243–88.
Robertson, N. (1984) 'Poseidon's festival at the winter solstice', *Classical Quarterly* 34: 1–16.
Robertson, N. (1992) *Festivals and Legends: The Formation of Greek Cities in the Light of Public Ritual*, Toronto: University of Toronto Press.
Roccos, L.J. (1995) 'The *kanephoros* and her festival mantle in Greek art', *American Journal of Archaeology* 99: 641–66.
Rohde, E. (1870) 'Unedirte Lucianscholien, die attischen Thesmophorien und Haloen betreffend', *Rheinisches Museum* n.s. 25: 548–60 = *Kleine Schriften*, Leipzig and Tübingen: Mohr (1901), 2: 355–69.
Romano, I. B. (1988) 'Early Greek cult images and cult practices' in R. Hägg *et al.* (eds) (1987) pp.127–34.
Root, M.C. (1985) 'The Parthenon frieze and the Apadana reliefs at Persepolis: reassessing the programmatic relationship', *American Journal of Archaeology* 89: 103–20.
Rosenblatt, P.C., Walsh, R. and Jackson, A. (1971) *Grief and Mourning in Cross-Cultural Perspective*, New Haven: Human Relations Area File Press.
Rühfel, H. (1984) *Das Kind in der griechischen Kunst: von der minoisch-mykenischen Zeit bis zum Hellenismus*, Mainz: Philipp von Zabern.
Sale, W. (1961) 'The hyperborean maidens on Delos', *Harvard Theological Review* 54: 75–89.
Sale, W. (1972) 'The psychoanalysis of Pentheus in *The Bacchae* of Euripides', *Yale Classical Studies* 22: 63–82.
Sale, W. (1975) 'The temple-legends of the Arkteia', *Rheinisches Museum* 118: 265–84.
Salviat, F. (1964) 'Les Théogamies attiques, Zeus Teleios et l'*Agamemnon* d'Eschyle', *Bulletin de Correspondance Hellénique* 88: 647–54.
Schachter, A. (1981) *Cults of Boeotia* I, London: University of London, Institute of Classical Studies.
Schachter, A. (1992) 'Policy, cult, and the placing of Greek sanctuaries' in A. Schachter and J. Bingen (eds), *Le Sanctuaire grec*. Entretiens sur l'Antiquité Classique 37, Geneva: Fondation Hardt, pp.1–57.
Schaps, D.M. (1979) *Economic Rights of Women in Ancient Greece*, Edinburgh: Edinburgh University Press.
Schefold, K. (1978) *Götter und Heldensagen der Griechen in der spätarchaischen Kunst*, Munich: Hirmer.
Schefold, K. (1981) *Die Göttersage in der klassischen und hellenistischen Kunst*, Munich: Hirmer.
Schmitt Pantel, P. (1977) 'Athéna Apatouria et la ceinture: les aspects féminins des Apatouries à Athènes', *Annales (Économie, Sociétés, Civilisations)* 32: 1059–73.
Schmitt Pantel, P. (ed.) (1992) *A History of Women in the West* I, Cambridge, Mass. and London: Belknap Press of Harvard University. (Trans. of *Storia delle Donne in Occidente* I: *L'Occidente*, 1990.)
Schuller, W. (1985) *Frauen in der griechischen Geschichte*, Konstanz: Universitätsverlag.
Seaford, R.A.S. (1984) 'I Corinthians 13.12', *Journal of Theological Studies* n.s. 35: 117–20.
Seaford, R.A.S. (1987a) 'Pentheus' vision: *Bacchae* 918–22', *Classical Quarterly* 37: 76–8.
Seaford, R.A.S. (1987b) 'The tragic wedding', *Journal of Hellenic Studies* 107: 106–30.
Seaford, R.A.S. (1988) 'The eleventh ode of Bacchylides: Hera, Artemis, and the absence of Dionysos', *Journal of Hellenic Studies* 108:118–36.
Seaford, R.A.S. (1994a) *Reciprocity and Ritual. Homer and Tragedy in the Developing City-State*, Oxford: Clarendon Press.
Seaford, R.A.S. (1994b) 'Sophokles and the Mysteries', *Hermes* 122: 275–88.

Seaford, R.A.S (1996) *Euripides' Bacchae*, Warminster: Aris and Phillips.
Sealey, R. (1990) *Women and Law in Classical Greece*, Chapel Hill and London: University of North Carolina Press.
Segal, C. (1986) *Interpreting Greek Tragedy: myth, poetry, text*, Ithaca, New York: Cornell University Press.
Sfameni Gasparro, G. (1986) *Misteri e culti mistici di Demetra* (Storia delle religioni 3), Rome: Lérma.
Shapiro, H.A. (1991) 'The iconography of mourning in Athenian art', *American Journal of Archaeology* 95: 629–56.
Simms, R.M. (1980) 'Eleusinian-Athenian cult and myth: their nature and origin'. Diss., University of Virginia at Charlottesville.
Simon, C.G. (1986) 'The archaic votive offerings and cults of Ionia', Diss., University of California, Berkeley.
Simon, E. (1959) *Die Geburt der Aphrodite*, Berlin: de Gruyter and Co.
Simon, E. (1975) 'Versuch einer Deutung der Südmetopen des Parthenon', *Jahrbuch des Deutschen Archäologischen Instituts* 90: 100–20.
Simon, E. (1982) 'Die Mittelszene im Ostfries des Parthenon', *Mitteilungen des Deutschen Archäologischen Instituts (Athenische Abteilung)* 97: 127–44.
Simon, E. (1983) *Festivals of Attica: An Archaeological Commentary*, Madison and London: University of Wisconsin Press.
Sinn, U. (1993) 'Greek sanctuaries as places of refuge' in R. Hägg and N. Marinatos (eds), *Greek Sanctuaries: New Approaches*, London: Routledge, pp.88–109.
Sissa, G. (1990) 'Maidenhood without maidenhead' in D. Halperin, J. Winkler and F. Zeitlin (eds), *Before Sexuality*, Princeton: Princeton University Press, pp.339–64.
Skov, G.E. (1975) 'The priestess of Demeter and her role in the initiation of women at the festival of the Haloa at Eleusis', *Temenos* 11: 136–47.
Smith, R.R.R. (1991) *Hellenistic Sculpture*, London: Thames and Hudson.
Snodgrass, A.M. (1980) *Archaic Greece*, London: Dent.
Sokolowski, F. (1962), *Lois sacrées des cités grecques: Supplément*, Paris: De Boccard.
Sokolowski, F. (1969) *Lois sacrées des cités grècques*, Paris: De Boccard.
Sommerstein, A.H. *et al.* (eds) (1993) *Tragedy, Comedy and the Polis*, Bari: Levante.
Sourvinou-Inwood, C. (1978) 'Persephone and Aphrodite at Locri: a model for personality definitions in Greek religion', *Journal of Hellenic Studies* 95: 101–21.
Sourvinou-Inwood, C. (1987) 'Erotic pursuit: images and meanings', *Journal of Hellenic Studies* 107: 131–53.
Sourvinou-Inwood, C. (1988) *Studies in Girls' Transitions: Aspects of the Arkteia and Age Representation in Attic Iconography*, Athens: Kardamitsa.
Sourvinou-Inwood, C. (1990) 'Sophocles' Antigone as a bad woman' in F. Dieteren and E. Kloek (eds), *Writing Women into History*, Amsterdam: Historisch Seminarium van de Universiteit van Amsterdam, pp.11–38.
Spencer, N. (ed.) (1995) *Time, Tradition and Society in Greek Archaeology*, London: Routledge.
Spivey, N. (1996) *Understanding Greek Sculpture. Ancient Meanings, Modern Readings*, London: Thames and Hudson.
Stears, K.E. (1993) 'Women and the family in the funerary ritual and art of classical Athens'. Diss. King's College, London.
Stears, K.E. (1995) 'Dead women's society: constructing female gender in classical Athenian funerary sculpture' in N. Spencer (ed.) (1995), pp.109–31.
Stengel, P. (1910) 'Haloa', *Real-Encyclopädie der Klassischen Altertumswissenschaft* 7.2: 2278f.

Stengel, P. (1920) *Die griechische Kultusaltertümer* (3rd edn), Munich: Beck.
Stillwell, R. (1969) 'The panathenaic frieze: optical relations', *Hesperia* 38: 231–41.
Thimme, J. (1965) 'Die Religiose Bedeutung der Kykladenidole', *Antike Kunst* 8: 72–6.
Thönges-Stringaris, R.N. (1965) 'Das griechische Totenmahl', Mitteilungen des Deutschen Archäologischen Instituts (Athenische Abteilung) 80: 1–99.
Thomson, G. (1966) *Aeschylus' Oresteia*, vol. 2, Prague: Czechoslovak Academy of Sciences.
Thrall, M.E. (1994) *A Critical and Exegetical Commentary on the Second Epistle to the Corinthians*, vol. 1, Edinburgh: T. and T. Clark.
Tréheux, J. (1988) 'Observations sur les inventaires du Brauronion de l'Acropole d'Athènes' in D. Knoepfler and N. Quellet (eds) (1988), pp.347–55.
Trendall, A.D. (1967) *The Red-Figured Vases of Lucania, Campania, and Sicily*, Oxford: Oxford University Press.
Trendall, A.D. (1973) *The Red-Figured Vases of Lucania, Campania, and Sicily* (Bulletin of the Institute of Classical Studies Suppl. 31), London: Institute of Classical Studies.
Trendall, A.D. (1978) *The Red-Figured Vases of Apulia*, vol. 1, Oxford: Oxford University Press.
Tresp, A. (1914) *Die Fragmente der griechischen Kultschriftsteller* (Religionsgeschichtliche Versuche und Vorarbeiten 15.1), Giessen: Töpelmann.
Tsantsanoglou, K. and Parassoglou, G.M. (1987) 'Two gold lamellae from Thessaly', *Hellenika* 38: 3–16.
Turcan, R. (1959) 'à Propos d'Ovide, *Fast.* 11, 313–330', *Revue des Études Latines* 37: 195–203.
Turner, V.W. (1969) *The Ritual Process*, London: Routledge.
Tyrrell, W.B. (1984) *Amazons: a Study in Athenian Mythmaking*, Baltimore and London: Johns Hopkins University Press.
Tzifalias, A. (1980 [1988]) Report on fifteenth Ephoria: Atrax, *Deltion* 35 B1: 291–4.
Tzifalias, A. (1988 [1993]) Report on fifteenth Ephoria: Atrax, *Deltion* 43 B1: 276–9.
Van der Loeff, A.R. (1916) 'De sciris', *Mnemosyne* n.s. 44: 322–37.
Van Gennep, A. (1909) *Les Rites de passage*, Paris: Librairie Critique.
Van Hoorn, G. (1951) *Choes and Anthesteria*, Leiden: Brill.
Van Sichelen, L. (1987) 'Nouvelles orientations dans l'étude de l'arrhéphorie attique', *L'Antiquité Classique* 56: 88–102.
Van Straten, F. (1981) 'Gifts for the gods' in H.S. Versnel (ed.), *Faith, Hope and Worship*, Leiden: Brill, pp.65–151.
Van Straten, F. (1987) 'Greek sacrificial representations: livestock prices and religious mentality' in T. Linders and G. Nordquist (eds), *Gifts to the Gods: Proceedings of the Uppsala Symposium 1985* (Boreas 15), Uppsala: Uppsala University Press, pp.159–70.
Vedder, U. (1988) 'Frauentod-Kriegertod im Spiegel der attischen Grabkunst den 4. jhr. v. Chr.', *Mitteilungen des Deutschen Archäologischen Instituts (Athenische Abteilung)* 103: 161–91.
Verbruggen, H. (1981) *Le Zeus crétois*, Paris: Les Belles Lettres.
Vernant, J.-P. (1980 [1974]) *Myth and Society in Ancient Greece* trans. J. Lloyd, Sussex: Harvester Press.
Vernant, J.-P. (1983 [1971]) *Myth and Thought among the Greeks*, London: Routledge and Kegan Paul.
Vernant, J.-P. (1991) *Mortals and Immortals*, collection edited by F.I. Zeitlin, Princeton: Princeton University Press.
Versnel, H.S. (1990) *Inconsistencies in Greek and Roman Religion I: Ter Unus*, Leiden: Brill.
Versnel, H.S. (1992) 'The festival for Bona Dea and the Thesmophoria', *Greece and Rome* 39: 31–55.

Versnel, H.S. (1994) *Inconsistencies in Greek and Roman Religion II: Transition and Reversal in Myth and Ritual*, Leiden: Brill.

Vidal-Naquet, P. (1986 [1981]) *The Black Hunter: Forms of Thought and Forms of Society in the Ancient World*, Baltimore and London: Johns Hopkins University Press.

Von Negerlein, J. (1902) 'Bild, Spiegel, und Schatten im Volksglauben', *Archiv für Religionswissenschaft* 5: 1–37.

Vorster, C. (1983) *Griechische Kinderstatuen*, Cologne: Wasmuth.

Walters, H.B. (1921) 'Red-figured vases recently acquired by the British Museum', *Journal of Hellenic Studies* 41: 17–150 and plate VI.

West, M.L. (1983) *The Orphic Poems*, Oxford: Clarendon Press.

West, M.L. (1992) *Ancient Greek Music*, Oxford: Clarendon Press.

Willetts, R.F. (1962) *Cretan Cults and Festivals*, London and New York: Routledge and Kegan Paul.

Wilson, N.G. (1983) *Scholars of Byzantium*, London: Duckworth.

Winkler, J.J. (1990) 'The laughter of the oppressed: Demeter and the gardens of Adonis' in *The Constraints of Desire: The Anthropology of Sex and Gender in Ancient Greece*, New York and London: Routledge, pp.188–209.

Wohlberg, J. (1968) 'The palace-hero equation in Euripides', *Acta Antiqua Academiae Scientiarum Hungaricae* 16: 149–55.

Woodford, S. (1981) Review of Loeb (1979) in *Journal of Hellenic Studies* 101: 221–2.

Zahn, R. (1970) 'Das Kind in der antiken Kunst', *Forschungen und Berichte* (from the Berlin Museum) 12: 21–30.

Zeitlin, F.I. (1965) 'The motif of the corrupted sacrifice in Aeschylus' *Oresteia*', *Transactions of the American Philological Association* 96: 463–508.

Zeitlin, F.I. (1982) 'Cultic models of the female: rites of Dionysus and Demeter', *Arethusa* 15: 129–57.

Zeitlin, F.I. (1990) 'Thebes: theater of self and society in Athenian drama' in J.J. Winkler and F.I. Zeitlin (eds), *Nothing to Do with Dionysos?* Princeton: Princeton University Press, pp.130–67.

Zeitlin, F.I. (1996) 'Signifying difference: the case of Hesiod's Pandora' in *Playing the Other: Gender and Society in Classical Greek Literature*, Chicago and London: University of Chicago Press, pp.53–86.

Zschietzschmann, W. (1928) 'Die Darstellungen der "prothesis" in der griechischen Kunst', *Mitteilungen des Deutschen Archäologischen Instituts* (*Athenische Abteilung*) 53, 17–47.

Zuntz, G. (1971) *Persephone*, Oxford: Clarendon Press.

INDEX

Acropolis, at Athens 37, 40, ch. 4 *passim*, 76
Actaeon *see* Aktaion
adultery 48, 125
Aelius Dionysius 158
Aeschylus 131, 155; *Lykourgeia* 130, 132, 138; *Oresteia* 18, 48, 49, 86–7, 134–5; *The Persians* 121; *Prometheus Bound* 87
aetiology 155–6, 162; *see also aition*
Agamemnon 48, 49
Agaue 134
Ageladas 74
Aglauros 102
Aigion, in Achaia 74
Aigion, Mount 74
Aiora, festival of 155
Aischylos *see* Aeschylus
aition, myth as 22, 23–4, 98, 101; *see also* aetiology
Aivatlar 36
Akropolis *see* Acropolis
Aktaion 132, 133
Alalkomeneus 24
Alkaios 74
allegory 156, 163
Alope 103
Althaea 107
Amazons 55–7, 67, 105–6
anakalupteria 64–5
anchisteia 117, 121–2
Andromache 96
Anthesteria, festival of 155
Antinoe 105
Antiope 108
Apemosyne 103
Aphrodite 2, 5, 18, 33, 58, 71, 76–8, 79, 80, 81, 84, 85, 89, 96, 97, 104
Apollo 2, 5, 18, 22, 53, 71, 72, 74, 75, 76, 77, 83, 85, 89, 100, 103

Apollodorus 53, 89, 158
Apollonius of Acharnae 159
Arcadia 15, 75
Ares 2, 105, 108
Arethas of Caesarea 157–8
Argos 15, 16, 17, 74, 106
Aristodicus 159
Aristophanes 149; *Acharnians* 132; *Birds* 20, 54–5; *Thesmophoriazusae* 17–18, 130, 132, 149
Aristotle 86–7, 125; *Generation of Animals* 88; *Politics* 88
Arkadia *see* Arcadia
arkteia, *arktoi* 33, 38, 40, 80, 101
Arrhephoria/Arrephoria, *arrhephoroi* 63–4, 100–1, 107, 151–2, 153
Artemidorus 132
Artemis 2, 4, 7, 14, ch. 3 *passim*, 71, 75, 76, 78–9, 80, 81, 84, 85, 89, 92, 96, 100, 102, 104, 129, 133; Artemis Apanchomene 31–2; Artemis Karyatis 28; Artemis Kithone 39; Artemis Kondylea 31; Artemis Limnatis 27–8; Artemis Lysizonos 34; Artemis Orthia 29, 40; and childbirth 34–5, 92; worshipped at Brauron 21, 29, 31, 33, 36, 37–8, 40, 41, 92, 101, 104, 107; at Mounichia 31, 101
Artemision 29
Asklepios 71, 72, 74–5
Asopos, river 23, 24, 105
Athamas 72
Athenaeus 57
Athene/-a 2, 5, 17, 22, ch. 4 *passim*, 71, 74, 75, 76, 77, 78, 79, 80, 81, 83, 84–5, 89, 96, 100–1, 102, 104; Athene Parthenos 49; Athene Polias 49
Athens 37–8, 40, 41, ch. 4 *passim*, 76, 86–7, ch. 7 *passim*, 149, 153, 158

INDEX

Aulis 31

Baanes 157–8
Balensiefen, L. 131
barbarians 55–6, 58
bears *see arkteia*
belts 34, 37–9
birth, of deities ch. 5 *passim*
Blundell, S. 91
body, female 80, 91
borders 27–30
Boreas, daughters of 100, 101
Bowie, M. 136–7
Brauron 21, 29, 31, 33, 36, 37–8, 40, 41, 80, 90, 101, 104, 107
Brumfield, A.C. 161
burial 116; *see also* death ritual

Callimachus, *Aetia* 78, 155; *Hymn to Artemis* 31, 78, 89; *Hymn to Delos* 100; *Hymn to Zeus* 74
Campbell, B. 62
Carrey, J. 57
Cassandra 103
castration 76–7
cattle, of Apollo 74–5
Cecrops *see* Kekrops
Centaurs *see* Lapiths
childbirth 33, 34–5, 39, 92, 101, 107, 117–18, 119–20; and male deities 85–6, 89; *see also* motherhood
childhood, bride's farewell to 14–15; of deities 5, ch. 5 *passim*; of mortal females 86–9, 93
children, in art 80, 90
choes cups 80–1
Cicero 116
Cithaeron *see* Kithairon
citizenship law, Athens 48, 53
civilisation 154–5, 156
Clearchus of Soli 57
Clement of Alexandria, *Protrepticus* 150, 151, 152, 157–9, 161
Clytemnestra 18, 48, 49, 132
Coronis *see* Koronis
cremation 116
Crete 74
Cyrene 33–4
Cyprus 77

Daidala, festival of 22–5
Danae 103

Daphne 103
daughters 149
death ritual 6, ch. 7 *passim*
De Polignac 27
Deiphontes 106–7
Delos 36, 75, 78, 79, 100, 101
Delphi 75, 84
Demeter 2, 8, 38, 81, 104, 108, 133, 134, ch. 9 *passim*
Demophon 134
Demosthenes 121
Despoina, temple of 133
Didymus 158
Diktys 108
Dionysius of Heraclea 160
Dionysos, Dionysus 2, 7, 71, 72, 73, 75, 83, 85, 89, 91, ch. 8 *passim*, 152, 155, 156
dirges *see* laments, women's
divorce 48
Dowden, K. 100
dowry 48
dredger-women 161–2
Durkheim, E. 96

Echinos 34–5
ekphora 113, 116, 117, 119, 122, 124
Eleusinian goddesses 134; *see also* Demeter, Persephone
Eleusis/Eleusinian myth 108, 151, 154, 155, 162
Eleutherna 36
Empedocles 137
ta enata 116
ephebes 38, 39, 102, 108
Ephesos/Ephesus 36, 79
Epidauros 75
epikleros 48
Eratosthenes 155
Erchia 18–19
Erechtheus 99
ergastinai 63–4
Erichthonios 65, 67, 101
Erigone 155
Erinyes (Furies) 18, 132, 135
Eros 14, 131
Eudoros 102
Euphranor 79, 89
Euripides 103; *Bacchae* 7, 129, 130, 134, 138, 139; *Ion* 103, 129; *Iphigeneia in Tauris/among the Taurians* 75, 104; *Medea* 133, 138
exegetes 159

INDEX

femininity 47
fertility 8, 149, 150, 151, 153, 154, 156
festivals *see* individual headings
Frazer, J., *Golden Bough* 149, 153, 154
Freud, S. 139
funeral speeches 117
funerals *see* death ritual
funerary legislation 115, 116–17, 122, 123
Furies, see Erinyes

Gamelion, month of 18–19
garments, offered to Artemis 35, 36–40, 41
Gello 40
gender, and the divine ch. 4 *passim*, ch. 5 *passim*, 96; in death ritual ch. 7 *passim*; inversion of 10, 108, 128–33, 139–40
Giants, Gods versus 55, 61, 67
Glauke 133
goddesses ch. 5 *passim*; femininity of 47, 87–8; in hellenistic period 89–92; masculine activities of 85; sexual statuses of 81–4; *see also* Aphrodite, Artemis, Athene, Demeter, Erinyes, Hera, Hestia, Iris, Leto, Maia, Metis, Moirai, Persephone, Selene, virginity
Golden, M. 87
Gorgon's head 67
grief, at funerals 121–3, 125

Habron the Exegete 159
Hades 133
Haloa, festival of 7, ch. 9 *passim*
Hector 96
Hekale 108
Helen 29, 40, 58, 100, 101
Heliodorus 155
Helios 61, 67
Hellenistic period, representation of goddesses in 89–92; status of women in 90–1
Hephaestus/Hephaistos 2, 17, 65, 67
Hera 2, 4, 7, ch. 2 *passim*, 64–5, 72, 74, 81, 103
Heracles 17, 98, 106, 133
Heraclitus 137
Heraia, festival at Olympia 20–2
Hermaphrodite 133
Hermes 2, 5, 71, 72, 73, 74, 75, 84, 85, 88, 91, 102
Herodotus 40, 53
heroes 3, ch. 6 *passim*
heroines 5–6, 21, ch. 6 *passim*

Hesiod 15; *Catalogue of Women* 102–3; *Theogony* 16, 60, 67, 74, 76; *Works and Days* 33, 67
Hestia 2, 61–2, 81, 84, 96
Hierophant, the 162
hieros gamos, of Hera and Zeus 16–17, 20, 25; Attic festival of 17–20, 25–6
Hippodameia 20–2, 108
Hippolytos 102
Homer 15; *Iliad* 16, 105, 134; *Odyssey* 103
Homeric hymns, to Aphrodite 76; to Delian Apollo 78; to Demeter 134; to Hermes 74
Hyakinthos 102
Hyginus 53
Hyperborean maidens *see* Boreas
Hyrnetho, eponym of Hyrnathoi 106–7

Icarius
inheritance 122
initiation 7, 14–15, 21, 22, 26, 29, 99, 100, 102, 107, ch. 8 *passim*; *see also* rites of passage
Ino 72, 108
inventories, of Artemis 37–40, 41–2
Io 17, 103
Iphigeneia 101, 104, 107
Iris 74
Isthmiades 108

Jacoby, F. 158
Jocasta 135

Kabeirion 108
Kalapodi 29
Kallimachos *see* Callimachus
Kallisto 30, 101
Kallynteria 107
Kaphyai 31
Karyai 28, 29, 30
Kassandra *see* Cassandra
Kearns, E. 40
Kekrops 53, 57; Kekrops' daughters 64, 65, 99–100
Keleos 108
Kephalos 99, 100
Kephisodotos 72
Kepple, L.R. 135
King, H. 31–2
Kithairon 23, 24, 134, 135
Klymene 108
Klytaimestra *see* Clytemnestra
Knossos 20

INDEX

Koronis 74
Kourotrophos 18
Kreousa 103
Kresilas 72
krokotoi 38
Kronos 74, 76
Kyme 105

Lacan, J. 7, 128, 135–7, 139–40
Laconia, Lakonia 15, 27
laments, women's 117, 121, 123–5
Lamia 40
Lampsake, eponym of Lampsakos 106
Lapiths versus Centaurs 55, 57–9, 67
legislation, funerary 115, 116–17, 122, 123
lekythoi, white-ground 114, 124
Lemnos 29, 40
Leto 71, 75, 78, 79, 84, 100
Locri 22
Loraux, N. 47, 87, 97
Lucian 8; *Dialogues of Hetaerae* ch. 9 *passim*; *Council of the Gods* 150, 155–6, 157
'Ludovisi Throne' 77–8
Lykosoura 133
Lysias 55

maenads, maenadism 7, 72, ch. 8 *passim*
Maia 74–5, 84
Mannhardt-Frazer hypothesis 153, 154
Mantinea 105
marriage, Artemis and 34; Athene and ch. 4 *passim*; Hera and ch. 2 *passim*; rituals of 13–15, 34, 114, 119, 120; *see also* weddings, and women, sexual statuses of
Megalopolis 75
megara (underground chambers) 151, 152, 157–8
Meidias Painter 75
Menander 19
Menelaos 58, 100
Menge 36
menstruation 32, 36
Metaneira 108
Metis 60, 76
miasma see pollution
Mikalson, J. D. 91
Miletos 38, 39
Minos 99
models, genital 152
Moirai 20
Mormo 40

motherhood 149; of heroines 102–4; *see also* childbirth
mourning *see* death ritual
Mynnia 80
mysteries 91; of Demeter and Persephone 134, 149, 150, 151, 162, 163; Dionysiac ch. 8 *passim*; Eleusinian 134; Orphic 129–30, 133

Naevius 133
Narkissos 133
Neanthes of Cyzicus 159
Neiaira 125
Neoplatonism *see* Olympiodorus, Plotinus, Proclus
Nonnus 137
nymphs 72
Nysa 72

Odysseus 102
Oedipus 135
Oenoe 74
oikos 47–9, 61–2, 116, 119, 120, 122, 123, 126
Oinomaos 20–1
Olbia 130, 133
Olympia 20, 33, 76, 77
Olympic Games 21
Olympiodorus 137, 142
Orestes 48, 49, 104, 132, 134–5
Orphism, Orphic hymns 134; *see also* mysteries
Ortygia 78, 79
Osborne, R. 59–60
Ouranos 76–7, 85, 89

Pallas 89
Panathenaia, festival of 51, 58–9, 67
Pandora 5, 67
Pandrosos 101, 104, 107
Panaetius 160
Papposilenos 72
Paris 58
Parsons, M. 138–9
Parthenon 5, ch. 4 *passim* 76
Parthenos statue 49, 60, 65, 66, 67
Patrai 30
Paul, St., *I Corinthians* 140; *II Corinthians* 141
Pausanias 20, 21, 22, 23, 24, 29, 30, 60, 65, 72, 74, 75, 76, 105, 133, 151, 152, 158
Pelarge 108

INDEX

Peloponnese 21
Peloponnesian Wars 40, 41
Pelops 21
Pentheus 7, 128–9, 131–5, 138–40
peplos, presented to Athene 51, 59, 63, 65, 100; presented to Hera 22
Pericles 48
perideipnon (funeral meal) 116
Perithoos 58
Persephone 22, ch. 9 *passim*
Perseus 108
Persians 49, 51, 55–6
The Persians see Aeschylus
Pheidias 51, 67, 76, 77
Phlegyas 74
physiology, female 32; *see also* body
Physkoa 21
pigs 151, 153, 154
Pindar, *On Delos* 78
pines 154
Pisa 20
Plataea 4, 22, 105
Plato 86–7
Pliny 79
Plotinus 137, 142
Plutarch 23, 24
Plynteria 107
Pnyx 8
polis, death ritual and the 122–3, 126; funerary legislation and the 116–17; in the hellenistic period 91; heroines and the 105–7; image of, in the Parthenon frieze 60; marriage and the 48–9; religion and the 3, 5, 25, 27–30, 104
pollution 115, 116, 117–18, 119, 120, 126
Polykleitos 72
Polymele 102–3
Pomeroy, S. B. 81
Pompeii, Villa of the Mysteries 131
Poseidon 2, 5, 18, 53, 56–7
Poseidonius/Posidonius 158–9, 160
Praxiteles 22, 72, 73, 91
priestesses 1, 5, 104, 107, 108
Proclus 142
Proitos, daughters of 108
Prokris 99
prothesis 113–15, 117, 118, 120, 121, 122, 124
Psamathe (Chione) 103
public/private 120–1, 123, 124–5, 126
public funerals 123
Python 75, 79, 88

rape 14, 102, 103
Rhea 74
Riedweg, C. 159
rites of passage 119–20, 122, 123; *see also* initiation
Robertson, N. 150, 159
Rohde, E. 150, 151, 157, 158

Samos 15, 17
Sappho Painter, the 116
satyrs 72, 130, 131, 132
Selene 61, 67
Semele 72, 103
Skirophoria, festival of 151, 158
Skopas 79, 89
Smyrna 105
Solon, funerary legislation of 115, 116–17, 122
Sophists 91
Sophocles/-kles, *Ajax* 133; *Electra* 135; *Ichneutae* 74; *Oedipus/Oidipous Tyrannos* 86, 135, 139; *Oedipus at Kolonos* 134
Sotades 159
Sparta 27–8, 76
Sourvinou-Inwood, C. 32
Stoics 160
Strabo 79, 105
strangulation 31–2

Tanagra 38
Tegea 74
Temenos, king 106
Tetrapolis 98
Thatcher, M. 62
Theocritus, *Idyll* 18, 100
Theophrastus, *On festivals* 159
Theseus 29, 40, 55, 98, 101
Thesmophoria, festival of 7–8, 9, ch. 9 *passim*
Thessaly 33, 34
Thetis 134
Thorikos 18–19, 99
Tinos 76
Titans 134, 137–8, 142
tombs 113, 116, 124, 125
Totenmahl reliefs 98
triakostia 116, 117, 118
'tripartite theology' 159–60
ta trita 116
Triteia 105–6
Triton 89
Trojans/Troy, sack of 55, 57–8
Typhon 17

INDEX

Uranus *see* Ouranos

Van Gennep, A. 122
Varro 53, 56–7; *Religious Antiquities* 159
Vernant, J.-P. 61–2
virginity, in goddesses 32, ch. 4 *passim*, 81–4, 85, 96–7, 107; in heroines 99; in women 14–15, 33; see also women, sexual statuses of, *parthenos*

weaving *see* wool-working
weddings, wedding banquet of the Lapiths 58; weddings and funerals 114, 119, 120; wedding procession, at Athens 48–9, 50, 64; *see also* marriage

wine 155–6
Woodford, S. 80
wool-working 36, 64, 65, 100, 104
women, sexual statuses of 13–14, 32–3, 104, 119; *gyne* (wife) 4, 8, 14, 2, 33, 119; *hetaira* 97; *nymphe* 4, 14, 33, 34, 119; *parthenos* (maiden) 4, 5, 6, 14, 21, 22, 23, 30, 33, 119, 100–2

Xenophanes 96
Xenophon, *Oeconomicus* 1; *Memorabilia* 57

Zeus 53, 60–1, 64, 71, 72, 74, 75, 76, 77, 83, 85, 89
Zeuxis 90